GLASTONBURY

Glastonbury

Ancient Avalon, New Jerusalem

EDITED BY ANTHONY ROBERTS

RIDER

London Sydney Auckland Johannesburg

DEDICATION

The editor wishes to point out that this book is his
personal tribute to a sacred and beautiful place. It is
dedicated to all those who have laboured (past and
present) to make the spirit of Glastonbury flourish.

First published in a limited edition in 1977 by Zodiac House
Revised edition published in 1978 by Rider
This edition published in 1992 by Rider
An imprint of Random Century Group Ltd,
20 Vauxhall Bridge Road, London SW1V 2SA

Random Century Group Australia (Pty) Ltd
20 Alfred Street, Milsons Point,
Sydney, NSW 2061, Australia

Random Century New Zealand Ltd
18 Poland Road, Glenfield,
Auckland 10, New Zealand

Random Century Group South Africa (Pty) Ltd,
PO Box 337, Bergvlei 2012, South Africa

Printed and bound in Great Britain by Clays Ltd,
St Ives PLC

A catalogue record for this book is available from
the British Library.

ISBN 0 7126 5373 2

Contents

Contributors

Mary Caine trained as an illustrator and has taught art in further education. She has painted large murals, and has contributed illustrations to this and other books.

For many years she studied the Glastonbury Zodiac, first discovered by Katherine Maltwood, and made further discoveries herself. She wrote a series of articles on it in *Prediction*, and a further series on the zodiac she believes exists around Kingston-upon-Thames. These were published in 1968/9. She contributed to the key overground magazine of the sixties, *Gandalf's Garden* and other similar periodicals.

She has written a book on the Glastonbury Giants and with her husband made a film about them, some of it from the air, which has been widely shown in the course of her lectures up and down the country. BBC Television also took her to Somerset to make a film about the Giants which was broadcast in 1976 on 'Nationwide'.

She has just completed her magnum opus on the Celtic Saints.

Donald L. Cyr was a scientist who worked in the ballistics field and was involved in various projects at NASA. He was also editor of *Stonehenge Viewpoint*, a speculative journal devoted to the study of prehistory via the techniques of astro-archaeology and comparative mythology. He has made numerous visits to megalithic sites in Britain and has written at length on Glastonbury.

He is a firm believer in the theories of Isaac Vail, an American cosmologist (a contemporary of Ignatius Donnelly, of Atlantis fame), whose 'ice canopy' hypothesis was given credence with the discovery of a similar cloud canopy around the planet Venus.

Donald Cyr is now retired and lives in Santa Barbara, California.

Jess Foster was a school-teacher, bookseller and author of many books and radio plays for juveniles. She founded the Pendragon Society in 1959 and was general secretary of the society from then until her death in 1979. She was also the editor of *Pendragon Magazine*. The society is now run by her daughter.

Aims of the Pendragon Society are: 'To stimulate interest in King Arthur and his contemporaries, and to investigate the historical and archaeological background of The Matter of Britain. Also, to study the significance, past, present and future of the Arthurian legends.'

Kenneth Knight was a researcher into the technicalities of occultism for decades. He made intensive investigations into the Hebrew Cabbala, tying the underlying gematria and geometry into the general canon of western-oriented geomancy. His articles appeared in several occult-angled journals such as *Torc,*

The Ley Hunter, Pendragon, etc.

He was a psychic of some sensitivity and also a talented painter who lived in the Glastonbury area for years. He died in 1980.

John Michael is a Welshman and was the proprietor of the Pentacle Bookshop, a major centre of occult literature.

He was an active member of the Pendragon Society and gave lectures on his researches into comparative aspects of terrestrial zodiacs and Welsh legendary. He was also a founder member of the Institute of Geomantic Research (IGR).

John Michell is the most celebrated of modern occult writers. His writings have revolutionized the conception of advanced culture in prehistory, while at the same time giving a true metaphysical/ philosophical interpretation to the 'magical' patterns of reality. He is ex-Etonian, ex-Navy and now resides in London.

John Michell is really best described as a mystical antiquarian in the fine tradition of Aubrey, Stukeley and Blake. He has conducted meticulous research in the Glastonbury area and is the discoverer of the patterns of the New Jerusalem in the Avalonian landscape.

Ann Pennick was an editorial assistant for the magazine *Arcana* and helped produce the underground periodicals *Oracle of Albion* and *Walrus.* She was the treasurer of the IGR and investigated subterranea, having a paper published in the Megalithic Visions Antiquarian Papers series, entitled *Dene-holes and Subterranea.*

Nigel Pennick was a micro-biologist but is now a prolific writer on all aspects of ancient mysteries. He has edited/published numerous books, journals and papers dealing with scientific aspects of geomancy, sacred geometry, prehistory, etc. He was actively involved with the group responsible for *Cambridge Voice,* a radical newspaper that touched upon various esoteric British traditions.

He claims to have discovered the East Anglian terrestrial zodiac around Nuthampstead and has published a pamphlet on this highly speculative field of research. He is a founder member of the IGR.

Anthony Roberts was born in Kensington, London in May 1940. He lived in Fulham until 1981 and was married with three children. He was educated on the streets and at numerous schools ranging from secondary through technical to art. His working career covered such diverse subjects as building-site labouring, exhibition designing, vagrancy and library research work for *The Times* newspaper. He travelled extensively throughout the British Isles, both on foot and by car, constantly seeking the atmosphere of the living past.

He moved to Glastonbury in 1981, and there spent the rest of his life reading, writing and experiencing the Glastonbury myths.

Anthony Roberts had many articles published in underground and speculative journals such as *It, Arcana, The Ley Hunter,* etc. In 1969 he founded Zodiac House Publications in collaboration with his wife Janet. In 1975 his book *Atlantean Traditions in Ancient Britain* was published. He went on to have *Sowers of Thunder* and *The Dark Gods* published by Hutchinson and continued to write and publish pamphlets and articles in series such as *Apocolyptic Archives* and *Anti-Feminist Papers.*

He is best described as a mystical anarchist in the Blakean tradition. He died on his beloved Tor on 9 February 1990.

Janet Roberts studied music before becoming seriously interested in the earth mysteries, especially around the Glastonbury area. She has had articles published in local newspapers and magazines detailing ley lines and terrestrial sculpture, and also produces and distributes all Zodiac House publications.

Since 1985 she has been running two Montessori schools, bringing up three children, and more recently learning to live without her husband, Anthony Roberts, who died in 1990.

Patricia Villiers-Stuart has been fascinated, since she was an art student in the 1930s, by the possibility that a united system could lie behind the complexities of life. An early attraction to William Blake was followed by a long search among many writers, from the mystical to the scientific. On the way she became interested in the problem of the labyrinth or maze. *The Language of Pattern* by Keith Albarn inspired her to apply some of his geometrical and numerical patterns to maze formations. These gave her a promising lead from which her research has gradually developed.

She was a member of the IGR. Oscar Nemon the sculptor was her husband.

Colin Wilson is a major English writer whose special preoccupations are with psychology, sociology and metaphysics. He was born in Leicester in 1931 and devoted his early years to refining his intellect and developing considerable critical faculties. In 1956 he exploded into the moribund world of literature with his brilliant analysis of committed spiritual rebellion, *The Outsider*. Since then his work has moved steadily towards a synthesis, incorporating the expansion of human consciousness through the blending of many separate disciplines: science, religion, music, etc. In 1971 he published a seminal work on magic, *The Occult*, and throughout the seventies he was moving further into the general, complementary fields of the paranormal and the earth mysteries. Colin Wilson has lectured in Europe and in America, where he was a visiting professor and has persued his interests in parapsychology ever since.

Landscapes in a Figure

JOHN NICHOLSON

In the front garden of a normal house on Wells Road, Glastonbury stands a four-foot high statue of Anubis. Anubis was an Egyptian divinity depicted as part-dog and part-cat because the animal was a jackal. The stone statue captures this ambivalence and the character of Anubis: poised, ears pricked, with a necklace around the throat and hanging down the chest to signify this is no ordinary creature. It is watchful. The special role in the Egyptian religion of Anubis was to guard the entrance to the Underworld.

To Anubis the souls of the dead came to be weighed. The god put the heart on one scale and a feather in the other. In the balance was your life. Had you been light-hearted or did you have a heavy heart? Had you loved and passed on love which makes the world go round? The love-filled soul whirled up like a feather but the heavy, egotistical soul fell like a brick.

The celestial role of Anubis was confirmed by its dog-like head. The most important star for the Egyptians was the Dog Star, Sirius. On winter nights you can clearly see Sirius under the constellation of Orion, the hunter. Sirius points, like a dog, towards an angel prince. The 'dog days' are the unbearably hot part of the year and it is in the hottest fighting you find the champion.

Is this house on Wells Road the home of an ancient Egyptian? Stranger things are found in Glastonbury.

This stone guardian, this Egyptian in an English garden, was the public face of the last home of Anthony Roberts, the editor and compiler of this anthology. It is appropriate to spend time trying to 'read' this peculiarity because Tony was saturated in such matters. If we begin to find some answers, we will enjoy this book much better.

Tony was greatly concerned with the idea of guardians. In Arthurian myth Glastonbury is the sacred home of a guardian. It is the realm of the mystical Fisher King, a wounded giant who - as the guardian of the greatest secret - acts as a kind of messiah. There is a selfless quality about his suffering which reminds us of Christ himself. His illness affects the land, which lies under a sympathetic sickness or spell. Since the Grail was in his keeping the universe can only be saved with his help. If this Arthurian figure of a guardian has Christian associations then what of Anubis? The garden-centre sold the figure as 'Egyptian hound'. But from the brief exposition above you see there is a huge importance in the duties of this hound. It performs the final judgement. It guards the entrance to the after-life, in heaven or hell. It is a great power with its own star and rules a season. These are attributes which Christianity gives to the archangel Michael. Over the chief court of our land 'flies' a golden angel, Justice, who is blind-folded. In one hand she holds scales, in the other an avenging sword. Here is the secular guardian.

Already we have traced a path through a multi-dimensional maze: Egypt, stars, angels, sympathetic illness, messiahs, secrets, Arthur and the Holy Grail. They all cross-relate and shape-shift: myth into Christian doctrine and out again as magic. How to see correspondences was considered the highest talent by Aristotle. All revolving around Glastonbury.

It is the sort of puzzle Tony loved. Especially when related to Glastonbury. He loved this place fervently since he believed, literally, that it was the centre, the omphalos, not just of myth or of his life but also of the fate of the universe. He believed that what happened here would determine the fate of mankind. So these characters and events were not only relevant on an abstract level. They inhabited the real world in the same way that the strange and supernatural sub-plot engulfs stories such as the trilogy by C.S. Lewis. In the final book, *That Hideous Strength*, the forces of evil have designs on the sacred wood in which a well and Merlin hide. The climax is consciously apocalyptic.

The daily world in which Tony lived in Glastonbury had similar qualities. It was not imaginary. The archangel Michael fought and slew the dragon - Satan. This evil angelic prince aimed to destroy the universe by imprisoning everything in matter, or - to use modern terms - to make materialism truimph. Earthly utopias would be eternal and therefore hells on earth.

Here we see how Tony moved into a sort of super-politics, or, if you like, supernatural politics or a political supernatural. He had been a fighter in the political sphere all his life but by the late 1960s he began to move beyond. But a warning is needed. It would be quite wrong to suggest that Tony 'progressed' from hard line activism to transcendent mysticism. That would be a linear distortion of all options! Nor was there some kind of warring co-existence. Rather there were no stages and no categories. No diagrams.

Tony was a passionate person. In his personal life he was notorious for his rhadomontades. His feeling and knowledge were legendary. They would surge out together in great waves to drown pubfuls of people until the door shut. But he never spoke from a platform, laying down dogma. He loved to argue face to face. It was this powerful presence which first attracted his wife to him and it proved their trial and strength. More than anything it is what she and his friends miss, that great passion which would flare up in rage, laughter or enthusiasm. One thing we were sure of, he would not blow cold. A small echo is in this book. For Glastonbury became the epitome of all Tony cared about. It was the essence of England, or Britain. Hence his political concerns did not die but transformed into something larger. His people and country were wrapped up in this small Somerset town and its surrounding mysteries. Here the word could be made flesh, here Tony could make 'portions of eternity' and walk among the pleasant hills where once walked Christ Himself.

But the more Tony tried to popularise Glastonbury the more he was repelled by the results. Instead of a place filled with transcendent beings the area was covered by a swarm of loathsome monsters! 'In the general mêlée of paranoia, euphoria, schizophrenia, messianic complexes and cheap, rip-off predatoriness, one begins to get the impression that something has gone very wrong with the 'dawning of the Age of Aquarius', ' Tony warned in his characteristically resounding, no-holds-barred way as long ago as June 1972. You can see his old politics peeping through when he condemned the 'hippy hierophants' for 'spiritual slumming'. The social divides in English society were reproduced by the new liars coming to Glastonbury. Also he objected to the setting up of authoritarian structures, 'a new hierarchy' peddling the same old 'fake spirituality and pretentious mumbo-jumbo'. For Tony could see through all the glib enthusiasm. He sternly warned that it was not the stirrings of a New Age but the 'last threshings of the current Age of Despair and Greed'. If the portrait Tony painted of the New Age gypsies enraging the locals rings true after 20 years, what can we say of his label for Thatcher's era - 'Greed and Despair'? But his purpose was not negative. He wanted to clear out the rot to allow the new shoots room to grow. He saw a 'unique opportunity to prevent disaster, not only to the people but to the place'. He saw the clowns as 'puppets of psychic forces', an idea he would elaborate in *The Dark Gods* in 1985. He quoted Blake - 'Awake! There are hirelings in the camp'.

These quotes from two of Tony's *Arcana* articles show how he was thinking about Glastonbury. At the time of writing he had been visiting for 9 years. The seed sown in *Arcana* germinated. Tony stuck out his neck against the new orthodoxy and earned new enemies. Twenty years later the accuracy of his warnings is self-evident, although his reputation is still vilified by those who he showed up as the despoilers of Glastonbury. Almost by default Tony had been made into a guardian himself. Which brings us to this book. The fights which his *Arcana* articles began would simmer on for years, indeed they still continue. But Tony wanted to show why he accused people of misconstruing Glastonbury.

Tony could not bear to see the eternal dream betrayed, packaged, monopolised and sold. 'Glastonbury' was meaningless if it could not generate better humans living better lives. This harmonious way of life must be available to everybody. Not the chosen few. So at one end of the argument Tony fought against snobbery and at the other he railed against those who sold the parody to the masses. He had only rage for the traders in ecstasies, the modern pardoners and relic peddlers. He was a protestant against the new Church. A true-born Englishman, he could never accept man-made authority.

I suggest this was the inspiration for this book, to provide the antidote. It peformed an act of spiritual cleansing. It was to show the true, canonical tradition of Glastonbury, the Glastonbury to which Tony belonged and in which he lived and died.

Therefore this book is another guardian. Nobody knew better than Tony the consequences of the role in which he was being cast. He knew the company he kept on both sides and he was as aware of the dangers as he was of the blessings. Some of the latter are seen in this book while the former are more visible in *The Dark Gods*. Tony lived surrounded by good and evil, just like Glastonbury. Even Anubis has undesirable neighbours.

This anthology was welcomed when it appeared. It was a trailblazer. The only predecessor had been a large booklet by the Research Into Lost Knowledge Organisation (RILKO), *Glastonbury, A Study in Patterns*, which was different in two major ways. It contained none of the syncretic myth in which Tony was steeped from Lovecraft, Lewis, Blake and Tolkien. Secondly, Tony's anthology was full of the most unlikely authors. Here were no stars like Keith Critchlow but housewives, a marine biologist, an art teacher, a US ballistics expert, a librarian, a bookseller, and a secretary from a firm making computers. They were disparate and expected no reward. They were taking on current monolithic orthodoxy, and, as we see now, the new orthodoxy which would replace it and be every bit as dogmatic. Tony was only too familiar with the way revolutionaries who came to power turned into worse tyrants.

No reward? How ironic this sounds 15 years later. The mysticism industry is now a major earner. 'New Age' has proved to be a marketing device which spans entire networks, particularly in America. Over there and now starting in Britain the consumers have choice between centres, foundations and belief systems. Check any of the glossy magazines, overflowing with adverts. Everything is now organised, highly businesslike and commercial. Is it any surprise that the fundamentalist Christian networks look askance? They see not only a rival in doctrine but also in business. In such an atmosphere what reason is there for denying proper acknowledgement to one of the founders of earth mysteries? Now that the man can no longer receive his due in person perhaps his work will be accorded a proper place. Let us hope the re-publication of this book marks the beginning.

For the rest of his life Tony continued to 'guard' Glastonbury. Neither side quietened down. The day before he died he finished an article on Glastonbury (see 'Glimpses of Eternity', page 18) about which he was very excited. As he wrote it he felt as invigorated as in the old days. His spirits revived completely, as usual he went from the dumps to the peaks. He was full of anticipation both for the changes in the world and his own life.

Neither side stopped. As I write, sitting in his chair and wearing his hat, this weekend has been yet another turning point for Glastonbury. A cluster of events have filled the place. But it is a rare moment when Glastonbury is quiet. For the seekers there has been a 'Cornference' - two days of talks about crop circles in which theories have been aired about this latest manifestation of the inexplicable. But there was something for the natives too, the Tor fair. The social split is today visible in the High Street. It is a strange contrast, a traditional small provincial town with shops selling things needed for everyday living - fruit, veg, provisions, mops - coexists with an international 'Disneyland'. Close enough to the Abbey entrance to fit into the stop-over time for the coachloads are alleys turned into 'The Glastonbury Experience' full of fortune-tellers and sillier. Commerce takes in the Christian and non-Christian in half an hour. Which is the most superficial? Shops have windows packed with books on related topics. How hard it is to believe that this anthology was made by two people in their front room in Fulham. The 'subject' is now bathed in stars. Gothic Image's windows promote no less than three new books launched this weekend!

Now there is such a quantity of works about Glastonbury why re-issue this trailblazer?

Because of its period charm? Haven't all the books on Glastonbury solved its mysteries yet? Or is it revisionism?

As we enter the 1990s the spirit of those pioneering days gets farther away not least because there is a vested interest to deny it. But a few of us remember and guard the memory while the inspiration burns as fiercely. In *Storming Heaven*, a history of the LSD 25 phenomenon, we are shown how another spirit, or acid, has become an antique. By the mid 1980s amazing experiments were taking place in creating or 'designing' mind drugs. Are there new generations of magic triggers, psychedelics? Indeed the term psychedelic is scorned in favour of new concepts in 'chemical consciouness engineering'. But when the dust cleared did the scientists learn anything about 'chemical consciousness engineering'? No, because the work of the real researchers was denounced as bad science and the dedicated workers vilified as charlatans. To quote *Storming Heaven*, 'a curious, almost Kafkaesque situation arose whereby those who knew the most about psychedelics were relegated to the side lines of the debate, while those who know the least were elevated to the status of 'expert'. And what followed was truly bad science, with politics and the laboratory reinforcing the worst sides of each.'

In February 1990 the synthesis of all Tony's explorations of Glastonbury, literally and metaphysically, was about to be put into his hands. John Michell, Tony's inspiration and friend, had been commissioned to write his book about Glastonbury. For Tony this was a fusing of all the parts, especially when John acknowledged Tony, as friend and Glastonbury scholar, by asking him to edit the text. Here was the ultimate acknowledgement of Tony's role not only as a scholar on Glastonbury but as a worker in the Michellean sphere.

It was a special moment. Globally the times were at a millennial turning point as the tyrannies of eastern Europe vanished cataclysmically. We discussed the murder of Ceausescu in December 1989 and were glad to see bloodshed. We looked forward to more – which has come in Yugoslavia. The heavens too were in transformation and a spectacular show was predicted for the weekend of 10 February. Where better to obseve than from the top of the Tor? (Tony had a hope that his 'trinity' would come together for the 'big one' at the turn of the century at an even more propitious site.) He had John in town, with the text which they would discuss next day, John's birthday. All portents were in conjunction. That evening they all came together for a roaring session which Tony said was the best ever. In the morning Tony made arrangements for the copying of his latest and thrilling article on Glastonbury. In the afternoon he took his younger son Michael up the Tor to watch the celestial sights. On the slopes he had a sudden massive heart attack and died instantly.

A giant megalith of Scottish granite stands at the edge of the cemetery, itself on the edge of the town. Again outsiders have placed Tony in the position of Guardian of the Threshold!

Some places or events transcend ordinary considerations. For Tony and many others Glastonbury is such a place. The spirit of the place changes people just as they can be changed by transcendent experiences such as shock, drugs or contact with an alien. These effects are outside human control. John Michell's book on Glastonbury emphasises that Glastonbury's spell is impossible to measure but it cannot be denied: 'the special character of Glastonbury is decreed directly by Nature'. He explains it affects visitors who recognise instantly 'the mystical quality of light over Glastonbury's landscape'. So the forces which change people are off the register of human measurement - they can only be experienced. How Tony would have loved this sly, wry dismissal of the entire basis of the scientific approach!

Can we say the same of certain people? We cannot deny they emanate. We call leaders 'charismatic' and we describe actors as having 'presence'. But what of the next step? We have plenty of recorded cases of people who exhibit even more extraordinary, non-human, physical behaviour. The most striking are those who fly, shine, burn, make their surroundings smell sweetly, see the innermost thoughts of strangers or simply are in more than one place at the same time. Occasionally we find a conjunction of place and person, maybe only because the one has affected the other.

Has Glastonbury been worn out by all these peak experiences? Has John Michell's book made Tony's redundant? We can answer that quickly. John never imagined that his book would appear *after* Tony's death. On the contrary, both looked forward to *both* their books working together for Glastonbury, just as they themselves had done for so long. Ironically John's book, like Tony's death, makes this anthology even more essential. We have extra reason for seeing what a turning point it marked. Zodiac House's edition was published 16 years before John's book. It was not commissioned and had no guarantee of success. Everything about it was both a risk and a labour of love. All the work was done in-house - literally. The determination and effort needed to assemble all these articles and illustrations, to type and design them, to arrange everything - we are close to a hymn.

John Michell offers another special quality of Glastonbury: 'Glastonbury has the power to attract and generate legends'. We could not have better proof of this claim than the emerging legend of Tony Roberts!

Although his reputation has begun to be re-evaluated in the 18 months since his death, Tony as a person remains the symbol of everything the liberals hate. Yet again Tony's guardian role is confirmed by paradox. The Michell book on Glastonbury appeared to a chorus of meanness and sniping which would never have got past the Guardian of Michell. The irony is the attack was blamed on Tony. John dedicated his book to his recently dead friend. That was too much for one feminist who considered any recognition of 'a man who ought to have died sooner' dragged down Michell and the book.

Perhaps we should remember that a Church Council held in the sixth century at Macon spent two days discussing whether a woman is a human being. In a universe populated by infinite hierarchies of angels and demons we may wonder at the minority interest of mankind.

But there are phenomena outside human control. The supreme irony is Tony is back in Glastonbury – among the women. Has he returned, Arthur-like?

A place like Glastonbury will obviously have no difficulty in accepting life after death. It accepts enough mystical and inexplicable phenomena. Tony was as convinced of the latter as he was sceptical of the former. No souped-up spiritualism for him!

If there are sites where Natural Law is broken surely Glastonbury is a primary target? Isn't the entire Glastonbury mythos based on the notion of another world, a world of death? Legends tell of fairy caverns (in Christianity, an infernal kingdom) which exist inside the earth. As we know the Tor itself is a huge artificial earthwork, it is easy to link both strands and postulate here is the glass mountain which guards the entrance to the underworld. There are many accounts of humans being taken prisoner and held in this nether region. Indeed Tony's stunt for 1990 was to mark one such famous alien abduction with a celebration - maybe even to spring the prisoner! Instead, as John Michell coughs, 'he goes inside himself!'

If Tony was level-headed and humorous in such matters even more so his widow, Janet. Therefore in the days and weeks following Tony's death she developed routine responses to devotees who persisted in telling her of their Tony sightings. He was on top of the Tor bellowing, Pavarotti style, *Jerusalem* (what else!). Or she would be with company in a pub when informed, 'He's with you now!'. 'Clear off Tony, I'm talking,' would be her response. All the more interesting therefore when Jan began to notice a qualitative difference. People she hardly knew, and who had never met Tony, people not known for any mystical inclination or need to curry favour, told her Tony was haunting their dreams.

'The dreams always began in the same way. It was hot, a very intense mid-summer heat, and I was walking down a country lane. I was not alone, I was with a person I knew to be Tony, even though this person had no physical form. He was in a very agitated state of mind. very angry with someone or something, though not with me. This anger rumbled away as we walked but occasionally it would explode with a volcanic intensity that terrified me.' People who knew Tony could confirm that the dreamer was right, but his anger was not personal and she need not have felt afraid.

In one dream Tony insisted the dreamer deliver a message: 'Tell Jannie to remember the dog'. Jan tells me Tony's private name for her was Jannie but who or what is the dog? The same person recounts another dream. 'Once he was half shouting at, half apologising to someone called May, whom he called an "old hag".' Jan agrees that this sums up his relationship with his mother, Mabel.

In a dream in January 1991, on the eve of fighting in the Gulf War, the dreamer was climbing the Tor. 'But it was different. Its sides were steeper, it had more of a pyramid shape, and its terraces were more sharply defined and less weathered than they are today.' On top was no Christian tower but a megalith and Tony. Again he had no physical form but was present as a huge and boundless spirit, full of energy and passion and anger, at the world and people who had ignored his warnings. 'We gave him no choice.' Tony struck the monolith which 'splintered into millions of fragments, and the whole Tor began to shake as though in an earthquake, as the hillside split open.

'An intensely white light poured out of the Tor and out of the light came a pack of huge white dogs. The dogs poured down the hillside and into Glastonbury where they began to devour its inhabitants. They attacked shoppers and tourists, they broke through shop windows and dragged people out of cars.' Tony watched 'quite calmly'. He told the dreamer it was impossible to stop - 'the forces of hate had already been unleashed'. She asked how she could 'escape'. He replied there was only one way and suggested she follow him. 'With that he turned and walked towards the light and into the Tor.' However she could not desert her children so she remained outside. She was in the world of the war which began in earnest next morning.

Another dreamer experienced Tony in the same role. 'At the bottom of Glastonbury High Street, by the Cross, people were digging a huge pool because John the Baptist was coming to town. Tony was exhorting people to leap off the edge. As there was no water this provoked terror. Tony was shouting that evil people needed redemption. There were screams as people jumped but they were unharmed.' Again Tony is cast as the stern messenger who sets a test worthy of The Final Judgement.

A third dreamer testifies that she was on her way from her children's school when Tony drew up beside her in a car. She recognised him, he was even wearing his familiar baseball cap. He was shouting, raging, in a fury, 'Get in! We've got to get to the Tor! They're after the Tor! We've got to save it!' She got in the back seat and they zoomed off. Suddenly it occured to her that Tony was dead so she asked the driver, 'Who are you?' Tony turned and it was not just Tony. She was struck by a pair of 'Blake-like eyes', radiating light and energy. 'You know who I am!' They continued speeding and she woke up.

Jan was also passed messages by an elderly friend of theirs who received visits from Tony. Tony was glad she recognised him. There was talk of guarding her and 'remember the dog'. The next night this woman died.

It may be relevant to record an inexplicable event on the Tor from the early 1970s. Tony and Jan were with Gino and his wife and daughter. Tony and Gino were fooling elsewhere in the mist and cold, playing hide and seek. The daughter went off home. The wives, neither of whom shared their husbands mystical enthusiasms, suddenly saw a big silver flash come out of the side of the Tor. 'There was an explosion of light then a ball of light. It went out and left a column of smoke.'

So here is the latest on Glastonbury and Tony Roberts: the Tor, a sense of cosmic urgency, warnings, tests - and 'remember the dog'. The hounds of hell who devour the unredeemed or Cerberus who guards the entrance to the underworld?

Even putting aside any other beliefs Christian doctrine has a well-developed topography of post-death worlds. The bourn from which no travellers return - Hamlet knew that was wrong which is why he was bothered. Christ came back after harrowing hell and destroyed the prisons. This is the promise of salvation on the last day.

But we have started enough hares. Readers of this book will soon appreciate why Tony Roberts is still a presence in his beloved Glastonbury.

Gentle reader, you are about to enter Glastonbury and its mysteries through the mind, soul and experience of Tony Roberts. This foreword has served as the guardian at the threshold, showing why this is an appropriate entrance. While he lived Tony believed himself a part of this ancient riddle. In death he has become inseparable. He is now and forever a piece of 'this holyest erthe'.

Glimpses of Eternity

A Visionary Voyage into the Glastonbury Zodiac

PRELUDE

The holy ground of Glastonbury holds many strange secrets. They are heavily festooned in the rich (often gaudy) accoutrements of myth and magic, but they all resolve themselves around a uniformly synergic nexus. This is that the Glastonbury terrain, with its physical and meta-physical alchemies, is a vast orrery and teaching environment for revealing (and enhancing) all that is spiritual in the nature of mankind. This blending of the physically symbolic with the symbolically physical this writer has termed the art of geomythics. In the powerfully weird environs of Glastonbury, geomythics forms an excellent decoder to the revealed mysteries of time and space.

The energies of Glastonbury's living landscape resurfaced on a grand scale at the beginning of the twentieth century. This is no accident. The twentieth century is a make or break time for humanity. As we now approach the imminent milennium, all the seeds of a New Age are burgeoning in the troubled yet still fertile soil of Gaia. A new synthesis of man, planet and cosmos is forming, and psychic power centres like Glastonbury are where this geomythical synthesis (synergy) is made magnificently manifest. To live in resolvent harmony with these alchemically solvent mysteries of the cosmos is the destiny and duty of the human species. At Glastonbury, the Ancient Avalon, all this is made perfectly clear to those who can eschew ratiocination and think with a loving heart.

One of the supreme mysteries of Glastonbury is its miasmic association with the Holy Grail. This numinous object, which is sometimes physical (in many forms) and sometimes meta-physical (in various ontological patterns), is said to be resonant in the Glastonbury/ Avalonian area. Indeed it is in ways that few are aware of, yet always in a strictly catalytic, geomythical context. In all myth, achievement of the Grail is said to afford glimpses of Eternity. This must mean a reconciliation between matter and energy, physical and metaphysical, destiny and fate, the sacred and profane, etc. etc. To do this it is necessary to perceive a rounded wholeness, a sense of universal vision. It must be noted that in all Grail legends the seekers traverse a magical terrain, a mythical landscape. They in fact quest through this landscape to achieve their Grail vision. It is this writer's contention

that at Glastonbury the Holy Grail manifests itself both microcosmically and macrocosmi-
cally - at the same time. It is postulated that the macrocosmic Grail is in fact the
geomantically far-famed Glastonbury Zodiac! Why? Because the Zodiac, in its incarnation
as an earthly manifestation of cosmic energies related through semiotic imagery, makes
a perfect geomythical symbol. It is a symbol of the unity and purpose inherent in canonical
Existence. Therefore the Glastonbury Zodiac needs careful attention. Alas, it has had little
of this synergic attention from the very people who profess spiritual and intellectual
awareness, and who live on it (and around it), and so this writing is now necessary to
clarify the situation somewhat.

First, reality is not what it was, as any contemporary particle physicist will quantify.
In Quantum Physics all is participatory, all is flux and all is cyclically connected. So the
great truths of mystical tradition are perennially renewed in fleeting terminologies,
today's 'science' being more fleeting than most scientists dream. Reality, which is the
full recognisance of Being, is a holistic construct synergistically fusing out of all the varied
constituents of Divine existence. Reality is not concrete, but cyclic and fluxous as the
alchemists were/are fully aware. The Holy Grail is the Sacred Centre: the generative flux
of the matrix of reality. It's what William Blake called 'The Starry Pole'. It is God's
kaleidoscope of dreams spinning in Eternity, threading inside and outside Time. The Grail
is the beckoning beacon of Spirit. It appears in times of need and crisis, holding up the
dimensions of Paradise as an ideal vision of structured, creational harmony. It fertilizes
and fuels the soul. It is a glimpse into the immortal heart of God.

All these functions are equally attributed to the Glastonbury Zodiac.

The astrological, psychological and spiritual lore encoded into the huge, shaped effigies
on the Glastonbury landscape are geomythical wisdom made gloriously extant. The
foolish contention that the Zodiacal figures are 'not really there' and are in fact a
ludicrously overblown Rorschach phenomenon shows a lack of wisdom, not to say
psychic acumen, that is truly staggering! Those who merely study maps and pronounce
the effigies as undecipherable should remember that they are looking at a landscape that
has been systematically violated over the last few hundred years. It's rather like someone
painting a 'page three' girl over the Mona Lisa! Thousands of years ago the Zodiacal
figures would have been much more 'physically pronounced' because the world was a
fairer, cleaner, purer place. Anyway, the Glastonbury Zodiac is a 'living' manifestation
of Gaian consciousness, and so is a subtle extrusion of telluric currents and earth-moulding
movements of a spiritual nature that is naturally geomantic in purpose and application. It
must be emphasised here that the Zodiac is a natural magical instrument: it is not and
never has been static. Humans have adapted and changed it, but they did not literally
create it. Life reigns universally and more than just homo sapiens are sapient!

Recent research into the more scientifically abstruse aspects of geomancy, now
somewhat prosaically termed 'earth mysteries', has revealed much about the strange
energies, properties and psychic realities that are keyed into the 'living' fabric of the earth.
Geological, geophysical and extra-terrestial interactions between earth and cosmos,
ranging far beyond the infra-red and electromagnetic, have revealed themselves in no
uncertain terms. Of course this has always been known (and encoded) in the Ancient
Wisdom. It was probably drawn from the Akashic Record, now known euphemistically as

the 'morphogenetic field'. It has always echoed through myth and folklore like the fairy notes of a long-lost but endlessly strong cosmic symphony. Some see astrology as a form of cosmic symphony, and that brings us back to the meaning and relevance of the Glastonbury Zodiac, the truly Avalonian Holy Grail.

As stated above, this meaning is totally linked to the spiritual destiny of the human race which has now reached 'critical mass'. By blending human consciousness through the magical geomancy of the Zodiac, neuronic links with the living planet can be achieved. Spirituality then bubbles up out of the human soul like crystal-clear water from a sacred spring. This analogy is deliberate and apt. Drinking the realised starry wisdom of the Glastonbury Zodiac is envigorating and enlightening. It produces a fully-harmonised transcendence, a real cosmic consciousness. In fact a genuine holistic awareness flows that gives beatific vision. But before this 'Grail' can be achieved, before wisdom can be distilled, a fructifying knowledge must be obtained. The latter half of this writing will now be devoted to briefly outlining crucial aspects of this knowledge. We will examine the physical Zodiac itself, investigate some corroberations of its existence, and then have a final look at the overall, star-filled vista of future hope.

THE ZODIAC

This vast earthly planisphere, as it is usually professed, is 30 miles in circumference (radius 10 miles) and contains constellation signs that cover the full Zodiacal range of star figures. Hills, land contours, streams, rivers and a myriad natural and man-made features form general aspects of signs of the Zodiac. No hill is more than 300 feet, and many effigies have folkloric connotations that tie in with the geomantic and astrological ambiences. This writer has discoursed at length upon the Glastonbury Zodiac for some decades, both verbally and in his books. It seems relevant to quote an apt Zodiacal passage from what many consider a work containing some shreds of geomantic wisdom. This Roberts précis of the Zodiac at least has the virtue of being reasonably succint. It comes from the book *Sowers of Thunder* (Rider & Co. 1978), a now hidden work of geomantic explicitness:

The Glastonbury Giants were rediscovered in the 1920s by the intuitive mental divinations of Mrs Katherine Maltwood, a sculptress and student of the inner Arthurian mysteries. She was investigating the intricacies of the "Perlesvaus", a medieval French Arthurian romance found in manuscript form at the Abbey and just translated into English by Dr Sebastian Evans. The setting of the "Perlesvaus" tale (in Celtic myth, "Peredur") was a symbolic landscape finally identified with the terrain of the Glastonbury region. This area of Somerset is almost unbelievably rich in ancient tradition (much of it giant-lore), and the countryside in which Perlesvaus enacts his symbolic saga conforms to the Vale of Avalon perfectly. Mrs Maltwood came to understand that the long, ritual journey of the Arthurian hero was associated with the immemorially old cycle of the Grail myth, another Christianization of pagan fertility lore and intricate initiation ceremonies. As she studied the larger Ordnance Survey maps of the area around Glastonbury's sacred pyramidal hill, the Tor, she began to see the shapes of astrological signs drawn on the surface of the earth with an uncanny precision.

First to be uncovered was the sign for Leo the Lion, its underbelly and legs drawn by the meandering river Cary between the village of Charlton Mackrell and the town of Somerton. The contours of head, mane, back and tail were defined by old roads, footpaths and low hills, the whole figure being absolutely unmistakable when seen from the air. Next to be shown was the Gemini form, here carved as a sleeping giant (Orion) and fashioned from the isolated twin hills called Dundon and Lollover. Gradually Mrs Maltwood's maps revealed more effigies, all in their correct astrological order, with the winter signs located to the north, the summer ones to the south. Eight of them are proportionally similar, being 6,000 yards in breadth, and are made up from geomantically adapted natural land contours, enhanced by earthworks, mounds, ancient tracks, watercourses and roads. It has been proven statistically that these figures could not exist by chance alone. Mrs Maltwood produced a number of books on her "giants" (including a full aerial survey) and she wrote in one of them:

> It has been computed that the chance of such a pattern being found on the ground to harmonize with the sky so closely is the order of 149,000,000 to 1 against. It must also be pointed out that both patterns correspond as to their north and south points; the signs of long ascension are also correctly larger for the most part than those of short ascension in the northern hemisphere.

The three human figures in this zodiac - Sagittarius (the Sun God), Virgo (the Earth Mother), and Gemini (the Divine Son/s) - form an equilateral triangle. Moreover the astronomical geometry, composed of solstice and equinox lines, is exactly as it should be in a technical planisphere of this nature. By scaling down the heavenly star constellations onto her maps, Mrs Maltwood found that the correct stars were located above the corresponding earthen effigies. This was the final confirmation of her discovery.

Mrs Maltwood dated the Zodiac to the Taurean astrological age of 2,700 BC. She found certain geometries and precise astrological alignments connected to the Taurus effigy whose head lies heavy on a tree-clad ridge consisting of Collard Hill and Windmill Hill (both 300 ft.). At that time the geomantic culture in Britain was highly advanced, constructing huge earthworks and many landscape patterns etched in stone. It appears that much work was done on the Zodiac during this period (a mini Golden Age), but of course the Glastonbury Zodiac as such did not leap from the earth in 2,700 BC. Many researchers taste an Atlantean flavour in the sweet airs of prehistoric Glastonbury, the famous Tor (Aquarius) being divined as a sculpted Atlantean Lion in its initial shaping. But we digress.

The Zodiac is a resolution of the manifested Gaian consciousness interacting with the flowing energies of the outer cosmos. This is the underlying rationale of the whole geomantic schema and is, incidentally, the basis for all that strange gnosis termed the Ancient Wisdom. The Glastonbury Zodiac is the Ancient Wisdom written in those four basic, magically alchemical elements: earth, air, fire and water. It is an immense ontological alembic, which is why it is analogised here with the morphologically supernatural Holy Grail.

THE INHERITORS

Earth Zodiac awareness has lingered on the fringes of human consciousness (and history) for thousands of years. Sometimes it is subtle, sometimes startlingly overt - but always it is there. Mystics, shamans and like visionaries instinctively respond to it. If we glance back into relatively recent history - a few centuries before Christ - we can begin a quick review of some of the more outward recognisances.

In the writings of the renowned historian Diodorus Siculus, who worked quietly while Julius Caesar was about his noisy conquering, there is found reference to the 'lost' writings of Hecataeus of Abdera. These histories were composed around 400 BC from much earlier writings. Hecataeus writes of a legendary northern island 'beyond the land of the Celts' (meaning Gaul), which can only refer to Albion. He says it is inhabited by the fabled Hyperboreans who worship Apollo (a late definition of the Sun God), and that it contains a wondrous, magical Temple to Apollo that is spherical in shape. Near this 'Temple' is a 'city' populated by musicians. Here is a fairly direct reference to the Zodiac and the

Druid college that flourished around it (there was a large Druid grove just behind the Tor).

In the fifth century AD, a Glastonbury bard, one Melkin (who was probably a Culdee, that is a Druido/Christian) made a prophecy that encapsulated much Avalonian lore. It was of course disguised in poetic terminology. In the poem, Melkin talks of local 'chanting spheres of prophecy' and there are other pointers to stars and Zodiacal reference. A little later, the illustrious St. Augustine (as given in Bede) discusses 'an ancient Church built by the hands of God himself that was in a certain royal island surrounded by water'. This Church/Zodiac was situated in the far west of Britain, and the royal island must be Glastonbury, its Tor-dominated mystical enclave then surrounded by brackish lagoons.

In the tenth century, St. Dunstan, who was originally an astrologer, alchemist and magician, inaugurated great earthworks and geomantic restructuring of the Glastonbury landscape. His earthworks helped to re-define some of the Zodiacal effigies, giving them more clarity and permanence. This psychic saint was fully aware of what he was guarding. Dunstan used a Griffin as his emblem, and a Griffin effigy exists in the Zodiac. The Griffin guards magical treasure always in an astronomical context.

In the sixteenth century two explicit references surface. One is from the prophet and alchemist Nostradamus, the other from the magician, scientist and alchemist Dr John Dee. Both were men of respected magical renown.

Much has been made of the validity (or otherwise) of Nostradamus' prophesies, but when all the controversy is stripped away it is obvious this wise man achieved genuinely-confirmed accuracy in some of his visions. His famous quatrains predict much, and in Book VI No 22 the following is uttered:

In the land of the great heavenly temple a nephew at London is murdered through a false peace.

The interpretation is interesting – and ironic. It was discovered (and interpreted) by the great Zodiac sceptic, in fact debunker, Geoffrey Ashe. Ashe is an Arthurian scholar who, naturally, lives and works in Glastonbury. He has recognised that the Zodiac might have a 'psychological' value, but little else. So much for his psychic acumen and intuition. However he has found the Nostradamus quatrain, no doubt helped in this by the very 'Gaian magic' he decries. His reading of the quatrain in fact validates the Zodiac. Let us now address ourselves to it.

By mentioning London, Nostradamus shows that the 'heavenly temple' must be in England. In the sixteenth century Stonehenge was neglected to a point of almost total obscurity and its astronomical implications completely eclipsed. It was thought to be a monument to Dark Age kings. No, the prophet means a Temple of the Stars, the Zodiac. The second half of the quatrain refers to the rebellion of the Duke of Monmouth against James II. James was Monmouth's uncle and he had him executed after the failed rising of 1685. The 'false peace' was the aftermath to this tragedy which was so cruelly enforced that James was bloodily dethroned a few years later. Incidentally, Monmouth and his army camped in Glastonbury Abbey on their way to Nemesis at Sedgemoor. Strange synchronicities here, but total vindication for Nostradamus and the Zodiac.

Dr John Dee was a court astrologer (and intelligence agent) for Queen Elizabeth I, but he was also a consummate scientist, mathematician, alchemist and wizard. He came to Glastonbury, staying at the ancient Sharpham Manor once owned by the Abbot, and there found books salvaged from the Abbey's recent ruin. Some of these now lost books must have discussed the Glastonbury Zodiac, because on the margins of a map Dee made of the area's sacred geometry, those Zodiacal lines were written:

. . . the starres which agree with their reproductions on the ground do lye onlie on the celestial path of the Soone, moon and planets, with the notable exception of Orion and Hercules . . . all the greater starres of Sagittaruius fall in the hind quarters of the horse, while Altair, Tarazed and Alschain from Aquilla do fall on its cheste . . . thus is astrologie carefully and exactly married and measured in a scientific reconstruction of the heavens which shews that the ancients understode all which today the learned know to be factes.

This is categoric recognition and the research for this was carried out by Richard Deacon, himself an expert in 'intelligence' studies under the name of Donald McCormick. In his biography of Dr Dee, Deacon quotes the above passage and mentions the map. This map now resides in the warily-guarded files of the Warburg Institute in their London library. The Warburgs have also had a long Glastonbury connection; two of them dying within sight of the Tor in recent years.

So the Zodiacal references slowly accrue. William Blake makes much of earth zodiac symbolism, 'Starry Wheels' etc., in the eighteenth century, and he was fully cognisant with Glastonbury's sanctity, weaving it into his great poem about Jesus' visit. Moving closer to our ruined age, we find the awakening quickening in pace and understanding. The occultist Madame Helena Blavatsky refers to four earth zodiacs in her writings; and the enchantress Dion Fortune, who lived and died at Glastonbury, states in her Avalonian testament *Avalon of the Heart* this great truth:

Do not let it be forgotten that there is a native Mystery Tradition of our race which has its nature aspect in the Sun-worship of the Druids and the beautiful fairy-lore of the Celts, its philosophical aspect in the traditions of alchemy, and its spiritual aspect in the Hidden Church of the Holy Graal, the Church behind the Church, not made with hands, eternal in the heavens.

Surely the last lines of this quote refer obliquely to the Glastonbury Zodiac?

We have seen how the true-minted Zodiac renaissance came with the inspired work of sculptress Katherine Maltwood in the early twenties. Since then this work has been refined and expanded by such brilliantly intuitive researchers as Mary Caine and Elizabeth Leader of the Research into Lost Knowledge Organisation (RILKO). In the early seventies an American professor, Dr Oliver Reiser, wrote an epic poem on the Zodiac entitled *This Holyest Erthe*. It gave much scientific validation to Zodiacal research and, strangely, prefigured the later studies of Lovelock, Sheldrake and Devereux in its examination of the 'living earth' hypothesis, morphogenetic fields and spheres of psychic energy which Reiser called 'the world sensorium'.

The current writer has expounded at length upon the Glastonbury Zodiac in three books and numerous articles since 1971. This has always been done in a magico/mystical context where, as this writing has hopefully shown, the insights can be more meaningful and enlightening.

CODA

The whole Zodiac concept is that it exists in nature, is recognised by man and is used to enhance spiritual growth. This is also the nature of the Grail. The Grail is noted in the old pagan mythos as an endlessly regenerating Cauldron of Wisdom. What is the Glastonbury Zodiac if it is not a cauldron of wisdom? Circular, glowing with life, all encompassing, richly symbolic yet physically manifest, the epithets fit the defined geomantic pattern. Here the 'starry wisdom' is arranged upon the ground for human edification. The Wheel of Heaven turns eternally upon the benignant face of the living earth.

But there is more. In the Inheritors section it was shown how the Greek historian Hecataeous knew of the Zodiac in 400 BC. Situated within this Zodiac he noted the 'city of musicians' who must have been its initiated guardians. Hecataeous named this remote priesthood as the Borads or Boreadae. The Glastonbury bard Melkin spoke of the "chanting spheres of prophecy" in the recent Dark Ages. The chanting of verses that had great astronomical import was a vital function of bards who sound like direct descendants of the Borads.

If this information is married to John Michell's studies of perpetual choirs, that is 'music' maintaining the balance of being at key sacred sites, mystical clarification ensues. Glastonbury has always been known as one of sacred history's 'perpetual choirs'. As Michell defines it in his book *Dimensions of Paradise*:

Plato was a respecter of tradition, a revivalist rather than an innovator, and the important themes in his writing were drawn from his knowledge of ancient science and sacred institutions of the past. His emphasis on choirs harks back to the days of priestly rule, when the calendar was regulated by the temple authorities and the procession of seasons and cycles was marked by an endless round of chanting and ceremonies. As the times changed so did the music of the temple, reflecting the movements of the planets. Their relative positions at any time determined the prevailing musical mode. At certain intervals, judged significant by the astrologers, when the planets repeated a particular formation, one cycle of temple music would come to an end and another begin. In response to this, subtle changes would become evident in religious symbolism and the forms of society. Thus the fluctuating moods of human nature were each allowed regular expression, in the course of a year and over greater periods of time. The institution of the temple was an attempt to perpetuate those legendary days when government was conducted through the influence of music rather than by means of a rigid code of law.

A relic of those days may be seen in the tradition of the Perpetual Choirs of Britain. In the Welsh Triads, verses which are thought to incorporate elements from ancient bardic lore, the sites of three of the Perpetual Choirs are named as Glastonbury, the Choir of Ambrosius or Stonehenge, and Llan Illtud Fawr which is the old Celtic sanctuary at Llantwit Major in Glamorgan. At each of the Choirs 2400 saints maintained a ceaseless chant, 100 for every hour of the day and night.

Because Glastonbury's 'perpetual choir' was situated within the Zodiac, in fact was the Zodiac, the musical aspect of its guardians is crucial. We have the Druid musicians, the Culdee bard (Culdees were great singers) and St. Dunstan, noted as a consummate musician. The songs of all the earth rang out from the Glastonbury Zodiac in a symphony of life, love and joy.

The 'songs' sung at these holy places of geomantic/celestial communion were magical resonances that channelled human input into Nature's cyclic function. Tuning in to Gaia in modern parlance. The antique 'city of musicians' was certainly of Druidical provenance.

Melkin and his fellow bards and saints 'chanted' their poetry to the spheres and these references span about a thousand years! Eventually the whole of Christian Britain was covered with tiny 'chantries', sponsored by more secular patrons, but all containing their magically-singing priests/prophets.

As all occultists know music/sound is said to be the magical secret that enabled levitation and the geomantic building of all the holy monuments of antiquity such as Zodiacs, the Great Pyramid and Stonehenge. The Christian Bible notes that in the beginning was the word - sound.

The 'music of the spheres' was integral to ancient Greek science and philosophy, which was largely inherited from prehistoric Golden Age sources. The music of the spheres at the 'perpetual choir' within the spherical Glastonbury Zodiac is a potent, magical alchemy unearthed here (or rather clarified here) for the first time in centuries! It helps to enhance the overall picture (or pattern) that makes up the holistic vision motivating human metaphysical impulse. This vision of geomythic interaction crystallizes perfectly within the parameters of Zodiacal recognition.

Because human magical input into the Gaian consciousness has fallen into abeyance, because the 'perpetual choirs' are no longer chanted at the key geomantic sites, our mother earth languishes in sickly somnolence. The Glastonbury Zodiac and the energies it collects, focusses and disperses must be recognised, preserved and re-channelled. The song must be re-awoken, the songlines re-established. The Zodiac and its contemporary 'chanters' are the guardians and enablers of True Spirituality. The 'chanters' are not all human and the Fisher King still lies wounded in Glastonbury town. Therefore disharmony is endemic.

Reconciliation and revitalisation must soon come to the Isle of Avalon if a harmonious New Age is to dawn. This can only happen when the Holy Grail is revealed and the right question asked - or sung. In the form of the Zodiac it is suggested - again - that the Grail is revealed. The human race can no longer afford to beg the question. The answer of course is obvious, but it seems only the non-human guardians are aware of it as they always have been. Listen to the Zodiac, blend in with its alchemies, sing its songs and all will then be REVEALED.

Imbolc 1990

CHAPTER ONE

Glastonbury - The Ancient Avalon
ANTHONY ROBERTS

In the far south-west of the British Isles, situated between the sea of the Bristol Channel and two low ranges of hills called the Mendips and the Poldens, there lies an enchanted area of land. It is an area that generates and guards a powerful magic. The county that contains this land is Somerset and the geographical designation of this sacred place has come to be known as the Isle of Avalon. This romantic and mysterious tract of country has a long historical pedigree, stretching back over countless millennia into eras of strange dreams and endless mystical revelations. Human beings who come to Avalon strong in the disciplines of the Old Knowledge are strangely transformed. They are fused into a form of cosmic consciousness that reflects the patterns of esoteric memory that are shaped into the very landscape itself. The focal point for the area and its arcane forces is Glastonbury, both the name of a town and the symbol of a great and holy mystery. The roots of this mystery have nothing to do with Christianity, which came late to the area, first as an inheritor, then as a usurper, finally as a destroyer. They are found through a synthesis of pagan ritual and natural, magical intuition, and they are so old, deep and strong as to be inviolable to all forms of fleeting desecration.

The key to the secrets of Glastonbury and the whole Avalonian complex lies within the contours of the landscape. Once this is realized the pattern assumes its correct perspective and balances into a satisfying coherence; magic and mysticism form a delicate equilibrial harmony that fluctuates between microcosm and macrocosm. This of course needs some elucidation. As in most tales of esoteric complexity, it is best to begin at the beginning, for the whole panorama is more important and beautiful at its start than in its later misunderstood manifestations.

The aura that surrounds the Isle of Avalon radiates a potent vibration; a vibration first stemming from the personalities and skills of those human beings who came to its environs during the so-called prehistoric days. Millennia before the advent of the Celtic Druids (c. 500 BC) there existed at Glastonbury a race of men who shaped the whole terrain to form certain mystical and astrological patterns. In the mid-1920s these patterns were rediscovered through the single-minded researches of a brilliantly intuitive woman,

Katharine Maltwood. Mrs Maltwood was a student of the Arthurian mysteries and Grail legends (both integrally woven into Glastonbury's later history) and she made her rediscovery while studying large-scale maps of the countryside around Glastonbury Tor. The Tor is a 522-foot-high mound that dominates the town of Glastonbury, which is built upon and around its lower slopes. The hill is strongly pyramidal in shape and has upon its green slopes the remnants of a seven-tiered labyrinth, while its summit is crowned with the ruined tower of a fourteenth century church. The Tor and its attendant companion, Chalice Hill, will be discussed later, but they are relevant here because they make up part of the Aquarian effigy in that stupendous group of prehistoric monuments known as the Glastonbury Zodiac. It was this example of ancient technology and magic that Mrs Maltwood found laid out upon the ground in giant forms, revealed only to those minds fired with the spirit of mystical revelation. She published several books on the subject (including an aerial survey) and the true proportions of this beautiful earth sculpture were made graphically apparent. The Glastonbury Zodiac is one of those great 'hidden works' that lies at the roots of all countries' lore and religion, blending physical and metaphysical into a divine coherence.

The form of this terrestrial zodiac, as Mrs Maltwood (and countless later researchers) have uncovered it, is circular with a circumference of thirty miles. Some of the effigies are two or three miles long (e.g. Leo, Sagittarius and Pisces) and they are all shaped geomantically from natural features of the land. The effigies are delineated by hills, earthworks, mounds, artificial water courses, old roads, footpaths, streams, and rivers. Notwithstanding this, they all tally with the appropriate star constellations that shine in the sky above them. In other words there was an organically real, natural formation of topographical features forming the basic outlines of the astrological signs which were adapted by shaping through geomancy to make the finished effigies realizable. Both mystically and physically the earth was moulded to conform to the harmonies of the terrestrial and celestial energy patterns. The grand design is fully apparent only at heights of 20 000 feet and it is obvious that an elevated form of spiritual technology was used to create it. An aerial perspective would have been essential to the logistics of the scheme. The date of this supreme achievement of antiquity is obscure. Some researchers push it as far back as the Atlantean era (10 000 BC) while others, with reference to such works as the Dendarah Zodiac from Egypt, date it to 7000–8000 BC. Mrs Maltwood suggested 2700 BC as a recognition point. Whatever the date of its initial shaping, the Glastonbury Zodiac set a permanent mystical mark on this area of the British Isles that was the fountainhead for all that followed. The later legends of the Round Table, giants, Arthurian quests for revelation and the secrets of a lost coherence and sanctity, all stem from the memory of this great work carved upon the face of Somerset by men of a forgotten era. They linked earth with heaven in a direct cosmological unity that created the harmony of a now-vanished Golden Age.*

With the permanent sanctity of the Glastonbury area secured by the zodiacal figures, it follows that down through the centuries men would be drawn to its lingering

*Evidence for the above statements cannot be dealt with in detail in this introductory article. Mary Caine and John Michael give more corroboration in their respective essays and the Zodiac crops up as a regular backcloth to many of the other pieces in this book.

Christianity: . . . finally as a destroyer.

atmosphere of magical potency. Sometime around 2000 BC a race of astronomer-priests came to Glastonbury and erected various earthworks and standing stones within the precincts of the Zodiac's hallowed ground. Legend recounts that they constructed some form of stone monument upon the summit of the Tor and that lines of single, free-standing menhirs were laid out on the surrounding slopes of adjacent hills. Recent work by Professor Alexander Thom, the foremost living expert on megalithic geometry, has shown that the men of 2000 BC were capable of creating complex structures in earth and stone that reflected precise mathematical, geometrical, astronomical and astrological knowledge. Professor Thom, a laconic Scotsman who was Professor of Engineering Science at Oxford, has examined the Glastonbury landscape and reached the conclusion that it was laid out to form a lunar observatory where eclipses could be predicted with great accuracy. He has computed that the positions of the stones fixed the declinational and azimuthal passing points of the moon as it rose and set behind the Black Mountains of distant Wales. This exact knowledge shows that the human beings who lived and worked at Glastonbury, at least in 2000 BC, had high cultural standards that must have been inherited from earlier people, handed down as a mystical-scientific system from a time when the two were co-terminous, not hopelessly fragmented as they are today.

Professor Thom's detailed analysis of Glastonbury's megalithic complexities are fascinating. He has produced significant data to the effect that the hills around the Tor were definite sighting points for long range observation into Wales. The moon's inclination of orbit as it passed behind various peaks of the Black Mountains was meticulously noted by the Glastonbury megalithic astronomers. Its major standstill point and even the complex perturbation wobble could all be worked out from stone observatories strategically placed upon the slopes of the Isle of Avalon. Writing in the book *Glastonbury: A Study in Patterns* (RILKO, 1969), Professor Thom states:

On the higher ground in and around Glastonbury the earlier Ordnance Survey showed about 30 'stones' but there is not much at present to show that these were Megalithic. A line of 5 stones is shown passing through the point 51003900 on the National Grid at an azimuth of about 298°. If it can be shown that this line is clear (or rather was clear) locally to the West then with the far horizon altitude of -0°, 2, it shows a declination of +16°·4. We find this declination at many Megalithic sites. It is that of the Sun at May Day and Lammas, two important days in the Megalithic calendar.

Evidence that the orientational line giving a declination of +16°·4 was clear about 2000 BC has recently been forthcoming. Climatologists and botanists studying the ecological conditions of the Bronze Age are now generally agreed that there was less afforestation than was once presumed and the atmosphere was free of all pollution, allowing sharper definition for the human eye.

The sacred connotations of Chalice Hill have always been indicative of hidden or buried treasure, even in their Christian manifestation (Grail or Chalice buried there) and this again is significant. Hidden treasures in or on hills are commonly found in numerous West Country myths. It is possible to interpret some of these myths in an astronomical context, as the work of Kenneth Knight shows,* so it is not improbable that a stone observatory was once situated upon the carefully rounded summit of the Tor's nearest neighbour.

At the foot of Chalice Hill lies the chalebeate spring named by the Christians as Chalice Well, the elaborate cover of which is carved with the major religious symbol of the Vesica Piscis. This curving, fish-like symbol forms the spring-point of religious architecture and it is used in the geometrical construction of all the more significant buildings of antiquity, including major prehistoric monuments like Stonehenge and Avebury. Chalice Well is more than a healing spring, however. Its sides are carefully constructed from great slabs of stone in the non-mortared style of masonry known as cyclopean. The bold megalithic construction of these stones was said by the archaeologist Sir Flinders Petrie to be of ancient Egyptian influence, while most modern researchers date it to at least the Bronze Age (2000 BC). Behind the central shaft, the stones form a perfectly polygonal chamber, and it is thought that ritual and sacrifice were carried out here at the correct seasonal times. Some authorities suspect that a willing victim was placed within the chamber, which was then quickly flooded from the main spring via a sluice. There are precedents for this in various European cultures in the Bronze and Iron Ages. That eminent astro-archaeologist, Sir Norman Lockyer pointed out that Chalice Well has been found (by measurements he carried out on midsummer day) to be

*See Kenneth Knight's two articles in this book.

Chalice Well

Note Vesica Pisces
on the lid's ironwork.

There are two chambers,
the inner one 5-sided.
Guesses at dating
their stonework vary.

It's other name, Blood
Spring, refers to the
legend that Joseph hid
the cup of the Last
Supper there.

It is radio-active, and
its iron content stains
its channel red.

Its flow is an unfailing
25,000 gallons a day.
Miraculous healings have
taken place here.

MARY CAINE

orientated towards the east, i.e. the summer solstice sunrise. This was (and is) a precise time of fervent religious celebration and ritual sacrifice in all lands.

Another ancient geomantic monument that has many odd, mystical connotations is the huge linear earthwork and ditch known as Ponter's Ball. It lies to the south-east of Glastonbury Tor on raised ground between what were once marshes, and it is nearly one mile long running exactly from marsh edge to marsh edge. Ponter's Ball neatly straddles the narrow isthmus of land that links the Isle of Avalon with the main high ground that rises eastward towards Shepton Mallet. The monument is so constructed that it seems to form an outward-facing boundary to the Sacred Isle and this is where its age and purpose become of great interest to the student of Glastonbury lore. There are two interpretations of Ponter's Ball, one strictly orthodox in form, the other of a more speculative nature, but both are highly complementary when they are studied comparatively. Even in the eyes of conventional historians, Ponter's Ball marks the outer boundary limit of a tremendous sacred enclosure. These earthwork enclosures, known as *temenos*, are found on the fringes of all the noteworthy pagan sanctuaries and the fact that the ditch of Ponter's Ball is dug on its eastern side (away from the Tor) enhances the possibility that the ridge was indeed a *temenos* of considerable importance. The earthen bank has spread a good deal over the centuries but is still thirty feet across and twelve feet high in places. The deep eastern ditch is now heavily silted up but its depth must once have been comparable to the mighty trenches that surrounded the stones and mounds of Avebury and Stonehenge. The whole structure could never have been purely defensive, for any reasonably intelligent invading army could have simply outflanked it.

The precise dating of Ponter's Ball is still somewhat ambiguous. That tenacious Somerset archaeologist, Dr Arthur Bulleid, excavated beneath the bank early this century and uncovered Iron Age pottery shards which he dated to about the third century BC. These finds at least secure the reputation of the Glastonbury area as a Celtic Avalon, but do not necessarily mean that the Celts who left their culinary expertise as a calling card actually erected the mound. The ditch also threw up shards of the twelfth and thirteenth centuries AD, but no one suggests the edifice was built by the industrious monks of the then thriving community at Glastonbury Abbey. Because of its size and careful geomantic positioning it is more reasonable to set Ponter's Ball in the Bronze Age or earlier, for adaptation by succeeding cultures is one of the key aspects of understanding the mystique of all the famous ancient sites, particularly the stones and earthworks.

It is this adaptive aspect that brings us to the more speculative answer to the riddle of this old straight embankment. Research into the mysteries of the Glastonbury Zodiac has found that the long, single horn that graces the head of the Capricorn effigy is perfectly delineated by the earthy orientational line of Ponter's Ball. Locally the earthwork has been alternatively termed the 'Golden Coffin', and it is in December (Capricorn's time) that the sun symbolically dies at the winter solstice. The link with the sun is important because Ponter's Ball is thought by some researchers to be a corruption of *Pontes Bel* or *Baal*, meaning the 'bridge of the sun'; *Bel* being a Celtic name for the sun-god and *Baal* being a millennia-earlier term for the perpetually regenerating life force symbolized by the golden sun. If the elongated, grassy embankment was originally the

The advent of the Celtic Druids.

horn of the goat effigy among the Glastonbury Giants, it is obvious that its later adaptation as a Bronze Age or Celtic *temenos* line would be perfectly in keeping with a form of ritually handed-on religious continuity.* The cultural ebb and flow around the Isle of Avalon has been spectacular to say the least, but it begins to appear that however socially diverse the incoming populations might have been, they always inherited the geomantic magic that lay in immortal stasis, graven into the landscape around them.

When the Bronze Age religio-scientific civilization waned, it was gradually replaced by the fiercer social patterns of the Iron Age (800 BC). With the mass arrival of the Celtic warriors into the lagoons and hillsides around the Tor (*c.* 500 BC) recorded history begins. Because of its vast antiquity and constantly preserved religious sanctity the Glastonbury area continued to attract, and incidentally mystically adapt, numerous tribes and cultures. Lake villages have been excavated at Meare and Godney (both only a few miles from the Tor) and the workmanship of the jewelled ornaments and terra-cotta utensils used in these villages again shows a high level of technological and artistic achievement. The warrior Celts received guidance, both religious and philosophical, from the Druid priesthood and here many see the first codification of certain rituals and practices akin to natural witchcraft (*wicca*). It is the Druids who were thought to have laid out the turf-banked maze, traces of which can still be seen winding up the steep face of the Tor. This seven-tiered processional path denotes the sacred importance of the Tor to the Glastonbury mystical schema and it is time to look at this artificially adapted mound in some detail.

If the Zodiac is the key to the whole Avalonian complex, then the Tor is the locus, the focal point, of the inner Glastonbury power centre. In Celtic myth the entrance to the land of the dead, known as Avalon, was always a high hill surrounded by water. It was also linked to Caer Sidi, the Fairies' glass mountain or spiral castle, where the supernatural power inherent in death met the natural energies that blended from terrestrial and cosmic interaction. Glastonbury in the Iron Age made a perfect Avalon. The low-lying levels between the Tor and the sea would have been largely under water, with numerous ranges of hills and large, grass-grown mounds rising from the shiny surfaces of interlinked lagoons. In Celtic mythology, Avalloc or Avallach was a deity associated with guardianship of the underworld (Avalon) and here the etymology of the name clarifies a little.† The Tor would have made a natural centre of worship, especially if a ruined stone temple then existed upon its summit. The sharply angled sides of this hill are shaped into a series of rounded steps, rather like the step pyramid at Saqquara, Egypt, and this is the legacy of the geomancers who created the whole zodiacal pattern millennia before. The name Glastonbury is thought to stem from the old British words *Yns-witrin,* which means

*If Capricorn's horn is Ponter's Ball and this marks the 'golden coffin' of the sun at the winter solstice, another interesting correlation arises. The moon has a vital midwinter alignment in the constellation of Capricorn, where, at the solstice, she seems to watch over the death and rebirth of her polarizing celestial counterpart. Professor Thom has shown that the old megaliths once situated around the Tor and Chalice Hill were certainly lunar-orientated; this brings even more cohesion to the anciently complex astronomical pattern.

†In Christian parlance this name was transformed to 'Evalake the Unknown'. Evalake was a wraith-like heathen prince who had mysterious powers and was mystically involved with the legendary forefathers of Christianized Glastonbury. The earliest chroniclers make him a magical being with command of elemental forces. Evalake is obviously Avallach in Christian disguise.

Isle of Glass (i.e. Caer Sidi, the glass mountain), the Tor dominating the whole of the high ground that rose above the waters in the form of an elongated, tree-clad island.

The ritual importance of the Tor lingered long in local memory and a church dedicated to that fearsome slayer of the pagan dragon, St Michael, was first built on the summit in the twelfth century. Traces of the megalithic stones that preceded it can allegedly be seen in the foundations of the subsequent church's remaining tower. The main body of this church was thrown down by a severe earthquake in the thirteenth century. Legend again has it that fragments of the original prehistoric stones were also used to hallow the foundations of the nearby abbey. The Fairy king, Gwynn ap Nudd, Lord of Annwn and sometime leader of the Wild Hunt, a cosmic manifestation that is universal throughout European mythology, was a localized Tor spirit. He was said to have a palace on the summit from where he rode out with magic dogs and spectral warriors on his regular collection of souls. Obviously a daunting spectacle to those not attuned to cosmic consciousness.

Another key event that linked the Tor to ancient ritual was the famous Tor Fair. The fair was held on the second Monday in September and it encompassed horse, sheep and cattle trading as well as drinking, games and general merrymaking. In 1127 King Henry I granted a charter to the abbot and monks of Glastonbury to hold the fair at the church of St Michael on the Tor. But the event was immeasurably older than this because the charter mentions that for two days the festivities had to take place at the site of the 'original' fair. This in fact was on the lower western slopes of the Tor's east–west axis, and just above the field used there still remain the large, broken fragments of an old megalith. This is a power stone that activates erratically early in the morning and late at night. Its power has been personally verified by the author, its manifestation being rather like a mild electric current running through the palms of the hands and spiralling up the arms.* On the twenty-five-inch Ordnance Survey map this still very active stone is marked and named, significantly enough, as the Living Rock!

The Tor Fair was a major local festival and in its earliest days the records state it lasted at least a fortnight. In 1850 the fair was removed to a site nearer the town, in fact to a large field behind an old public house which is called the Fairfield Tavern today. Although the date now varies between September and October this true festival of the people is celebrated in Glastonbury even now. Its earliest recorded mention is in a Saxon edict of King Ine; the Celtic observance and the broken stone seem satisfyingly to locate a Bronze Age perspective. Two other points can quickly be mentioned. First, the old fairs of England were often located near or utilized mazes, and the labyrinth on the Tor is now an established fact. Second, the axis of the Tor (on which the power stone directly lies) is orientated on a major ley line that runs across Britain from St Michael's Mount, Cornwall, through St Michael's, Burrow Mump, the Tor, Avebury circle, Ogbourne St George, and countless other minor sites linked to the dragon and his saintly slayer. Glastonbury Tor is the predominant earthwork along this straight line of mainly elevated holy sites. This sacred hill is recognized as a vast repository for both free-flowing psychic power and

*Personal excavation has discovered other small fragments of broken megaliths scattered around the lower slopes of the Tor. These are in evidence particularly on the hill's western flank, but they are very well hidden, some being below ground level.

symbolic psychological stability, a realized unity between life and death. Its brooding strength radiates a dual purpose: generation of direct magical forces and reconciliation between the many states of consciousness that fertilize the basic impulses of human metaphysical perception. As the architect and psychic Bligh Bond realized, it is indeed a 'hill of vision'. Haunted by spirits, the abode of fairies and demons, the Tor casts an awe-inspiring 'shadow of heaven' across the surface of the earth.

Fairy fairs or gatherings are always cropping up in folk-lore and there is a large body of tales recounting the adventures of farmers, cowherds, milkmaids, etc., who come upon these events by accident. The Fairy fairs were held at certain sites that were traditional to the 'good people', a well-known West Country venue being that near Pitminster in southern Somerset. At these seasonal fairs the Fairies danced, sang, ate, drank and sold livestock just like any normal human gathering. The sites are all adjacent to either mazes, mounds, stones, hill-forts or earthworks, and the later human fairs at such places were probably another directly inherited esoteric tradition. The Tor fair, linked as it was to a maze and megalithic stones, not to mention the hill's association with Gwynn the Fairy king, culturally fits into its magically topographical surroundings in a completely satisfying manner.

The memory of Fairy fairs at places of proven historical importance magnifies the magical and ritual aspects of the sites themselves and sets them firmly in the context of a carefully applied geomancy. The supernatural Pitminster Fair actually manifested itself on the slopes of Black Down Hill, situated between the villages of Pitminster and Chestonford near Taunton, and this hill still bears traces of ancient barrows and earthworks. The Fairies who frequented this fair were described as being of 'man-like' stature, and the most common sighting by mortals was at the crucial time of the midsummer festival. A significant time if one thinks of the antique summer solstice celebrations, recognized even now by the numerous adherents of what is sometimes termed the Old Religion. Trezidder Lane, near St Levan, Cornwall, is also remembered as the site of a seasonal Fairy fair; this lane is part of a ley orientation* as well as being surrounded by numbers of standing stones, cromlechs and barrows in its immediate environment of the megalith-packed Penwith peninsula.

There are no definite connections in folk-lore between the Tor fair and the Fairies (except that the fair's oldest site was on the slopes of Gwynn ap Nudd's Caer Sidi, or Fairy Mountain). But when the maze and the megaliths are blended into the pattern, the importance of this hallowed mound is made physically clear in a historical yet decidedly geomythic frame of reference.

The maze on the Tor and the rituals of the Druids mark the end of Glastonbury's organically spiritual purity. The long interregnum since then has been led first by the Christians, then by the 'reality-trip' materialists, and now by the neo-Christian cults that proliferate there today.

When Christianity first tentatively approached Glastonbury during the first century AD, it came in the form of thinly disguised pagan legend; e.g. the tales of Joseph of Arimathea, the planting of his staff on Wearyall Hill, the burying of the grail/chalice containing

*Author's research.

The holy thorn that flowered from his staff.

Jesus' blood on Chalice Hill, etc. The embryonic Christian ethos was forced to embrace much pagan ritual to survive, so strongly were the old ways of thought and worship planted in the brains and souls of the people.

The Joseph-of-Arimathea legend is remarkable both for its tenacity in local memory and its weaving together of various pagan/Christian themes. In the Glastonbury region, 17 March was always celebrated as St Joseph of Arimathea's Day and a church in Langport (All Saints) has a stained glass window depicting the aged saint on his way to founding the first Christian church in Britain. The absorption of fertility themes is seen in the tale of Joseph's thorn staff (the thorn was a foremost symbol of pagan magic and mythology), his carrying of the Holy Grail, and in the little-known rhyme associated with St Joseph's Day itself. This rhyming couplet carries a simple incantational force ideal for oral chanting:

> If Saint Joseph's day is clear,
> We shall get a fertile year.

The famous thorn still grows at Glastonbury, and it burgeons forth on at least three religious sites. There is a large tree in the parish churchyard of St John's off the High Street. Another tree lies in the Abbey grounds, and a small bush is in the original place on the upper slopes of Wearyall Hill (the Pisces effigy in the Glastonbury Zodiac). This thorn is a genuine Levantine variety, and is a freak hawthorn or applewort. It actually stems from the Near East and only flourishes in the immediate vicinity of Glastonbury.

Its botanical name is *Crataegus oxyacantha.* Normally it cannot be struck, only budded. It flowers around 5 January (old Christmas Day) and blossoms are still sent to the reigning monarch in a continuation of a truly old tradition of magical and ritual recognizance.

The legend that Joseph of Arimathea was sent by St Philip to bring the Gospel to Britain is well-established in local folk-lore but has little extant historical documentation. The complexities of its origin are too involved for any elaboration here, but there seems to be a lot of circumstantial evidence in favour. This peripatetic 'uncle' to Jesus was supposed to have left the Holy Land sometime after 60 AD and to have ended up at Wearyall Hill (for the thorn-planting miracle) in 63/64 AD. The local king, Arviragus, supposedly gave Joseph and his followers twelve hides of land around Glastonbury and they then built the first temple to the new religion in the British Isles. The building was circular and from its alchemical fluidity of dimension great magic grew. In the author's opinion, it must have replaced a pagan shrine of even greater cosmic efficacy, for it was established early Christian practice to build churches, etc., on the sites of those potent monuments to past religious devotion.*

One of the most important geomantic aspects of the Joseph legends lies in the journey (quest) made by the man and his twelve disciples across the Somerset landscape. Most of the myths state that final landfall was made in the vicinity of what is now Bridgwater Bay (after a disastrous excursion into Wales) and that from there the small band was 'called' across the marshes to the looming majesty of Avalon's holy Tor. As if this was not enough for intuitive geomantic divination there is an almost unknown reading of the legend peculiar to the area around Crewkerne. This reading is quite specific in its imagery. The old folk-tale was collected by E. J. Watson and told afresh in his locally famous work *The Legend of Crewkerne.* The story was actually printed in full in the *Somerset County Herald* of 1920. In essence the myth relates how Joseph and his disciples were led to a straight track that marched across country following a route of antique ancestry, a route originally used by Phoenician tin traders. This old straight track was marked by small grassy mounds (barrows?) and in one place ran directly through an earthwork known as Cunnygar. Every five miles the pilgrims rested and one of their number thrust his staff into the ground to sanctify the line and mark the way. At certain unspecified points they erected crosses and on one hill Joseph set the Holy Grail on a standing stone; its light blazed out, illuminating all the surrounding woodlands. When they finally reached Wearyall Hill only Joseph retained his staff which, when thrust into the ground, burst forth as an instantly flowering thorn tree. It was then recognized as a mystical reconciliation between the magic of the old gods and the miracles of the new.

That briefly is the Legend of Crewkerne; all the facts are exactly as given in the tale, only the richness of writing has been of necessity removed. The ritualistic perambulation of Joseph and his people bears much relevance for students of ley hunting and even has metrological overtones in the placing of the staves at five-mile intervals. It is interesting that Joseph planted his staff on Wearyall Hill, not the Tor. As stated above, Wearyall is part of the triple Piscean effigies in the Zodiac and it must be noted that the sign of the fish was one of the first Christian symbols linked to the magic of the Vesica Piscis.

*Refer to the famous letter (as given in Bede) from Pope Gregory to Bishop Mellitus written in 601 AD.

Equally fascinating is the knowledge that with the inception of Christianity, the world entered the zodiacal age of Pisces, an age now in the process of violently dying from self-inflicted wounds induced through spiritual treason. By planting his staff on such a geomantically and astrologically apt spot, Joseph of Arimathea was recognizing the zodiacal signature that permanently sealed the sanctity of the whole Glastonbury landscape. Even if the legend is not strictly 'true' it has a symbolic, metaphysical strength that transcends physical reality and reaches directly towards an understanding of Glastonbury's more ethereal cosmic correspondence. The area has always been seen to have a zodiacal or heavenly ambience, linking the stars with their patterns reflected on the earth.

The star-like aura of the Zodiac lingered in Christian consciousness in a variety of ways, few of them really overt. The mystical dimensions of the great Abbey incorporate certain zodiacal/astronomical symbolisms in their numerology and the east–west line of orientation, which forms the Abbey's main axial alignment, is part of a major ley line that links Glastonbury with Stonehenge (a solar and lunar temple) and Canterbury Cathedral (site of another megalithic astronomical observatory.* A certain subtle corroboration is found in a suitably mysterious passage contained in the history of the Abbey, written by William of Malmesbury in the twelfth century. William was a famous scholar and historian of mixed Norman/Saxon descent. He was a native of Somerset and his books are models of well-marshalled facts, succinct clarification and good historical judgement. In his definitive work on the subject, *De Antiquitate Glastoniensis Ecclesiae*, William of Malmesbury includes the following short passage:

This church, then, is certainly the oldest I know in England, and from this circumstance derives its name (vetusta ecclesia) ... In the pavement may be seen on every side stones designedly inlaid in triangles and squares and figured with lead, under which, if I believe some sacred enigma to be contained, I do no injustice to religion.

This guarded statement was obviously designed to protect William from any charges of heresy, a continuously favourite pastime among the squabbling clerics of 'full-steam' Christianity. The passage refers to a mosaic pattern that was drawn into the stones of the St Mary Chapel (originally St Joseph's Chapel, for Arimathea), a building of great mystical importance that marked the site of the original foundation by the Christians of the early first century AD. This pattern must have been a direct reflection of esoteric Christianity and it seems to have enshrined a memory of the overall geomantic schema that dictated the correspondences between the Abbey's dimensions and the surrounding design of zodiacal, prehistoric and Celtic landscape geometry, i.e. effigies, mounds, stones, leys, etc.

The continuous psychic reminiscence of the above surfaced again during the early years of this century through the researches and archaeological work conducted at the Abbey ruins by Frederick Bligh Bond. This erratic Bristol architect and mystic made some astounding cabbalistic discoveries during the course of his excavations, tying the dimensions of the building into numerous explicit interpretations of ancient science, mathematics and astronomy. The technique of automatic writing was employed by Bligh

*This is proved in Professor Lyle Borst's book *Megalithic Software* (Twin Bridge Press, 1976) and John Greed's *Glastonbury Tales* (St Trillo, 1975).

Bond (to the hysterical disapproval of the dry ecclesiasts) and 'contact' with a fifteenth century brother of the Abbey led to a passage in Bligh Bond's book *Gate of Remembrance* that bears a remarkable resemblance to the words of William of Malmesbury. If Bligh Bond's findings are valid the zodiacal aspects are here totally proven from an apparently unimpeachable source! The astrally contacted brother stated:

That which the brethren of old handed down to us, we followed, ever building on their plan. As we have said, our Abbey was a message in ye stones. In ye foundations and ye distances be a mystery – the mystery of our Faith, which ye have forgotten and we also in ye latter days.

All ye measures were marked plaine on ye slabbes in Mary's Chappel, and ye have destroyed them. So it was recorded, as they who builded and they who came after knew aforehand where they should build. But these things are overpast and of no value now. The spirit was lost and with the loss of the spirit the body decayed and was of no further use to (us).

There was the Body of Christ, and round him would have been the Four Ways. Two were ybuilded and no more. In ye floor of ye Mary Chappel was ye Zodiac, that all might see and understand the mystery. In ye midst of ye Chapel he was laid; and the Cross of Hym who was our Example and Examplar.

Braineton, he didde much, for he was Geomancer to ye Abbey of old tyme.

In examples such as this the everlasting magic of Glastonbury continues to work its ageless spell over minds, bodies . . . and souls.

Glastonbury's early links with Christianity are always of an ambiguous nature, with many of the saints and mystics associated with the area showing marked undertones of strange powers, origins and practices. For instance, there is a tale that the Irish St Bridget came to Glastonbury around 488 AD and that she passed some years in meditation on the 'island of Beckery', where there was an earlier chapel dedicated to St Mary Magdalene, a holy shrine of great sanctity. When St Bridget returned to Ireland she left the ancient chapel with her name and certain personal relics – her wallet, her rosary and her oak staff. These then became imbued with miraculous powers. The 'island' of Beckery is located due west of the Tor and is a low, mounded ridge lying near the gently meandering River Brue. It has always been associated with religious magic, and Arthurian myth states that the great king had a potent vision of the Holy Grail in its tiny chapel. St Bridget was reputed to possess many powers over natural things: it was said that 'animals and birds obeyed her call' and that she could work miracles with milk and butter that paralleled Christ's feeding of the five thousand. The legends of Beckery remain, but alas, all traces of the chapel (and much of the mound itself) have been systematically destroyed by the relentless march of progress and industry over the last couple of centuries.

The Bridget legends are particularly interesting when it is remembered that St Bridget was the Christian incarnation of the mighty pagan fertility goddess, Bride. The cult of Bride or Brigantia was solidly tied to childbirth, sacred wells, crops and the vegetation cycle throughout pagan Ireland, England and western Scotland. The goddess was also guardian of the hearth fires, which linked her symbolically to that life-giving furnace, the sun.* Those British sacred centres that are situated on mounds or hills are usually

---

*The great pagan Celtic festival of 'Imbolc', celebrated on 1 February, was dedicated to the goddess Bride (Bridgid) and was connected to fertility through its emphasis on sheep. The Christian adaptation is obvious, as the official saint's day for St Bridget is also fixed on 1 February. In ecclesiastical art, St Bridget is portrayed with two of the foremost symbols of her pagan predecessor: she usually has a cow at her side and a flame above her head. Greatly venerated, she is still the patron (after St Patrick who, incidentally, was a visitor and incumbent at Glastonbury) of Ireland.

connected with some form of sun ritual, be they pagan, Christian, or intermediary through the Culdees and the heretical Gnostics. The obvious fact that St Bridget was 'Bride' Christianized reveals yet again the new religion's debt to the centuries of complex worship that had developed at Glastonbury in a more natural and all-embracing manner – in fact, via a vast pagan cult that fulfilled every psychic, religious and ecological need through its ever changing, but ever constant pantheon of archetypal gods and goddesses. These prime elemental forces are always symbolic of highly practical applications of a strange but realizable power. It is a power that is miraculously in tune with the rhythms and energy flows inherent throughout nature; a power that links stones and stars, earth and heaven, man and cosmos. It is the unifying power of a holistically geomantic magic – the living pulsations of the spirits in and around the earth.

After Joseph the Arthurian mythos became entwined in the pattern, for the quest for the Grail stemmed subconsciously from the memory of Glastonbury's earlier marvels, back to thorn magic, the maze on the Tor and the Great Round Table of the Zodiac itself. The Arthurian knights traced the barbed but sacred paths toward achievement of the Grail, and the hidden symbolism of this is self-evident in the light of what is written above. At the summit of the Tor the achievement of the Grail is still possible for the dedicated and spiritually enlightened seeker.

In this brief study of Glastonbury folk-lore and legendary history, we have discovered, hidden deep at its roots, the poetically coded messages that have filtered down from the lost eras. They have manifested themselves through the constantly recurring patterns of myth, magic, and the intuitive insight that once illumined the minds of the ancient seers. From this insight, handed down through the generations as oral tradition and written wisdom, couched in poetry, ritual, music and prose, the geomantically active 'presence' in the British Isles is enshrined and perpetuated as a regenerative dream in the consciousness of men. The highly developed intuitive sciences of the past pose a perpetual enigma to the closed minds of our own era, which resound with empty materialist bravado. This results in the constant decrying of the sacred mysteries as a desperate defence mechanism against ultimate truth. When these mysteries are approached with an open mind, strong in its understanding of the psychic realities of psychological and metaphysical interaction, the veils of the mysteries can be lifted, and the natural structure of the ancient world can be revealed in bright patterns that illumine the soul and transform the basic contours of human consciousness. The esoteric tradition native to the British Isles was carefully preserved by the various mystical orders who succeeded the megalithic and Bronze Age wizards, to be finally codified in incantation, ritual and poetry by the ancient order of Druids. They then transmitted much of it to the early Christians who gradually replaced them at the beginning of the last astrological age. In this way, there was preserved into modern times some of the vital magical heritage so carefully developed by the giants of the past, which is so essential now to our understanding and resurrection of a nearly ruined world.

It can safely be assumed that the Glastonbury region is one of the holiest centres on the face of the earth because so many religions and cultures have met and meshed around its fields and streams. The true Glastonbury atmosphere, embracing zodiac (astrology), maze (psychology) and Grail (cosmology) is defiantly universal, never dogmatic or parochial. These triadic images symbolize respectively heavenly glory, earthly complexity and a linking gateway to the wonders of the Higher Worlds. They all combine to form a psychic representation of the Cosmic Temple on earth and this is physically realized in the landscape geomancy around the Isle of Avalon, with Glastonbury Abbey and the Tor as the key sites.

The strengths of the Avalonian mythos remain because they are based on the energies and harmonies contained within the original structure of Creation. Something vibrant and beautiful watches over the hills of Glastonbury, for this section of the English landscape is the Dream of the Gods made real.

Recommended Books

Fortune, Dion. *Avalon of the Heart*. Aquarian Press, 1971.
Greed, John A. *Glastonbury Tales*. St Trillo Publications, 1975.
Hawkins, Desmond. *Avalon and Sedgmoor*. David & Charles, 1973.
Lewis, Lionel Smithett. *St Joseph of Arimathea at Glastonbury*. James Clarke, 1976.
Maltwood, Katharine. *A Guide to Glastonbury's Temple of the Stars*. James Clarke, 1964.
Michell, John. *City of Revelation*. Garnstone Press, 1972.
    The View Over Atlantis. Sago Press, 1969.
Powys, John Cowper. *A Glastonbury Romance*. Picador, 1975.
Roberts, Anthony. *Atlantean Traditions in Ancient Britain*. Rider and Company, 1977.
Watson, W. G. Willis, ed. *Calendar of Somerset Customs, etc*. Somerset County Herald, 1920.
Wilcock, John. *A Guide to Occult Britain*. Sidgwick & Jackson, 1976.
Williams, Mary, ed. *Glastonbury: A Study in Patterns*. RILKO, 1969.

CHAPTER TWO

The Glastonbury Giants or Zodiac:

An Arthurian Reflection

MARY CAINE

The secret source of Avalon's mystique, the bubbling fount of all its legends, the magnet that drew so many saints, kings and pilgrims, is all the more mysterious for being invisible. This is the Glastonbury Zodiac, claimed by its discoverer Katharine Maltwood as at once the oldest and biggest of all Britain's antiquities. This great geomantic circle of giant effigies, ten miles across and thirty miles round, has so far been totally ignored by cautious Establishment archaeologists. It is Too Big to be Seen, Too Good to be True!

Modelled in relief by hills and lesser contours, outlined in part by streams which follow these round, the effigies are essentially *natural* – yet the outlines have been completed by man through the ages, by roads, paths and canals, and embellished by tumuli, ramparts and lynchets at the nodal points.

Preposterous? Maybe, but there on the map are the twelve signs of the zodiac in correct order in a circle, guarded by a great hound to the southwest, all of five miles long.* Can this be chance? It has been calculated that if the odds against two signs being right with each other are two to one, the odds against twelve being in correct relationship are nearly 480 million. And if we study their exact form the odds get even longer. Thirteen heads for instance face west; the winter signs are to the cold north, the summer signs to the sunny south, and when the planisphere is superimposed to scale on the map, *the zodiacal constellations fit over their earthly counterparts.* The figures are designed in proportion too, eight of them being 6000 yards across. Two fish of Pisces match in size; so do the two birds and the two twins. The only human figures form an equilateral triangle across the circle – a Trinity of father, mother and son(s). Of these Sagittarius the sun-god is the largest (five miles across); Virgo the earth-mother is four miles long; and Gemini, their son(s), smaller still. Gemini must signify Man himself, split in two: half earthly, half-divine; half conscious, half subconscious; half mortal, half immortal; always struggling against himself to make his sundered psyche whole.

There are in fact so many refinements and accuracies of design that there is no way of

---

*A second hound effigy has now been discovered by Janet Roberts, lying west from the circle and of similar shape to the Great Dog of Langport. It is discussed in her article in this book. (*Ed.*)

doing justice to them all in this article. Typical of these refinements are Aries' head and Virgo's wheatsheaf. The wheatsheaf marks not only the exact line of the sun's ecliptic path on the superimposed planisphere, but also its exact width. The star which falls in the centre of Virgo's wheatsheaf marks 20 September, the Christian festival of the Blessed Virgin's birth. The central (or equinoctial) line of the ecliptic passes through the burial ground of Glastonbury Abbey, then through the point of Aries' head, and is also grasped between the fingers of Gemini's upraised hand. Joseph of Arimathea planted his thorn-staff dead on the line on Pisces' Wearyall Hill . . . and so on.

Beside all this, there are about a hundred significant place names and a rich crop of local legends which in both cases only make sense in the context of the starry giants. If Chance can design like this she deserves a ticket to the Chelsea Arts Ball!

KATHARINE MALTWOOD

Katharine Maltwood, FRSA, a sculptor and a Catharine indeed, discovered the Glastonbury Zodiac about 1925 while drawing an illustration for the *High History of the Holy Grail.* This was a Norman-French MS which had just been translated into English by Sebastian Evans. The original manuscript may well have been written at Glastonbury Abbey so clearly does it describe the local terrain; if not, at least its monkish or knightly author knew the area well, for he tells us in fact that his tale was taken from Glastonbury Abbey. Mrs Maltwood surmises wisely that he was a Templar. She had been asked to draw a map of the itinerary of the Arthurian Grail Quest round Avalon, and, as she tracked a knightly encounter with a lion to Somerton on the six-inch Ordnance Survey map, Leo himself leapt out at her with a roar, his underside entirely drawn by the river Cary, his back outlined by ancient Somerton Lane, his mane tangled by woods in *Cat*sash Hundred. Then she saw a giant baby modelled by Dundon and Lollover Hills nearby. Too much! The Vale of Avalon, she knew, had long been haunted by a lion and a giant. From their relative positions an astrologer friend suggested a zodiac, and soon the whole grand consortium was carefully uncovered.

After some ten years of research, her books, *Glastonbury's Temple of the Stars, Enchantments of Britain,* and an *Aerial Survey* (a selection of aerial photos of the effigies) were published by John Watkins. James Clarke now publishes the first two titles.

Katharine Maltwood died in Canada in 1961, having been laughed at or ignored by all the very best universities. (They laughed at Schliemann too when he said he had discovered Troy.) Her home, Thatched Lodge in Vancouver Island, is now a museum housing the many treasures she and her husband amassed during their world-wide travels; it also possesses many of her notes, letters and manuscripts.

She was a remarkable woman – handsome, talented, mystical and dedicated. Her sculpture was enshrined in a temple-like studio which readily inspired her many visitors with awe. These sculptures were also strangely prophetic of the zodiac she was later to find; her *Wounded Centaur, Magna Mater,* and *Plucking Feathers from the Eagle's Tail* read like a list of her yet-undiscovered Glastonbury effigies. She appears as the heroine in a book written by a friend, a Mrs Barrington of New York, writing under the pen-name

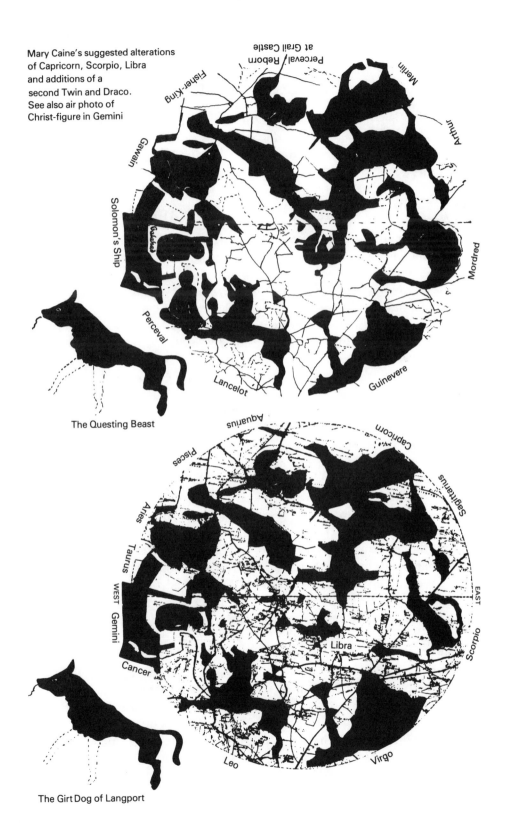

Mary Caine's suggested alterations
of Capricorn, Scorpio, Libra
and additions of a
second Twin and Draco.
See also air photo of
Christ-figure in Gemini

Perceval Reborn
at Grail Castle

Merlin

Fisher-King

Arthur

Gawain

Solomon's Ship

Galahad

Mordred

Perceval

Lancelot

Guinevere

The Questing Beast

Aquarius

Pisces

Capricorn

Aries

Sagittarius

Taurus

EAST

WEST

Gemini

Libra

Scorpio

Cancer

Leo

Virgo

The Girt Dog of Langport

of Adams Beck. The book, *The House of Fulfilment* (Fisher Unwin, 1927), will reveal something of her character to those who wish to know her better.

She's dead but she won't lie down, for already a multitude of young enthusiasts are following the mystical trail she blazed – fired by the strange magic of her Zodiac. If it was the sculptor in her that responded to this nature-sculpture, modelled in relief on the very earth, it was the *Cathar* in her, the mystic in Katharine, that attuned her to its philosophical and astronomical teachings, still vibrating faintly on a wave-length no one else could then hear.

ARTHUR'S ROUND TABLE

Here, Mrs Maltwood said, was the original Round Table of Arthurian legend, with Arthur, Guinevere, Merlin and the chief knights still seated majestically round it as the zodiacal effigies. Had she not been led to it by following the knightly Grail-Quest? *La Queste del San Graal*, another Norman MS, supports her, saying that 'the Round Table was made on the advice of Merlin, not without great significance, and signified the round world, the round canopy of the planets, stars, and many other things.' Malory's *Morte D'Arthur* also says that it could feed four thousand people and 150 bulls. *So this magical board must have been remembered in Norman times as a large tract of land endowed with starry significance.* The legends say that it belonged to King Leodegrance of Camelot, Guinevere's father, who gave it as her dowry when she married Arthur. But Camelot is Cadbury Castle, overlooking the effigy of Virgo. Is Leodegrance not Leo? Is Virgo, identified by the nearby village of Queen Camel, not Guinevere, Camelot's multi-faceted Queen?

It has often been noted that Arthurian legend contains all the elements of archetypal sun myth. Mrs Maltwood went further, showing that the four heroes of the *High History* – Gawain, Lancelot, Arthur and Perceval – typified the four seasons of the year, both in their characters and in the nature of their adventures. She cited the famous medieval clock at Wells Cathedral as evidence for her idea; there Arthur and his knights joust on the hour in solemn roundelay when the bell is struck by Jack Blandifer, who, by his name, can only be the sun. This clock is said to have been cunningly made by a Glastonbury monk.* Here, certainly, Arthur is connected with time, with the hours and seasons.

Merlin, the legends insist, made the Round Table. And Merlin was seen as the hoary inheritor of still hoarier Druid lore. The Druids were famous astronomers as well as philosophers. It is extraordinary that no one before Katharine Maltwood put two and two together and realized that the Round Table was a *table of measurements*, charting the movements of the earth and heavens! Yet there is vastly more to it than that. The ancients were not simply astronomers in the modern sense of the word; their philosophy was based on astrology, which included the effect of the stars on human character and events – a comprehensive system which embraced evolution and its purpose in a grand cosmology undreamt of by modern science. With them, myths and maths were united in a splendid space–time scheme which made glorious sense of the human situation and its ultimate goal. Today with all our science we are left with only the maths, and though

*This was the celebrated Peter Lightfoot who made other time-pieces for various ecclesiastical establishments during the fourteenth century. (*Ed.*)

these run into billions of light-years they shed little light on the great questions which have always tortured the most intelligent – namely, 'Why are we here? What is it all for? Has the universe indeed a purpose at all?' With all our knowledge most of us can no longer make sense of our basic situation.

Zodiacs have always existed, since the dawn of all civilizations all over the world, to answer these questions. But with the passage of time their figures have been to some extent distorted or altered, so that their original message can now hardly be read. We have not wondered enough about the zodiac pattern as it has come down to us through Chaldea, Egypt and Greece. Few of us have even speculated whether these figures, imaginatively projected on to constellations, have a story to tell at all. The Glastonbury Zodiac, with its slight but significant changes in the interpretation of some effigies, restores the original message loud and clear. Surely it is no accident that Arthur's Round Table has been traditionally associated with the Vale of Avalon, where this great terrestrial Zodiac, once known and valued, has for so long lain forgotten. The very Quest of the Grail can now be seen as the search for the hidden effigies; for each knight, an initiate in the Ancient Mysteries, in searching for his own sun-sign was trying to find – himself.

To substantiate these claims we must study and quantify the effigies themselves. The few changes from the zodiacs with which we are familiar are changes in interpretation rather than in actual shape. Cancer and Libra for instance seem at first sight to be missing, and only reveal themselves later, slightly displaced westward from their normal positions, and in disguise. Cancer appears as a ship, Libra as a dove. Aquarius is not a waterman but an eagle or phoenix, and a mighty whale or sea-monster is added to the two fish of Pisces. But these changes allow us to read the zodiac as never before, and make sense of this ancient and seemingly incomprehensible menagerie. It is noticeable that in every case the familiar original shape is kept; Cancer is a crab-shaped ship; Libra a scales-shaped bird; Aquarius a bowl-shaped phoenix like the early Aquarian waterpot of Chaldea. The whale has the important job of pulling the sun-god at Sagittarius down into the sea, and Sagittarius himself makes new sense of the senseless centaur, being revealed here as a mounted figure with a splendid pair of buttocks of his own, who is being dragged off his horse, thus obscuring his mount's neck and most of its head. It certainly looks as if this may be the origin of all centaurs, in this, the first of all the antique zodiacs.

THE EFFIGIES

The Girt Dog of Langport

If this circle conceals the ancient Mysteries of Britain, it is not surprising to find them guarded by a huge hound – perhaps the first Cerberus of all. (Arthur's Dog, the old Welsh historian Nennius tells us, was called Cabal, a name that certainly denotes the Mysteries. Here too is Gwyn ap Nudd's dog Dormarth, 'Death's Door', another revealing name preserved for us in an old Welsh poem.) This huge creature, five miles long from nose to tail, guards the main western approach to the underworld mysteries from the Bristol Channel down the Parrett River. This river in fact draws the whole of his underside.

He is a Grail-Quester too, appearing in Arthurian legend as the Questing Beast, his belly gurgling 'like thirty couple hounds'. The river Parrett along its belly explains this somewhat antisocial characteristic, for it gurgles noisily at the spring-tide bore, like the Severn into which it flows. Moon Drove is situated at the dog's mouth.

He is the best attested effigy of all, appearing in the ancient Somerset wassail song as the 'Girt Dog of Langport' who 'burnt his long tail' (see *Oxford Carol Book*). Some twenty-three place names no less, perhaps more, proclaim him – his tail, delightfully, is at Wagg! Two Head droves are on his head, Earlake Moor is by his ear, and Othery too (Greek *otis* is an ear). Names like Curry Rivel, North Curry, Curland and Curload all remember him well, for a cur was once a guard dog. Places like Helland, Hellard and Hellyar's Farm seem to preserve his function as the underworld's gate sentinel, and at Oath Hill initiates doubtless took vows of secrecy before sailing with thumping hearts up the Parrett into the sacred circle. Starsland Farm, west of his nose at Hedging, proclaims that the Star Temple is near. What sighs of relief when they emerged safe and sound at Paradise, on the dog's tail. But take courage pilgrim; he is not only girt (great), but also girt (tethered), for Leazeway drove runs to Little Hook on his neck.

His nose is Alfred's Burrow, Athelney, a three-tiered mini-tor or mump, twelve miles south-west of Glastonbury Tor. Cadbury Castle, also terraced, is twelve miles south-east of the major Tor, making a great geomantic triangle. More medals for Chance, that arch-designer? Was Alfred, in burning those famous cakes at Athelney, performing a time-honoured ritual by throwing them into the river Tone (the girt dog's tongue) as a 'sop to Cerberus' before entering the sacred circle as an initiate? So Mrs Maltwood surmised. Burnt barley cakes were often used in the old solar rituals. 'Saxon' Alfred was at least half Celt, as his ancestors' names proclaim; and an old Celtic poem tells of an ancient royal secret passed down from kingly father to son 'on the bank of the river of Spectres'. Mrs Maltwood may well be right, as usual. It was a hot time for the dog, with Alfred defensively burning his nose and the rampaging Danes sacking Langport on his hind leg.

But long before Alfred, the Sumerian hero Gilgamesh seems to have undertaken zodiacal adventures, travelling to the far west to sail up the 'river Parutti to the place where the Star-Gods dwell' in search of eternal life. Here too came Hercules, to the land of the Hyperboreans in quest of the Mysteries, and strangled Cerberus. And westward-sailing Ulysses, and Jason, and Joseph of Arimathea . . .

Aries

Where to break in on a magic circle? Shall we begin with Sagittarius, who is Arthur, king of this Round Table, then proceed to Guinevere (Virgo), and from there to their Geminian son(s)? No, let us begin with the first sign of the zodiac and thus preserve the correct order of the seasons.

Aries is the spring sign, and in Arthurian legend he is Gawain – bold, promiscuous, rash, who leaps without looking, then wishes he hadn't. He is blustery March winds and April showers of remorse; like the spring sun, he has courage, but little understanding and no staying-power. It was said of Gawain that his strength waxed until midday, then rapidly waned; it seems he must have had to fight all his battles before lunch. It was

Gawain who, without forethought accepted the Green Knight's challenge to cut his head off only to find that the challenger picked up his head from the floor, and replacing it, challenged him to have his own head cut off in a year's time. Poor Gawain! The honour of Arthur's court demanded that he keep his appointment; he was lucky when the dreaded hour came that his mighty opponent generously let him off with only a lightly grazed neck. Courage counted here. The older knight has compassion on his youth and thoughtlessness, commending him purely on his courage alone.

That Gawain is Aries is hinted at by Arthur, who says of him, 'Thou art the first to move this Quest . . .' It is also typical of Aries that though he began it, he failed to finish it. He simply got bored with it, being too young to understand the full implications.

He has to learn the hard way, and leaves a trail of devastation and weeping damsels behind him – the Waste Land of Arthurian legend is all Gawain's fault. It came about because, on a visit to the Grail Castle, he was privileged to see the Grail procession but failed to ask its meaning. He was too immature to comprehend such matters, and was ignominiously ejected from the castle to learn wisdom in the fullness of time. Only later did he return, sadder and wiser, to ask what the Grail (and indeed life itself) was all about. He had, all unknowing, been a candidate for succession to the sick and ageing Fisher king, and had failed the test. In consequence the maimed king grew worse, and the land which depended on his well-being became more waste. Gawain's story is a very acute parable of youth, for whom the outer world of materialism and the senses is all there is. Yet the Mysteries are patient with the young, for only there lies any real hope: Gawain appears in old poems and mumming plays as a peerless doctor able to revive the dying sun-king, as spring revives the dying sun. Even peerless doctors sometimes begin like some medical students we have known!

The zodiacal effigy emphasizes his youth: he is a hornless lamb, his head reverted at Street like the Christian Paschal lamb, not a ram. Does the place name Asney on his tail mean Agnus Dei? Yet this young ram has seen battle, as befits a sign ruled by Mars; his haunches, defined by high ground, are scarred with prehistoric fortifications (lynchet patterns). It is remarkable how well the fields define these haunches for Nature herself has carefully assisted in the design. Local people still tan sheepskins on his golden fleece – for this is really Jason's Ram. The dragon Draco guards the fleece, and Medea with her rejuvenating cauldron lurks at Virgo, as we shall see as we progress around the circle.

The effigy is all drawn by a triangle of ancient roads, its underjaw at Street being the Portway, a road which leads on to Aries' back and to the old British tidal port of Dunball on the Parrett. How apt that Street should be famous for its shoes! Clarke's and Moreland's both have factories there. His feet, tucked under him, are drawn by Ivythorn Hill where a large Neolithic flint scraper was found. Three upright stones mark the entrance to the path that defines his bent-back forefoot. The road outlining his chest and the back of his head is the old tin-track from Somerton to the Mendip Hills, through Glastonbury.

The *High History* describes Aries accurately, saying that 'the King of Wales was lord of this land' (a reference to Walton Hill, his haunch) and mentioning a tower there on a high rock. This tower still stands on Walton Hill. It is older than the Normans, having been rebuilt in 1192 as a corn-mill.

It is merely chance that a *youth* hostel, the only one in the Zodiac, should be on Aries' Ivythorn Hill? Is Chance, that fickle jade, at her subtle tricks again?

Taurus

This same old road, Ivythorn Hill, leads on to the smaller effigy of Taurus, drawing its neck on Collard Hill, actually its collar. Only the head and forefoot of this effigy appear, a feature copied in many ancient zodiacs. His horns are clearly terraced by lynchets on Hatch Hill. His eye was once a pond at Trays Farm, but has now alas been filled in. Chance would have it that a rifle range was once here, by the old bull's eye! It is indeed a bull's-eye, for if we take a line from four little field-strips on Taurus' foot almost due east–west, it passes through his eye to Sagittarius' eye and on to the village of Stone in Scorpio in the east. Mrs Maltwood dated the design of the Zodiac by this line, which shows the position of the Royal Star Cross in 2700 BC, in fact the equinoctial line. The star Aldebaran in Taurus falls on the little field-strips and the star Antares falls on Stone in Scorpio where, by its name, a marker stone must once have been set. These two stars form the east-west arm of the Royal Star Cross. The archer draws a regular bead on the bull's-eye! It is only one of the astonishing refinements of design that one discovers as one researches into this strangely well-co-ordinated Star-Temple.

The Pleiades stars fall on earthworks on the highest part of Collard Hill. Someone has added a third horn here to Taurus' head, for the Hood Monument, a tall stone obelisk, dramatically crowns him. Earthworks coil around his ear.

Taurus' lone foot stands on the top of the ship's mast; here is the bull of Hu the sun-god, who in Celtic lore 'strained himself to pull the vessel (Avanc) out of the lake, so that his eyes started from their sockets, and he dropped down dead'. This is perhaps a reference to the cutting of the original dykes by means of yoked oxen, thus irrigating the flood-lands of the ship and at the same time drawing its planks. Arthur too is credited with drawing the Avanc or sea monster out of the lake with oxen, one of the Mighty Works of Britain. This bull it seems created both whale and ship, it being one of the key effigies in the circle.

In Arthurian legend he must be Sir Ector, young Arthur's benevolent foster-father. For Taurus, under Venus in the kindly month of May, is the builder, the provider of shelter, the foster-father to Gemini's young sun-king whom in the zodiac he overshadows. Hector – Protector. Is he not also Joseph the Carpenter, bending over the Gemini babe in the manger stars of Cancer, with the ass of the Asella stars in the same constellation? In the Hebrew calendar Joseph certainly corresponds with Taurus. The Taurean Age (c. 4000–2000 BC) was the acknowledged age of mighty earthworks (Avebury, Stonehenge, the Pyramids, etc.). Was Mrs Maltwood wrong to ascribe the recognition and development of this vast nature-temple to this comparatively recent period?

Gemini

In the *High History* followed by Mrs Maltwood, Gemini is Arthur's valiant son Lohot (the low hot sun?). Like his noble father – like all sun-gods – he is ultimately doomed to die. It was a fatal habit of his, so says the *High History*, to lie down and sleep on any giant he happened to kill, thereby recovering his strength. As he lay on one victim, envious Sir Kay happened by, cut off his head and claimed credit at Arthur's court for killing the giant, who had, he lyingly asserted, first decapitated Lohot. As Sir Kay showed Lohot's bloody head to woeful Arthur and fainting Guinevere, two suns simultaneously flooded the windows of the hall with light from either side. We can hardly avoid understanding the *High History's* hint that two doomed sun-gods, father and son, were present in that hall at that fatal moment.

But what a perfect picture of the Gemini giant in our Zodiac! For lying on or within Mrs Maltwood's giant babe is a Christ-like figure, his hands bound above his head, his hair and beard uncannily drawn by woods on Dundon Hill's British Camp, his eye its dew-pond, his face perfectly profiled by prehistoric fortifications. His head lolls in sleep like Lohot's, or in death like Christ crucified. (The lolling head is said by Christians to account for the angle always built in to medieval churches between chancel and nave. Here it would seem is the original reason for this curious architectural trait.) It satisfactorily accounts for the strange name Lollover Hill on Gemini's lower body. It also accounts for Lohot's weird habit – the *High History's* author knew his effigies well. So, one imagines, did William Blake, seer, Druid and bard, when he wrote, 'And did the Countenance Divine Shine forth upon these clouded hills?' Blake was well aware of the continuing Glastonbury mystique.

Was this intuition on the poet's part, or did he know the Ancient Secrets of Britain? I can only say that when I joined the London Order of Druids, I found that William Blake was celebrated as Chosen Chief of that Order for forty years – a fact that appears in none of his academic biographies. It was there, incidentally, that I first heard mention of the Glastonbury Zodiac. But Blake was conversant from his boyhood with the story of Christ's coming to Britain; his earliest engraving at the age of fourteen was *Joseph of Arimathea landing on the Rocks of Albion*. Though Blake was ostensibly a Londoner, two ladies claimed kinship with him on the strength of their common descent from Admiral Blake (see Mona Wilson's *Life of Blake*). As the admiral was born at Bridgwater, practically on the Glastonbury Zodiac, I am inclined to accept the claim of these two ladies, the more so since my own family descends from the prolific if unmarried admiral. But whether one accepts all this or not, Blake's visionary preoccupation with Druids and the Mysteries of Britain is self-evident from his poems and pictures. Has not his beautiful poem *Jerusalem* been called our second national anthem?

In Arthurian terms our Christ-like Gemini figure is obviously Galahad, the Christ-like knight. But this name, which appears late in Arthurian legend, is only a variant of the earlier and more obscure Lohot. Other variations, like Galehot and Galahaut, proliferate in the legends. Galahad, I venture to suggest, is simply Lohot in the galley or ship. Just to muddle things however, Galahad, when he does appear, is not Arthur's son but Lancelot's, begotten unlovingly on Elaine (Helen, the perfect woman) in an attempt to produce the perfect man, an exercise in metaphysical eugenics! It is plain that Arthurian legend is actually describing the Son of man portrayed in the timeless Gemini effigy. And it is interesting that the Druids, long before the time of Jesus, called their dying young sun-god Hesus or Esus. To pronounce his name accurately we must call him Yesse, as the Welsh still pronounce Jesus. He was to the ancients not only the Son of God and man, but the very essence of ourselves. It was a Roman writer that told us that the Druids worshipped a Trinity – Belinus, Taranis and Esus – so, like the name Jesus, their

Mary Caine's messianic figure contained within Mrs Maltwood's Gemini child.

names are in Latin form. Belinus was Bel the Celtic, Sumerian and Phoenician sun-god; Taranis, though taken as a male thunder-god, can only have been Tar-Annis or Black Annis the Witch and earth-mother; Esus was obviously their son. As Taliesin said in the sixth century, 'Christianity may be a new thing in Asia, but there never was a time when its basic precepts were not taught in Britain; we always had the Word.' Druids called him the woodcutter, Christians, the carpenter.

Did lion and Gemini giant name the lost Arthurian land of Lyon-Esse? Say 'yes' and affirm the holy Name. Yes, Tor on Celtic Dartmoor remembers the Mysteries of Britain and drowned Lyonesse, the British Atlantis.

Christ-like, our effigy hangs between two robbers, for Gemini is ruled by Mercury, god of thieves. He is the good thief of many myths, stealing salvation for humanity from the reluctant gods and paying for it with his life, like many a poet, artist, inventor or mystic through whose ultimate sacrifice we all have gained. His name Ysus recurs in the pre-Christian mysteries of Dion *Ysus,* in questing U*lysses* or Odysseus, and in the star-gazing Essenes who taught John the Baptist and no doubt instructed Jesus too.

I eventually found the missing second twin, his head near his brother's, within Mrs Maltwood's griffin. No doubt both are there; the griffin is a minor character in the *High History.* In Greek myth Pollux the immortal twin saves his mortal brother Castor. In Arthurian myth Galahad saves Perceval by his example. Perceval the mortal twin makes, like ourselves, every mistake in the book, but by faithfully following Galahad (whom he can never quite catch) he at last becomes worthy of the Grail, and together they sail away in Solomon's ship beyond mortal ken.

In our Zodiac you can see Perceval seated in yogic posture, trying to raise his consciousness by process of transcendental meditation.

The Ship: Cancer?

Is this Cancer in disguise, or the star-ship Argo Navis, also belonging to this part of the sky? Perhaps both, for there's no crab to be seen. A crescent-shaped ship cradling a baby symbolizes Cancer's watery, moon-ruled, maternal sign so well that we may send the crab scuttling into the sand for shame; it simply cannot compete.*

If you object that Cancerians walk sideways, as they are known to do, well, what tacks sideways better than a ship? And what Cancerian would not prefer to be signed by it than by a morose crab? But Cancerians are possessive – they have crab's claws! Yes, but what is more tenacious than a ship's hold with crew and cargo battened under hatches to withstand a storm? One can think of many young sun heroes who started

---

*Various Gnostic medallions portray a crescent ship with high, upcurving prow and stern and a crouching baby in the middle. Sometimes the prow and stern are carved to represent zodiacal figures. There are always stars positioned in the sky above the vessel and its youthful occupant. One specific gem, illustrated in C. W. King's *The Gnostics,* shows a baby in a ship with the planks clearly demarcated. The curving prow is carved as the head of a griffin-like bird with a crescent moon above it (the traditional Cancer sign), while the stern is shaped as the head of an ox with a four-pointed star above it, representing the sun in Taurus. The griffin-bird effigy in the Glastonbury Zodiac lies in the sector that comes under the jurisdiction of Cancer and is resting at one end of the vessel that carries the Gemini child. The Taurus effigy is situated at the other end of the rhine (canal)-drawn ship! It's an interesting corroboration of mythical, not to say historical, continuity. (*Ed.*)

life precariously in a tide-washed cradle, ark or boat; none who was sea-borne on a crab. The moon rules Cancer; this half-moon boat is the moon-boat of Isis, the crescent moon of Mary, the Cauldron of Ceridwen, the Celtic mother earth-goddess. It is at once moon, womb and tomb, a totally feminine symbol.

It is entirely man-made, deliberately it would seem, yet the dykes that draw the ship's planks drain a crescent-shaped marsh that claws round Gemini's hills, so it is still a topographical response to the zodiacal environment's bidding.

This in Arthurian legend is Solomon's ship, made by Solomon (Sol) and his wicked wife the Moon to preserve the secret wisdom until a man worthy of it should come. The unworthy who invaded it met with instant death. At last Galahad boards it, and is inspired by the three mysterious spindles that hang above its rich bed. These are doubtless a memory of the Druidic 'three bars of light', the *Awen* or Logos which inspired Celtic seers, the *Duw-A-Digon* of the earliest Druids.

Can we doubt that its cargo of wisdom is the very zodiac itself, on whose space–time measurement all civilizations have been founded? Solomon was famous for his deep occult wisdom, learnt doubtless from Phoenician Hiram of Tyre and the mysterious Sumerians. Solomon hid the ark in the rock of the temple at Jerusalem; its measurements were sacred, being based on Noah's mighty ship. And were the animals of Noah's post-diluvian ark not the zodiac menagerie, brought from sinking Atlantis to found new civilizations in the east?

Mrs Maltwood found that the ship's plank on which Gemini sits measures exactly one-thirteenth of the circle. Here it conceals the thirteenth moon-month of the Druids, right on the moon's own sign. The name Emblett Lane on Gemini, she says, may come from the Greek *embolos,* an intercalation.

'Sale piece' on the ship's short mast may recall a sail, despite its current spelling. Redlands and Liver Moor both refer perhaps to Gemini's liver or kidney shape. Chaldeans regarded the liver as the seat of life, and used it for divinatory prophecy, as may be seen from the stone livers, carefully inscribed, in the British Museum. Christ and Prometheus are mythologically one. Prometheus' punishment for benefiting humanity was to be chained to a rock and have his liver clawed eternally by a vulture. One recalls the perpetual red wound on Gemini's thigh. Could the eagle-headed griffin-bird be pecking at it?

According to local legend, a ship once sailed up under the lea of Street and then disappeared. A magical ship once berthed at Minehead too, without captain or crew; it is anually celebrated in the Sailor's Horse procession from 1 to 3 May. The 'horse' is an upturned *boat,* and used to sport a cow's tail, thus including Taurus in the festivities. The procession once celebrated the spring, for the equinoctial line through Taurus' foot runs down the ship's mast, making it the first Maypole. As the Minehead horseboat prances, they still sing:

> Awake, St. George our English Knight-O!
> For summer is acome and winter is ago,
> And every day God gives us His grace
> By day and night-O!

Leo

When the star Aldebaran on the bull's foot marked the spring equinox of 2700 BC the star Regulus on the lion's tail marked the summer solstice. Lug the Celtic light-god is Leo; his Welsh form, Llew the Long-Handed, means Leo of the Longest Day. In Arthurian legend Leo is Lancelot – a name also meaning 'lance of light'.

We have already seen that Guinevere's father Leodegrance is Leo, but he is only a minor character in the legends. Who but Lancelot, most magnificent of Arthur's knights, can match the summer sun's fiery splendour? (As the number of Round Table knights varies in different accounts from 24 to 366 – all calendar numbers – we can expect to find duplication of the original twelve signs. Galahad and Perceval are not the only twins for instance; Balin and Balan are equally bound together, as are the young Arthur and his envious foster-brother Sir Kay. Their tales have all proliferated from the original story of the twins.)

The sun rules Leo; in astrological anatomy it also rules the heart – and here is the noble Lancelot's only failing. It was his heart, burning with faithful ardour for Guinevere, that betrayed both his king and himself, and brought about the ruin of the glorious Round Table. His consuming passion for the earth-goddess, all too earthy, also denied him the vision of the Grail. (Was Lancelot-Leodegrance an irresistible father-figure to Guinevere? Or did the earth-goddess simply prefer her sun-gods hot? Mystical Arthur after all, was the ageing, wintry sun in decline, a symbol of waning powers.)

Fathers who fail put their hopes in their sons, so it is interesting to see the second twin I found in Mrs Maltwood's griffin springing from Leo's paw at Somerton. The hope-star Sirius falls on his heart, and earth responds with a welling spring at Grove Steyning Ford. Lancelot's son was the chaste, ethereal Galahad. And though we have identified Galahad with the Christ-like twin, as indeed we must, the two Gemini figures are really one. The name Lugshorn on the second twin's head definitely shows that he springs from Leo.

Nature herself adorns our Leo's mane with thick woodland and Saxon kings built their palace at Somerton on royal Leo's paw. The sun's own sign beams on the Summer County's old country town; a lion adorns its mellow market hall, and Red and White Lion inns, the Globe, the Unicorn, all proclaim memories of the zodiac. The lion and the unicorn! Here it seems, is the origin of the supporters of our Royal coat of arms. The lion is the southern or summer zodiac sign; the unicorn or Capricorn, the northern-most or winter sign. True, these supporters only appeared when James VI of Scotland, our James I, joined the Scottish unicorn to the English lion. But the marriage was inherent in myth; the poet Edmund Spenser had already in Elizabeth's reign said 'the lion and unicorn support the crown' in his mystical poem *The Faery Queen*. And how did the unicorn become Scotland's symbol? Through Jane Beaufort of John of Gaunt's family, the Earls of Somerset – her badge the unicorn, who married the first James of Scotland! John of Gaunt, a major historical figure steeped in Plantagenent and Templar mysteries, must have known of the zodiac. Shakespeare, putting the impassioned speech, 'This other Eden, demi-paradise', into his mouth, knew it too and knew that John of Gaunt knew it. For in Somerset is indeed another Eden, with Adam–Arthur and white

Guinevere. Her serpent Draco is still coiled about the Tree of Life, whose Somerset cider-apples are stars which even now can give knowledge of good and evil. Here too are their sons Cain and Abel who still fight out the long battle of human evolution.

In the sixth century, long before Shakespeare and John of Gaunt, however, Taliesin knew of the lion. For what else can this passage of his describe?

If ye are primitive bards, according to the discipline of qualified instructors, relate the great secrets of the world we inhabit . . .. There is a formidable animal of the city of Satanas which has made an inroad between the deep and the shallows. His mouth is as wide as the mountains of Mynnau [Snowdon]; neither death shall vanquish him, nor hand, nor sword. There is a load of nine hundred rocks between his two paws; there is one eye in his head, vivid as the blue ice.

This can only be a vast nature-effigy and Leo, oddly enough, is the only one with paws. Somerton must be the 'load of nine hundred rocks' between them; it was there in Taliesin's time, for Roman villas and marble quarries liberally besprinkle the area. The city of Satanas is of course the domain of the underworld, and of our Zodiac. Much of Taliesin's poetry describes it, and he never tires of taunting pretentious bards with their ignorance of Britain's great Secret.

Leo, significantly enough, lies in *Cat*sash Hundred; Catsgore lies between his feet, while Catsham is inscribed on Sagittarius' helmet nearby. This lion-cat, one suspects, was Britain's heraldic sign long before fiery Richard the Lion-heart wore it. It was, says Waddell in his *Phoenician Origin of the Britons,* the royal sign of the metal-working Catti or Cassi, who left so many 'Cat' and 'Cass' names about Somerset. They came he says from the Caspian, northern Sumeria.

The Romans seem to have inherited Leo with the metal-trade. A ruined Roman villa on his ear retains the odd name Maggotty Paggotty. Here, speculates Mrs Maltwood, sun-worshippers whispered their prayers to Father-Mother god into his ear. In a Romano-British cemetry at Charlton Adam on Leo's tail, lion's claws have been found!

Leo is also the 'Cath Palug' hunted by Arthur in Celtic myth. *Cath* means 'lion-cat'; *pa* is an old Sumerian word for 'month' and Lug's month was Lughnasad, August. Here is calendar-myth: Celtic Arthur was hunting Leo, the Lion of August, round Somerton, the Sumer-town, in Somerset, the Sumers' seat!

Virgo

Virgo – Virgin soil – is an earth-sign. Here is the goddess of nature, whose magic names are legion, her worship world-wide. She is the ancient triple goddess of the earth, the sea, and the three-phased moon, who nurtures, seduces, mothers and kills the life she bears, mourning over the dying sun-king's funeral barge like triple Isis or Arthur's three queens, weeping like the three Mary's at the empty tomb. All women in one, she is both kind and cruel: smiling at spring and harvest, a screaming hag in winter, a malevolent *femme fatale* in the dark phase of the moon.

In the Glastonbury Zodiac she appears as beldame or witch, perhaps the first witch of all, equipped with her broomstick and tall bonnet. Beneath her head, Annis Hill proclaims her as Black Annis, Tar-Annis, the mother goddess of the Druidic Trinity. Ansford at

Part of the Virgo effigy showing the double mystical aspect of interpretation through physical structure, the Maiden (Corn Goddess) and the Hag (witch).

Castle Cary resoundingly echoes this name. Perhaps the broomstick is also a trident, making her the original British Anna, Britannia, whose wheel is the zodiac (she appears already on Romano-British coins). Or is it a wheatsheaf she holds out to her son? Gemini's mouth is nourishingly stuffed with corn from an old tithe-barn at Dundon. And as the river Cary draws her from top to toe she can only be Mother Cary, Britain's half-forgotten old sea witch. (Charles Kingsley portrays her lovingly in *The Water Babies.*) The Cary rises at Castle Cary in Seven *Lady* Springs – opposite the *Britannia* Inn!

Mother Cary's chickens are flying round the Zodiac at Aquarius and Libra, her favourite being Davey Jones, the Libran dove located at Barton St David. He is mystically the Logos rising from the head of the dying Sagittarian sun-king, who announces the coming Virgin birth. After harvest Virgo's stars descend below the horizon, and the new sun of the winter solstice rises from this point – in her arms. It is the birthday of Christ, the new sun too. In Templar times the Virgin Mary, whose birthday is celebrated by the church in September, appeared as Virgo in cathedral zodiacs. (Judging from architecture, the Church had its finest hour when it embraced astrology; its fortunes have not flourished since it disowned its starry origins, and its Virgin disowned the polarizingly unpleasant but necessary virago.)

The name Babcary on the pregnant Virgin's womb solves the vexed problem of the Virgin Birth. Virgin soil is ever pregnant with life. At Babcary Post Office I asked if there were any local legends, and was told that 'a royal child was hidden here, long ago'. The obliging postmistress knew nothing of the Zodiac and its Virgin until I told her later. I have read another version of this tale - that Henry II was hidden here from King Stephen as a boy - but this was in Templar times when the Zodiac was known. Perhaps this version too is a Zodiac myth in disguise, since historians continually assure me that the Angevin was not in England in his boyhood.

With her nutcracker jaws and wrinkled robe cruelly drawn by the Cary river, our Virgo is no fashion-plate - Rag Lane on her throat seems fair sartorial comment! But the place names Annis Hill and Ansford indicate not only Black Annis and Britannia, but also St Anne, mother of the Virgin. And she, Cornishmen still stoutly affirm, was a Cornish princess before being rescued by Joseph of Arimathea as she wandered pregnant and turned out of doors by her husband. Under Taurus' - Joseph's - protection, she went to the Holy Land and married Joseph's brother, giving birth to the Virgin.

Celts, poets to a man, never understood the gospel story in an exclusively literal, historic way; they heard far more complex overtones. St Anne to them was really Mother Nature. No wonder there are so many St Anne's Hills dotted about the countryside. Like Henry Moore, they saw her breasts in rounded hills, suckling her teeming progeny with sparkling streams, pure as *Liebfraumilch*. They put a tumulus, Wimble Toot, on the nipple of Virgo's breast, drawn by the Cary, and doubtless celebrated harvest festivals here, laced with snake-goddess oracles. *Wimble* means 'augury'; *Toot* or *tot*, we are told, meant a look-out mound or meeting point, but first it meant 'teat' as any tot could tell you, or any sailor if you stood him a tot of rum.

Look carefully at Mother Cary's face in the air-photo and behind the witch's profile there appears a full face, young and beautiful. There are dips for the eyes that still flood after rain and a deep ditch for her smiling mouth. This, alas, has recently been filled in and planted with potatoes! Old Cary–Ceres hunted the earth for her lost daughter Persephone; she should look within, to find herself, eternally young, perennially lovely, endlessly mysterious.

Stickle Bridge clearly emphasizes her broomstick or wheatsheaf. If she is Ceres, Koré, Cary, is she not also Kerin whose cornucopia named all Cornwall, ancient Lyonesse? Canonized by the early church as St Keyne of Cornwall and Somerset's Keynsham, she was known as a determined Virgin who turned all Keynsham's snakes to stone - hence Keynsham's limestone spiral ammonites! Keinton Mandeville on the wheatsheaf hints at his identity. Snake-goddess, royal virgin - who can she be but Virgo?

At least ten place names proclaim her: Downhead is just south of her head, while Queen Camel acknowledges her as Guinevere, queen of Camelot. But in Arthurian legend she is both Perceval's chaste sister and the dark enchantress Morgan-le-Faye, which befits her triple aspect. Perhaps as Guinevere, beloved of Lancelot du Lac, we may also see her as the Lady of the Lake who received Arthur's sword of the spirit at death. And in this first Garden of Eden she is of course Eve, mother of all – and of all ill and evil – as the people of Yeovil and Yeovilton, Ilchester and Ilminster once knew. All yeoman are her husbandmen, tempted like Leo–Lancelot at Charlton *Adam,* in this garden of Universal Myth.

Libra

Here at Barton St David, Davey Jones hurtles down from the dying sun of Sagittarius to Virgo's earth-sign. Hurtle is right, for Hurtle Pool is on his wing. Davey Jones is right, for the church near his head is dedicated to St David of Wales, and both David and John (or Jones) are names meaning 'messenger from God'.

David of Wales had a pet dove that led him to the spot where he founded St David's cathedral; the dove was a symbol of his inspiration by the Holy Spirit. So this bird, says Mrs Maltwood, is David's dove, the Holy Spirit of the Christian Trinity, yet drawn and contoured in Avalon long before. And indeed, Druids revered the *Awen,* 'White Wings', which inspired their bards to say 'Duw Dovydd [God's dove] gives me a ray of inspiration, as it were from the Cauldron of Ceridwen.'

This sun-ray from the godhead quickens the womb of mother earth, just as the dove flies toward the Virgin Mary in many an old Annunciation scene. And St David of Wales is said to have been born of a chaste nun, in fact of St Nunn of Cornwall's Altarnun, during a sea storm (the dove's descending splash?). His father King Seint was obviously far too saintly to have had anything to do with it. Clearly the old Celts understood the Zodiac picture and its multiple meaning in Celtic Christianity. Other names, Gosling Street and Silver Street on the bird's body, raise other white-winged images, like Mother Cary's sea-birds, Leda's or Lohengrin's swan, and Mother Goose's gander whose golden eggs were actually inspirational ideas.

Here too is the Logos or Word, moving over the face of the waters at the creation, calling all into form and life – Noah's dove, willing to begin all anew after the Flood had washed the first human errors away. Its body and wings make the Druid's broad arrow, the three bars of light (a mark still used on government property today, and till recently stamped on convicts' clothing, perhaps reminiscent of the mark of Cain!).

The three primary colours, the three primary chords ... three coloured spindles hung over Galahad's bed in Solomon's ship of Arthurian legend: the Trinity at work. 'God breathed His name,' said the Druids, 'and all Creation sprang into being. And One were the hearing and the seeing.' Light and sound. In physics, science is discovering that three forces of electricity, with a hidden fourth which they call 'charm' lie at the basis of all created matter. It is all there in our ageless Zodiac in a physically poetic symbolism.

Note that the important Plough Stars of Great Bear fall on the dove. Chaldeans called these seven stars *Wul mo sarra* – 'The lord Bel [Wul], Voice of the Universe'. Our dove is indeed the Logos, or the seven holy words of creation. Are these not the seven words from the Cross also? From the dove's outstretched wing (Mrs Maltwood's), trace two lines with a rule down the ship's two masts, then bisect these with a third. It pierces

Gemini's bent head, his ear, his eye, his mouth, his heart, and a red wound in his groin. Here surely is the origin of Galahad's spindles, of the wounded and Christ-like Fisher king: the very image of Christ himself, pierced by the lance of Longinus on the Cross. Arthurian legend perpetuated the unitive teaching of Avalon's Star-Temple through Celtic Christianity, though when Celtic teachings were suppressed, it had to be esoterically transmitted in code.

This invisible arrow is preserved also as Arthur's sword Excalibur, thrown at last into the lake by Bedivere who, by his name, knew Arthur the sun's true grave. It is also Robin Hood's last arrow shot into the forest at his death; for Robin Hood, the Sagittarian archer with his Merry Men and Maid Marion, again is a Templar code for Britain's Zodiac Secret.

Arthur in Welsh means both 'bear' and 'ploughman'; sufficient clue to his high, starry origins. The Great Bear or Plough is a twenty-four hour clock, doing duty for the dead or absent sun in the dark hours. Celts called the Plough Arthur's Chariot or David's Chariot, for it carried the sun's spirit through the night until it finally came again.

The dove also appears in Grail legends, flying through the hall before the Grail procession and filling it with unearthly light. Some see phallic symbolism in this mysterious pageant – the lance held erect by youths, its point dripping sacred blood-drops into the Grail Cup, borne by young damsels. No doubt, at one level, they are right. But the dove intends us to raise our eyes to a higher, more cosmic meaning. The purely phallic interpreters forget the dove of the Spirit and the fact that chastity was essential in the knight who hoped to see the Grail. The catharsis he sought was ultimately of the spirit, not the flesh.

Libra's dove (and what Libran would not prefer to be signed by this aerial messenger, peaceful, inspirational communicative?) is suspended equinoctially at the last quarter of the year, the quarter of maturity and higher mind. Its displacement, I suspect, is a hint to those who can read the signs. Cancer too is slightly displaced. Are these two signs connected? If so the secret they convey is that of the Grail procession, male and female, yin and yang, the foundational secret of creation. Here Libra is the penetrating male, Cancer the receptive female vessel, like the four Grail hallows of lance into cup, sword into stone. By this device, both zodiac and Grail legend tell us, evolution works tirelessly to produce ever higher and more complex forms of life. Not only physically, but psychically – for the more complex the ganglia, the higher the consciousness. And as this cross-fertilization extends through the amoeba and the mammalia, into man and thus into the realm of ideas, the evolutionary engine slips into an overdrive, into a higher, faster gear. Among men, ideas and ideologies can sway world populations on a scale that dwarfs all previous evolutionary gains among the animals; dwarfs even Leo's power conquests, his long civilizations of Egypt, Chaldea, Assyria, Greece, Rome. The time-scale shortens continuously until it seems that the human race can be converted almost overnight to truer ideas of social justice, of greater hope for all. We are increasingly impatient of imperfection and failure, constantly seeking an equilibrial balance of perfected harmony.

The sun seeds not only life, but increasingly, ideas and inspiration on the earth. The dove of the Logos is still at work, and working faster than ever before. We have arrived at a point when peaceful Libra's academic notions of justice and idealism are over taken by zealous reformers and militant political activists – even terrorists.

Scorpio

Scorpio is the revolutionary, ruled by red Mars. But he is also the self-analyst, as critical of himself as of others. He must find the truth and establish it, cost what it may. Libra dreams of the Holy City, the new Jerusalem; Scorpio starts excavating its foundations in the middle of the High Street, regardless of the destruction and chaos he causes, regardless even of his own death in the process. The scorpion in myth stings himself to death with his own venomous tail.

He is Mordred in Arthurian legend, Arthur's envious nephew-son by his sister Morgan-le-Faye. Incest! But do not blame Arthur – with only one woman in the zodiac he can hardly avoid it. Virgo must be at once mother, sister, wife. Morgan-le-Faye the witch plots her son's rise and his father's fall. Her husband, King Lot of the Orkneys, is another light-god, swept into Arthur's orbiting Round Table like another old Celtic sun-god. Perhaps he represents the Northern Lights? Perhaps, too, he accounts for the name Lottisham on our Scorpio effigy.

Mordred works secretly to divide the Round Table over Guinevere and Lancelot's affair, and eventually succeeds. He stages the fatal Battle of Camlann, aiming to abduct Guinevere, queen of the land, and then reign with her. Shades of Oedipus! But Oedipus too is ancient solar myth, a fact obscured by the recent Freudian furore.

Mordred, that penetrating Scorpionic critic, seizes on the one weakness in the noble Arthurian fellowship to bring it down; the lovers, all too human, give the Devil his chance. Yet in killing Arthur, Mordred is killed himself. The glorious pageant comes to an end with a bang. November is still the month of purging bonfires and fireworks, and significantly, it rhymes with 'remember'. Would the Round Table be remembered today with such nostalgia, would it keep its inspirational power, if it had simply faded away? The most memorable sunsets are those that bathe the sky in blood, and Arthur is best remembered in the splendour of his passing (*Morte d'Arthur*).

Two enemies assail the sun-god in this zodiac; the whale or *Avanc* (apathetic matter, chaos) resists the Supreme Artist's struggle to mould it into form, and by sheer dead weight drags the Creator down into the deep; and Scorpio (human free-will, pride, passion and envy) attacks him treacherously from behind. He is truly caught between the Devil and the Deep.

Scorpio is indeed deep, always working his plans in secret. He is the most elusive sign in this whole Zodiac, and the least satisfactory of Mrs Maltwood's original figures. I have attempted another using her main lines, but standing him up the other way. Scorpio, the water-sign, like Pisces and Cancer, is naturally subject to floods. Many banked ditches indicate possible claws, but these are suggested rather than fully outlined. Fourfoot and Bridgefoot Bridge on the Fosse Way seem to indicate that he once had four feet, as scorpions should. Scorpio is the sign of death, the Eighth House of the zodiac, and we avoid the thought of death. Perhaps this too has caused the effigy to be forgotten. Even the marker stone at Stone seems to have disappeared. One place name however is significant, though it can only be seen on the six-inch map – Hell Ditch. It runs from Arthur's eastern arm as if to save him from his enemy, a hope as forlorn as Canute's, for November's sun is inevitably doomed to die. It reminds us of Blake's epitaph: 'I was buried near this dyke, that my friends may weep as much as they like.' Was it once a wailing wall for mourning sun-worshippers? Throughout myth all sun-gods must harrow hell.

Arthur's funeral barge is said to have floated down the river Brue from Salisbury Plain, where the battle of Camlann was fought. How right that he should enter Avalon through this death sign, for the Brue traces Scorpio's southern boundary – my figure's tail, Mrs Maltwood's figure's southern claw. At either bank are the churches of East and West Lydford – Lud the light-god's ford. At East Lydford's ruined church, open-lidded graves yawn, for Arthur is not there. He has risen! 'Unknown,' sang the bard, 'is the grave of Arthur.'

The river Cary draws four southern signs, the river Brue four northern ones, an extraordinary feat of 'chance'. The Brue, river of rue, outlines Arthur's enemies – scorpion, Draco's dragon, the whale – thus encompassing his ruin.

Yet Scorpio is a light-god too: he is Lucifer, whose name means light-bringer. Fallen from heaven to earth he must, by scathing self-analysis, win his way back to his first home. He is the very symbol of man and his aspirations. The ancients said that Scorpio was once the brightest sign in the sky, till his star fell. Once he was signed by an eagle, now by a scorpion – venomous creeping thing. So he cannot rest until he has regained his wings. Take courage, Scorpions! You too may become eagles, but the way is hard.

Alford church on his tail has some significant old pew-ends: a dragon-like scorpion, stinging its own head with its tail in an agony of self-examination; a Paschal lamb (Aries); a pelican in its piety (Aquarius). They indicate Scorpio's way back – using his great strength in self-sacrifice.

Ditcheat's church has a superb medieval mural of St Christopher, who is surely Scorpio on his regenerating path. Christopher, a soldier under Mars like Scorpio, abused his great strength serving one conqueror after another, attempting to find an invincible king worthy of his power.* At last, disillusioned, he became a hermit on a torrential river's bank, humbly carrying travellers across on his broad back until one stormy night he carried a little child over the water. But its weight increased until Christopher, staggering, felt he had the world itself on his shoulders. It was the Christ-child, the invincible king at last! Christopher, like Scorpio, must cross the river of death, turning his back on the world to find himself. Ditcheat – the name is intriguing. Ditch at what? The ditch at the eastern gate of the Zodiac; the ditch dividing the world from the Otherworld. Note too the name of Ditcheat's inn, the Green Tree. Here Christopher's staff becomes the holy thorn of Joseph of Arimathea, who, legend states, also bore the Christ-child across the waters to Britain.

'But', scholars will exclaim, 'Ditcheat is near the Fosse Way, which itself means ditch or dyke. No nonsense here about the zodiac.' Yet the Fosse Way runs across Scorpio straight as a die, neatly dividing the eastern world from western Avalon. To the Druids,

---

*St Christopher was also recognized as a pagan giant who suffered conversion. (*Ed.*)

east symbolized the world, west the Otherworld. The Fosse Way itself is part of this numinous pattern. Virgo, *the world,* lies east of its line. Not for nothing does the *High History* describe her as 'the damsel beyond the bar'.

Scorpio, man himself, is at the judgement bar and Libra's judgement stars fall on Scorpio's tail. The *High History* knew this, describing him as Callixtus, a dead hermit whose misspent life was the subject of an intense struggle between devils and angels. Take heart, Scorpions: Callixtus scraped into heaven by a whisker!

Sagittarius – Arthur

Just before the battle of Camlann, Arthur has a disturbing dream which describes Sagittarius' position in this Zodiac with some accuracy. This doom-laden vision occurs at the end of *Morte d'Arthur* and elsewhere. He dreamt he sat, robed like a king, in a chair fastened to the Wheel of Fortune, high above dark waters infested with serpents and other deadly monsters. Suddenly, at midday Dame Fortune frowned, turning her wheel, so that he fell 'up-so-down' amongst them, each creature seizing him by a limb. This piece of evidence, if there were no others, is enough to identify Arthur and his Round Table in Avalon with this Zodiac – for here Sagittarius the sun-king hangs upside-down on a wheel, menaced and gnawed by Scorpio and the Piscean leviathan. And is he not performing Somerset's first somersault? Up to Dickens's time, a somersault was always termed a 'somerset'.

'Arthur' as a solar title stretches further than the Vale of Avalon. To the Egyptians, he was Osiris, Ausar, his son Horus (the hour) also bearing his name, Arueris. To the Persians, Assyrians and Medes, he was Ahura, Asser, Ashur, the sun, ruling by night as Sagittarius the glittering Archer. It seems he was taken to these culture centres in very ancient times, his figure being badly copied into a centaur. But this, as we have seen, he is not, being a kingly figure in adversity, dragged over his mount's neck to set sun-like below the horizon. The very earth contours proclaim the declining sun of Sagittarius in November and December; his horse is recognizably modelled by the Pennard Hills, while Arthur's body lies below in the plain of Baltonsborough. These names are eloquent, 'Pennard' means Arddur's hill-top, while Baltonsborough remembers another well-known sun-god, Bel or Baal. Even the prosaic name West Bradley on his leg has a secret: it was once Bodelege, or body-leg! Canters Green and Breech Lane on his breeches loudly proclaim the horseman, and Arthur's Bridge on his horse's tail leave no doubt that he was remembered when place names were given out.

Arthur in the legends too is plainly in decline; his glories are all in the past, and when he or Guinevere are insulted, as frequently happens, he has to rely on younger knights to seek redress. He is moreover cuckolded by Lancelot yet bears no malice, having learnt the generous detachment of the zodiac's Ninth House of higher mind. He is indeed the wise and patient philosopher-king.

Arthur resides in English hearts more than St George, our patron saint, has ever done; how welcome then to find them both identified by this splendid effigy. Both exemplify the same virtues of chivalry to the weak and of strength only used against evil. Both wrestle with the dragon, and our Sagittarian effigy's arms are also outflung in the patronal Cross of St George. 'George', like 'Arthur', means gardener, ploughman; Adam too cultivated the soil. All are symbolized by this one figure in the western/Eden-garden; here is man, or God in man, wrestling with the earth and crucified on the cross of his own dual nature, animal and divine. Here is also Cornwall's Phoenician St Michael – and Scotland's enigmatic St Andrew, who, according to apocryphal legend was a dragon-slayer too. Andrew represents the androgyne man of the Mysteries, uniting the virtues of both sexes in himself, like Indara (Indra), sun-god of the wandering Aryan tribes.

What patron saint, what national symbol, does not derive from this archetypal Zodiac? Their patronal crosses, combined in the Union Jack, make the spokes of Britannia's wheel. Arthur's name, passing into our everyday language in words like 'heart' and 'hearth', betrays the central place he holds in our subliminal affections. Two of his Celtic names are in fact shown here, for *Hu* (pronounced He) was the sun-god giant who led the Cymric Welsh westward to Britain 'across the hazy sea in the Age of Ages'. He has countless names but all denote the same Sun, worshipped by all for its *ard*our, for its *ard*uous labours on behalf of creation. *Per Ardua ad Astra* should really be translated 'with Arthur to the stars'. He hides in another Phoenician title, *Hercules Melk-Arth* (Melk = king, Arth = Arthur), for what were Hercules' Twelve Labours but the passage of the sun through the twelve Houses of the Zodiac? The stars of Hercules indeed fall upon Sagittarius' effigy and Hercules, at least in myth, came to Britain's Star-Temple to find its Eden-garden apples of wisdom. It is recorded that he travelled from Greece through Illyria and on to the river Po, making a bee-line for Britain!

The river Brue runs down our Sagittarian effigy's forehead until, at Baltonsborough Flights, a little waterfall, it rushes out like life-blood into the wing of the dove, his departing spirit. Many things tumble into place with the water as one muses at this poetic spot in the landscape. Here the sun-god yields up his spirit, which flies to the earth-goddess to ensure that the new God-man shall be born, to die for his people in his turn. It is the flight of the spirit of Bel, the God-name spread by the Phoenicians, heirs of the lore of sunken Atlantis, right across the world from west to east.

Capricorn

Arthur's leg descends into the horn of Capricorn, sign of old age and frozen wintry earth, ruled by Saturn, old Father Time. This horn, an Iron or Bronze Age earthwork three-quarters of a mile long, is still locally known as the Golden Coffin.* The Zodiac explains why. Arthur it seems is not only between the devil and the deep – he also has one foot in the grave and it is the grave of the dying year. But in the zodiac the grave is not the end, and Capricorn's frozen horn is a cornucopia in which the seeds of the coming spring are stored over the winter solstice. The new sun-gods of most religions, including Christianity, are said to be born at this seminal time. Zeus, said the Greeks, was suckled by the goat Amalthea with her cornucopia horn in the Cave of the Rising. For this service Zeus later translated her to the stars as Capricorn.

*Its more general name is Ponter's Ball (*Ed.*)

But this Capricorn is not just a goat, however mythological; its horn, single and straight, betrays the unicorn, the wintry north pole of the lion–unicorn axis. And the unicorn, though we are accustomed to see him as a king of horse, still betrays his Capricornian origins in his goatish beard and cloven hoofs.

Our Capricorn is also the White Hart, a mysterious creature who, with the unicorn, has been hunted through the forests of myth by every prince of folklore. Here in Avalon they could run both to ground, cooling their feet in the Hartlake, their hearts thumping from the chase at Hearty Moor. Both creatures symbolized secret knowledge, an esoteric philosophy, a church disestablished, indeed oppressed by the lion of the Establishment. They stand for the elusive Truth surviving in adversity as only those under Saturn *can* survive. The White Hart, found by St Hubert and other saints in the deepest part of the forest, had a crucifix between its horns; this is secret Christianity, the essence of the Mysteries.

And this makes sense when we realize that Capricorn here must be Merlin the Druid, by whose ancient wisdom the Round Table was made and the Grail Quest begun. The Druids were always people of the forest and the grove. Like his pursuers, our Capricorn also seeks the Grail; his nose is pressed ardently against the Tor, that hill of self-fulfilment. For goats must climb mountains; his back leg in the swamps of the White-lake river is launching itself for the final leap from Launcherley Hill which will gain him the Grail-vase or waterpot of Aquarius. (In legend a goat has long haunted Glastonbury Tor.)

Capricorn under Saturn, old Father Time, represents man in the whole course of evolution, heaving himself with great persistence and against insuperable difficulties out of the primeval swamp; his powerful shoulders show boundless potential, his back legs are lost in amoebic slime. He is Pan, oldest of the Greek gods, animal or goatish man; horned and cloven-footed, some have even seen him as Satanic. And truly, such power, like any power, can work either way. But see how he is helped by Sagittarius, the sun-god or divine man, whose effigy penetrates him at three nodal points – the intuitive back of the head, the heart, and the bowels or sex organs. With these intimations of immortality he can no longer be merely animal; his mystical antlers or unicorn's horn (the brain beyond the brain) will not let him rest, despite the diabolical horns and cloven feet. (As these still betray him they have been given to Merlin's father, who was said in Arthurian legend to have been the Devil.)

But Merlin, all-wise adviser to Arthur – a goat? Why certainly. Remember how the love-besotted old wizard told the enchantress Vivien all his spells, and how she, tiring of him, used them against him to lock him up for ever in an oak? What a warning to all ageing philosophers! Perhaps this also hints at ageless wisdom locked in the Druidic oak?

On Glastonbury's Glass Mountain, Capricorn is due to see himself reflected in all his goatish imperfection, die of self-loathing, and be reborn. He is the Jewish scapegoat, loaded with all humanity's sins. But on this mount of transfiguration, of resurrection, he will at last reach a new level of consciousness. The Tor completely overawes the Vale of Avalon. Terraced like a ziggurat in the seven steps to perfection, it is unmistakably a holy hill, the focal point of endeavour and achievement for the whole transcendent landscape. This pyramid of earth and stone is really a spiritual beacon.

Aquarius

At this magnetic point we may expect all threads to come together, to be woven into a single strand that gives revelatory significance to the whole. And so we find that Aquarius for Mrs Maltwood was Perceval. But he is no longer the boy from the backwoods of the second twin, the gruff Griffin, the ingénue who made every mistake in the book, like Gawain. Here at the Tor, purged by all the sequential zodiac Houses, by all the adventures and experiences of the Grail-Quest, he has at last become worthy to see the Grail unveiled. As Galahad always was, so Perceval has become. From the thoughtless lad who broke his mother's heart and left her dying, the adventurer who took all he was offered and rode off, the rake who would kiss the girls and leave them crying – he has become the very 'parfit gentil knight' to whom damsels and crones could apply for help without fear or favour, a man who would take on fifty miscreants single-handed on their behalf. But Perceval's transformation is not achieved without much suffering. As he begins to see himself as he is, he goes mad with horror and wanders in the wilderness like a wild man of the woods, covered in shaggy hair. But at the point of death (surely in Capricorn) he is rescued and brought to the Grail castle – brought to himself!

Perceval is a marvellous portmanteau name. It can mean 'pierce the veil' (or the Vale of Avalon), like the eagle eye of Aquarius' Phoenix, or 'perceive all', as all may do from the Tor. He is also called *Par-lui-fet* (in the *High History*), the man who has made himself. For he has perfected himself at last, and can thus be Ganymede, the perfect man of the Greek mysteries who was always identified with Aquarius.

The Zodiac is no mundane vicious circle. Here, at its northernmost point it can become a mystic spiral – but only for those who like Ganymede can soar to Olympus on eagle-wings. And Geoffrey Russell has found just such a spiral on the Tor, cut by its seven terraces in the form of a 'Cretan' maze. (It is doubtful if Crete was the first to use this ancient mandala or brain-pattern to indicate the course of human evolution; much more likely that it was brought from neolithic Britain to Crete and the Middle East. Ancient examples cut in stone are found in Dublin's Hollywood Stone and at Tintagel; penitential mazes were long habitual all over Europe and would seem to be indigenous.)

The Druids taught that man's true goal was the sun – though this was but the first of seven heavens which he was destined to attain spiritually. They saw its shining orb 'as an assembly of pure souls' (as an old Breton legend puts it) radiating out their light and energy to vitalize and sustain the whole solar system. For those whose vibrations had reached the required pitch, Aquarius symbolized the escape hatch from the circle of earthly lives; it is the phoenix, dying on its self-made funeral pyre and reborn from its own ashes, the sunward eagle destined for higher realms of endeavour.

Ancient Egyptians held that 'a soul might make its transformation into the phoenix that flew to Heliopolis, city of the sun' – obviously agreeing with the Druids on the important question of ultimate human potential. Maybe both derived their teachings from this timeless circle, itself a survival from Atlantis, as much evidence seems to show. (Gemini for example must be the original Atlas, titan king of Atlantis, bearing the ecliptic or starry universe on his upraised arm; his ship the original ark of Noah, bearing its cargo of zodiac animals to seed new civilizations on the foundation of their accurate time measurements and psychological-cosmological knowledge.)

Actis, son of Sol the sun, was one of several brothers distinguished for their learning and knowledge of astrology. Out of jealousy however they killed Tenages, the most brilliant of them, and had to flee. Actis went to Egypt and founded Heliopolis, to which city the phoenix, a calendar bird, was said to fly every 500 years to renew himself by self-immolation on top of a pyramid. How interesting then to find Actis Fields just south of pyramidal Glastonbury Tor! The graves of Arthur, Guinevere and even St Patrick are all said in old chronicles to have been marked in Glastonbury Abbey's grounds by pyramids. There is a further identification of the national saints and heroes of our islands with the calendar – for the Abbey grounds on the Aquarian phoenix's tail lie directly on the sun's ecliptic path. St Patrick's Day, 17 March, is round about the vernal equinox.

The Tor itself has often been seen as an artificially adapted step-pyramid. *Pyre-amid* on which our phoenix burns! Its pyre was legendarily made of cinnamon and other spices so do not be surprised to find Ashwell Lane and Cinnamon Lane nearby. For here is the *High History's* burning castle, from which the story's hermit prophesied that a flame should be kindled that would burn up the whole world and bring it to an end. An Aquarian Age prediction? Yet never fear; in Aquarius' end lies its new beginning.

The star Fomalhaut falls on Crab Tree Drove just west of the Wells road and north of our phoenix effigy. Draw a line from here south to Christian's Cross, on Leo's tail, to find star-fall for the star Regulus. This is the north–south axis of the Royal Star Cross, whose east–west arm (Aldebaran on Taurus' foot, Antares at Stone on Scorpio) we have already seen. These said Mrs Maltwood, marked the compass-points in 2700 BC; thus she dated the Zodiac's recognition and development to this period.

Glastonbury Abbey's arms, she said, commemorated this calendar cross by a green tree with horizontal branches, stricken, lopped and bare. This tree of life appears in many Arthurian legends by a magical fountain (Chalice Well). Those who dared to drink from it were soused by an instant and violent hailstorm, which stripped the tree of all its leaves and left the presumptuous knight more dead than alive. A typical lightning-strike from Uranus, ruler of Aquarius! In some tales a giant mounted knight, clad in rusty armour, would rise from beneath a great stone slab and trounce the initiate who dared to drink this self-revealing water of life. This knight surely can only be Arthur–Sagittarius, situated nearby.

The eagle–phoenix, resurrection bird, as its crest of lynchets denotes, is raised entirely on Avalon's highest hills. Its west wing is drawn by two old roads to Wells, round and over Edmund Hill; its east wing by the Edgarley–Wick road, emphasized by terraces sweeping round Southdown Hill. Its breast, delightfully, is drawn by Paradise Lane. It is indeed a water-carrier, holding the water of life, Chalice Well, in its curved beak. Here, they say, Joseph of Arimathea hid the chalice of the last supper which contained the Blood of the Crucified, and nature responds by growing crimson, algae-like clots of blood in its waters. They indeed run iron-red and are credited in times past with many miraculous healings – hence the name Blood-Spring. The flow from the Aquarian water-pot or chalice is unceasing; its water both blood and wine.

The avian creature, its beak turned to peck its own wing, may well be the origin of the

The Aquarian effigy symbolized here in one of its oldest forms – the rejuvenating Phoenix. It is set around Glastonbury.

medieval 'pelican in its piety', who drew its own blood to feed its brood, and was thus a symbol of the self-sacrificing Christ. But it's as an eagle that this effigy seems best remembered locally. Medieval eagles are everywhere. One is carved high on the Tor's old tower; another carved on Glastonbury's magnificent tithe-barn, reminds us that its four evangelistic creatures, bull, lion, eagle and man, were once the four cardinal points of the compass. A third appears on a house at Wick on the eastern wing. Our Aquarian eagle, the greatest of them all, turns his head westward to see the sun set in the Severn Sea like all the other effigies. Sunsets from the Tor are well worth a backward glance!

Pisces

This dual sign under Neptune and Jupiter, symbolizes enlarged consciousness. On its higher side it produces the mystic – the initiate like Perceval who is ready to leave this earth for a better world. On its lower side it can produce drink and drug addiction, dissolution, even confinement in hospital, prison or asylum. Pisces must enlarge his consciousness by hook or by crook; his is the Twelfth House of self-undoing. Thus it provides shelter for those who fail the Aquarian Grail test (and who can fail like Pisces?), a place where they can return to the earthly Wheel of Lives to try again, beginning as all life begins, in water. One fish in this numinous circle is thus set high on Wearyall and Fisher's Hill; the other is low, by the ram's head at Street. How apt too that Glastonbury Abbey, most haunting, most otherworldly of all sacred ruins, should lie between Aquarius and Pisces' mystical northern fish. It is a very monument to dissolution; a monument also to mystical religion – Celtic or Grail Christianity. Yet on its greensward Arthur's empty grave gives promise that man, like the sun his exemplar, will rise again and again until he achieves patient evolution's aim.

Joseph of Arimathea, they say, came to Wearyall Hill with twelve companions and thrust his staff into its soil as they rested, wearied all. Here it took root and flowered at Christmas and Easter until cut down by a furious Puritan, who was blinded by a flying chip. Luckily other sprigs were budded from the parent thorn, and all flourish still flowering, incredibly, at Christmas. (Nature willingly assists all Zodiac myths, as we have seen.)

They also say that Joseph brought the chalice of the Last Supper with him, fleeing from persecution as a witness to the Resurrection – another empty tomb. Legend has it that Arviragus granted Joseph and his band twelve hides of land round Glastonbury to maintain themselves. Here, the tale goes, Joseph built a little church of wattles, round in form. Some, echoed by William of Malmesbury, averred that it was not Joseph, but the Lord himself that built it, 'for the salvation of men'. Whoever the builder was, William remembers how sacred was its reputation, and that its floor was inlaid with a pattern of triangles and squares, of which he says, 'If I say it contained a holy mystery I do no injustice to religion.' The twelve hides? The twelve animal-hides or hidden zodiacal figures. The little wattle round church? The vast nature–temple in the Avalon marshes. Built by the Lord himself for our salvation? Why certainly, as I hope all of the fore-going makes plain. The triangles and squares? The triplicities and quadruplicities of the Zodiac. William of Malmesbury, Templar-inspired, undoubtedly knew the great Secret, the disestablished unicorn church in hiding; but for fear of the established church he had to couch his description in a careful code.

Joseph of Arimathea or the Phoenician tin-trader who brought Christianity to this island, whoever he was, also knew the Secret. For he landed on Pisces, the first sign for Christianity, planting his staff right on the ecliptic line as a calendar-peg to mark the new religion of the dawning Piscean Age. (In every case the first Christian churches were founded in Phoenician spheres of influence or colonies.) To Phoenicians the teaching was not so much new as a restatement of the ancient Mysteries. They must have been well aware that they were in a sense bringing coals to Newcastle – that this was the perennial philosophy's first home. Yet the mission was necessary, and timely. It shows in fact split-second timing, for the Druids, long the guardians of these ideas, were decimated by the Romans on Mona in 61 AD. Joseph, or 'another man of the same name', arrived to tend the languishing nature-temple in 63 AD. So at least the legend goes. This fascinating blend of history and legend is far too coincidental to be taken merely as chance or accident. Yet it is of the essence of myth that having explained everything on a metaphysical level, one suddenly comes to see that it may well be true on a purely literal one as well. For myth is not fiction; it is eternal truth. And what is eternally true must always be acted and re-enacted in time and place in terms of actual flesh and blood,

Well may Joseph, the wealthy man of the gospels, have obtained his wealth by tin-trading in Britain. Well may he have brought his nephew, trained most likely with his cousin, John the Baptist, by the astrological Essenes, to see himself in the Geminian messiah; to learn his part and see his counterpart in Britain's first and greatest open university.

Joseph mediates between all three of Avalon's mysterious legends, making them in essence one. He joins the Zodiac to the legends of his coming with the Christ-child and the Grail by landing in the only astrologically possible place. By the Grail he unites these myths to Arthurian legend; he is indeed cited in these and in many old genealogies as ancestor (through his son Josephes) to Arthur and all his knights. It is, it seems, something of a family business. But are we not also descended from this stock – is the Quest of the Grail not ours by right of inheritance?

The fish of Wearyall Hill is the only sign of the circle that is readily recognizable from the ground; it looks like nothing so much as a great fish, dolphin, whale or salmon, rearing out of the sea-level moors around it. It is the one visible clue granted to the pilgrim on the quest. Here surely is the Celtic Salmon of Wisdom of the 'Mabinogion'. In Arthurian legend it is King Fisherman's castle, reached by crossing the Perilous Bridge (*pons perilus*) over the river Brue, river of death; and from here, it is said, Arthur's sword Excalibur was ritually flung into the waters. There were three bridges in the legends, razor-narrow, vertiginously high and frail. Traces remain in actual fact of three bridges here, carrying the ancient road from Somerton to Glastonbury and the Mendips across the treacherous marshes of the whale.

For here we are on the whale's tail, that great leviathan that drags Arthur's setting sun down into the deep. Three place names confirm him – Hulk Moor on the tail, Plunging on the body, and Wallyer's (whale's) Bridge on the jaws that mangle Arthur's arm out of all recognition. Who wins this eternal battle between light and darkness? Arthur was swallowed by a great fish, says Layamon's *Brut,* and coughed up again in three days. Whale's jaws, optimistically, hang like a victorious trophy on Glastonbury Abbey's gate.

I found a serpent's head projecting from the whale jaws, a head that turned, like those of the other effigies, westward. It lies near Mrs Maltwood's serpent head in the legend-haunted confines of Park Wood. Though it is a newcomer to her circle its credentials are good; when I placed the planisphere on the map the stars of Draco curved along its neck. Arthur is undoubtedly tangled with the dragon Draco! I suspect this circumpolar dragon has seven heads, for the seven pole stars. One is on the ominously named Black Acre Rhine, the others you may find for yourself. They are all there.

The guardian King Fisherman should not be left unsung. Pierced by a lance in the groin – that is, impotent – he languishes in his castle awaiting a knight who could ask the vital, and vitalizing question: 'To whom serveth the Grail?' Admittedly in its garbled (perhaps intentionally garbled) form it is difficult to know just what this means, so perhaps it is not surprising that he had to wait so long for someone to ask it. However, we do know basically what was meant: the Fisher king needed to find a successor to whom the outer world of the senses was not all there is; one who could ask questions about the purpose of life. He dies happy at last in Galahad's arms, having found such a king among men. Some versions say Perceval cured him, in others it is even Gawain.

Who is he? Variously named Pelles, Pelleas, Pellinore or Avallach, even Evalake, he is the old sun-king of Avalon's apple orchards, whom the Greeks later adopted as Apollo Meleatas, the apple god. (Apollo's mother Latona was a Hyperborean, that is a Briton, for Hecateus plainly stated in 400 BC that the land of the Hyperboreans was here.) On Avallach's health the well-being of the land depended. He must be cured or, alternatively, a young and worthy successor found. Pierced Christ-like in the thigh, he is the personified sun, ever-dying that we may live. But sun-myth is not so primitive or naive as we have thought.

Evalake is All-Consciousness, languishing until his creation can raise itself to his level. Like Gemini in the ship, from which he must derive, he fishes for the souls of men. He is thus that highest part of ourselves that we constantly ignore, betray, mangle and mutilate. For consciousness is not only Evalake's but evolution's aim — *and this is what the Zodiac is all about.* This above all is its message, the core of that marvellous 'Hyperborean wisdom' so revered by the ancient world. It was to learn the purpose of life that Gilgamesh, Jason, Perseus, Odysseus, Joseph, even perhaps Jesus, sailed across half the world in Solomon's ship or argo.

The zodiac pattern is written not only in the stars, but on human form and character, on animals, plants and even minerals. It is also, it seems, inscribed on the very face of the earth itself – perhaps all over the world. Many suggested and possible new zodiacs are being found, as at Kingston, Nuthampstead, Pumpsaint, Prescelly, and Durham. *It is, I suggest, a pattern made by the forces or laws of creation in their own image,* inscribing themselves on all created matter, as if they, the tools of the creator, left their characteristic mark. It is not only a pattern in space, but in time; history, examined with this sequence in mind, betrays the same design. But that is another story!

The association with ancient roads of the zodiacs so far found suggests that they may be nodal parts of the geomantic ley-system, itself pointing to electro-magnetic currents, little understood and quite untapped. What a surging powerhouse lies beneath our feet! A similar powerhouse of mental and spiritual vitality also lies within us, could we but learn to know ourselves. And here again the zodiac offers each a personal dossier of enormous, limitless potential in our horoscope.

Can modern psychology offer a place and purpose in a larger co-ordinated scheme for every individual? Dare it be so frank with our failings, so knowledgeable about our individual course? Does science itself dare point to a reason and purpose for the universe and its myriad individual parts? No. Only religion dares do this, and it is dying, for it has relied too long on unquestioning faith, and now finds itself in a period when people have been educated to demand reasons for their beliefs. Man is, or must try to be, a reasoning being, so 'faith' in the sense of accepting blind dogma is being thrown out of the window.

Yet for sanity and even health we need a sense of purpose, a vision. It is still true that 'where there is no vision the people perish'; truer for those with imagination and enquiring minds than for those without. Mental hospitals are tragically full of such sensitives. We used to think that all our social ills were due to poverty, but it becomes apparent that we need more than materialistic security. Never have we been so enraged at the seeming futility of life, so depressed by the mocking finality of death.

At such a desparate juncture the zodiac reappears, its therapeutic existence endorsed by nature itself. A natural phenomenon, it invites rational investigation. It even promises to add to our knowledge of scientific laws. It reconciles science with religion, and sundered and warring religions with one another, by restating old and misunderstood dogmas in revelatory terms which make new and illuminating sense. It shows order and aim where we had supposed only accident and chaos, pointing a path not only through this life but beyond, towards ever-heightening realms of beauty and consciousness.

It is perhaps the rational religion for Aquarian man. For now dawns the Age of the Phoenix, the escape-hatch of the zodiac. Is evolution preparing a new leap in consciousness in our time? There are many signs that it may be – general literacy, instant communication, instant global travel, travel beyond the globe. But the burning castle threatens too, and globally; never has the human race been so dangerously inflammable. The very terror of the times forces the ultimate questions upon all but the cynic, the frivolous, or the apathetic. 'Who am I?' 'Where am I going?' 'What is it all for?' It is to answer such questions that this Zodiac appears. Yet is has *always* been there; it is rather our changing level of consciousness that has brought it into view once more. Airborne, we see more than the plodding, earth-bound traveller. Yet the traveller lost can heighten his view by climbing a hill, and *orientating his map with the aid of the sun or the patterns of the stars.*

Recommended Books

Caine, Mary. 'The Glastonbury Giants' (twelve articles in *Prediction,* 1968–9).
Evans, Sebastian, trans. *The High History of the Holy Grail.* James Clarke, 1969.
Malory, Sir Thomas. *Le Morte d'Arthur.* Everyman.
Maltwood, K. E. *A Guide to Glastonbury's Temple of the Stars.* James Clarke, 1964.
Reiser, Oliver L. *This Holyest Erthe.* Perrenial Press, 1975.
Roberts, Anthony. *Atlantean Traditions in Ancient Britain.* Rider, 1977.

CHAPTER THREE

Somerset Legendary Geomancy

JANET ROBERTS

'The whole of China south of the Great Wall was formed to a single design, in which the topographical features of the landscape were artificially moulded to produce their conformity with the required pattern.' Thus states John Michell in his book *The View Over Atlantis*. It is open to conjecture whether Britain falls into this incredible category but certainly, looking at the area surrounding Glastonbury, we do find many fascinating examples of terrestrial geomancy on a pretty large scale.

Take the Tor itself. Rising out of the flat Somerset marshes is a marvellous conical hill with a circular maze path winding its way to the top, to the remains of St Michael's church;* members of the Old Religion and ancient geomancers would eye the countryside beneath them from the slopes. Obviously the church was a later Christian adaptation as the original mystic schema involved numerous megalithic stones, and you can find remnants of these scattered around the lower slopes of the hill. Over 500 feet tall, the Tor is an island promontory rising at the end of a saddle of land that reaches back to Shepton Mallet. Its current shape is recognized as partially artificial, built up and sculpted by men who could tune in to the very patterns of nature, working in harmony with the natural rhythms and psychic contours.

Now, if men existed who could do feats of 'spiritual engineering' to this extent, it comes as no surprise to find nearby one of the finest terrestrial zodiacs in the country. Ten figures depicting the astronomical signs of the zodiac and three constellation effigies all within a thirty-mile circumference have been etched into the ground, to be seen strictly from above as the figures are so vast. To build this 'temple of the stars' must have taken much energy and planning. Hills had to be raised dozens of feet higher, rivers diverted, earthworks and ditches as well as paths and trackways designed to fit the picture – all conforming to the grand design of stars burning in the sky above them.

Many people disbelieve the fact that our ancestors could think about such scientifically

---

*Many churches built on pre-Christian holy sites are dedicated to dragon saints, the most popular being St Michael, the archangel who slew the dragon of paganism with his fiery sword. St Michael sites nearly always occupy elevated positions in the landscape. (*Ed.*)

esoteric things, let alone build giant working monuments to enhance their lives and souls. It's hard to accept the fact in this Newtonian era that the Ancients were far more knowing and more organically skilful in engineering than we are today, and on a religious basis to boot!

The Glastonbury Zodiac was rediscovered in the twenties by Mrs Katharine Maltwood. She only discovered it by ranging over the area looking for the more mystical Arthurian landmarks. Its verisimilitude is borne out by the key fact that all these effigies are in conjunction with the appropriate stars in their corresponding constellations.

We now have the majestic Tor and the huge terrestrial Zodiac around it. If the old geomantic genii produced all this, could there be anything else of similar nature lurking in the Somerset marshes? The visitor to central Somerset will notice the way the flat marshland which predominates suddenly gives way to beautifully shaped hills and isolated humps of green, luscious turf, turning the area into a marvellous vision of balanced landscape engineering. The locals are far more aware of this geomantic aura than they make out. I happened to be poking around a piece of land over near Wells Cathedral one day when the farmer whose land I was on came over to see what I was doing. I mentioned my interest in antiquarian matters and he suddenly lowered his voice; almost reverently he told me that the line of low hills bordering the road and his land had been man-made 'Gawd knows when'. He was waiting for me to laugh as obviously most people would, but luckily, being reasonably conversant with the facts of geomancy, I knew what he meant and told him so.

About twelve miles as the crow flies from Glastonbury, we find Burrow Mump at Burrow Bridge – a smaller replica of the Tor with its processional path winding up to another ruined St Michael's church. If you check this conical mound on a large scale OS map you will see it forms the very definite snout of a huge earthen effigy. This figure is known as the Girt Dog of Langport, an animal existing in obscure Somerset myth. Its underlying jaw and throat are depicted by the river Parrett while its ear stands on a hill in the district of Earlake Moor. So the answer is yes, there is something else lurking in the marshes! Within the contours of the head is a very clever construction of rhines (old waterways) marking out the structure of the beast's face. Once seen on the map you will have no doubts as to the existence of this great dog.

THE ALLER DRAGON

All that has been written so far is fairly common knowledge in the field of geomantic research – that is why I haven't gone into too much detail. It was the Great Dog that made me think that perhaps there could be certain 'guardian figures' surrounding the major effigies in the Glastonbury Zodiac. I knew that the area nearby had a legend in which a man called Hext finally slew a huge, fire-breathing dragon that kept flying between the villages of Curry Rivel and Aller. Near the village of Aller there is supposed to be a patch of grass that never grows, marking the spot where the dragon breathed his fire upon the earth. It's interesting to note that the church here is dedicated to St Andrew who, according to the Apocrypha, has various connections with dragons and serpents.

Many people have wondered why Alfred should have chosen the tiny village of Aller to Christianize Guthrum and the Danes. It is hinted in some writings that Alfred was an adept king, very knowledgeable of the ancient rituals and geomantic structures surrounding the Somerset Levels. He may well have been aware of the area's dragon legend; he also no doubt knew how much the Danes respected the fire-breathing beast. Thus, a pact of peace made at Aller would be doubly binding, as Guthrum would not dare go against the serpent power. And remember, the dragon was a symbol the Danes sailed under – they always decorated their long ships with the dragon motif.

Looking from Aller church over Oath Hill towards the village of Curry Rivel, there is a large area of typically flat Somerset moorland. Suddenly rising from this is a ridge of small humped hills, sporadically but beautifully tree-covered. Consulting the large-scale OS map, I discovered what seemed to be a definite dragon's head outline where the ridge started to climb out of the marshland, to become Red Hill. Could the name have something to do with the fact that dragons breath fire? The contour lines and old pathways continued to meander their way along the ridge outlining a rather abstract, but serpent-like figure for about nine miles, where I found not a tail but another head, albeit more worm-like. So, what I had actually come across seemed to be a double-headed dragon. This latter head area was etched out by Crimson Hill tallying with Red Hill to the east. At the western mouth of this creature stands a major cross-roads at Hatch Beauchamp and there are three large prehistoric standing stones embedded in the earth, in one instance propping up a pub on the corner. Nearby there is a church within the grounds of a country estate right where the dragon's eye should be situated.

About one and a half miles north-west, just off the figure, stands a small picturesque church at West Hatch. In my search for clues I thought it would be a good idea to check all the churches upon and around the suspected effigy for any dragon clues. This ancient holy place was very useful, being perfectly sited on a raised circular mound and again dedicated to St Andrew. Around the outer fabric were carved several dragon gargoyles with large claws, leathery wings and huge bulging eyes. Inside the church I found a stained glass window to the right of the altar depicting a red and gold dragon entwined to give the effect of a double-headed serpent. Obviously this was just the sort of thing I was looking for, being at least circumstantial corroboratory evidence.

My next ecclesiastical visit was to St Martin's at Fivehead which I originally thought might be part of the tail-end of the creature. The building is very old, again sited on a raised circular mound, with many lanes homing in on the church from all directions. Apart from its interesting location, all it had to offer was a large portrait of St Martin holding his wheel with emanating rays (the dragon and the disc are often combined in ancient symbolism).

About one mile south of Fivehead the village of Isle Abbots sits in lonely isolation out on the moor. There is only one road to and from it, with some charming cottages leading to the large church of St Mary the Virgin. The tower is positively alive with magnificent statuary displayed in filigree-carved niches. On the left-hand side of the tower were two prominent dragon saints; St Michael, having slain the dragon which circled around his sword and feet, and St George. Both were upheld by winged, god-like figures reminiscent of the central effigy on the Gateway of the Sun at Tiahuanaco. On the other side of the

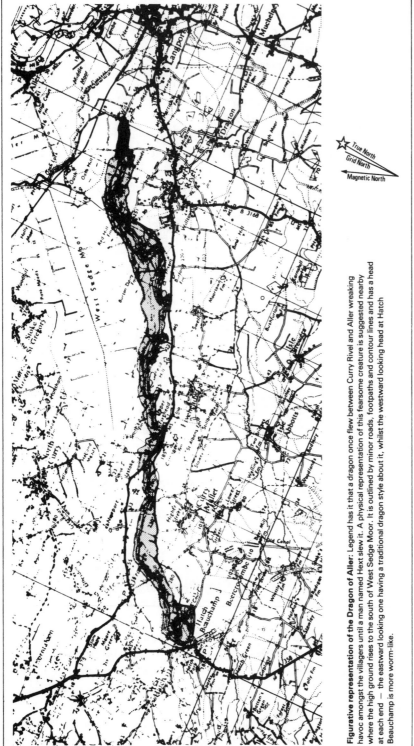

Figurative representation of the Dragon of Aller: Legend has it that a dragon once flew between Curry Rivel and Aller wreaking havoc amongst the villagers until a man named Hext slew it. A physical representation of this fearsome creature is suggested nearby where the high ground rises to the south of West Sedge Moor. It is outlined by minor roads, footpaths and contour lines and has a head at each end — the eastward looking one having a traditional dragon style about it, whilst the westward looking head at Hatch Beauchamp is more worm-like.

tower was another dragon saint, St Catherine, depicted holding the wheel on which she was martyred. But it is within the church that a most significant clue comes to light.

The font, according to church records, is Saxon with Norman carvings. Closer examination reveals that two sides of the font seem to be carved in a much older style to that of the Norman coats of arms and fleur-de-lis, etc. The pre-Norman carving depicts a serpentine-like creature, which fits nicely with my theory. The church blurb describes it as 'a dragon reversed by baptism' – possibly a vague reference to the Alfred/Guthrum peace pact. There is another dragon situated between a sword and a fleur-de-lis, with horn on head and a scorpion's tail, but this is a Norman variation on a theme. They were obviously keeping the serpent idea alive. The church was built in the thirteenth century by monks of Muchelney Abbey, but to have a font with carvings of such antiquity embellished upon it only goes to show that this site had been in business long before the monks came on the scene. Buildings came and went over the centuries and it seems possible that this strangely carved stone had always been there, and, rather than destroy it or build it into the church walls, some enterprising mason adapted it to become a font. More speculatively, perhaps it could have been part of a stone circle that existed on this very ancient site thousands of years ago.

South of the effigy head that looks eastwards is the large village of Curry Rivel. Situated on a rising piece of ground, the church there is dedicated to St Andrew. On its outer fabric there are no less than four large dragon gargoyles. Inside there is a stained glass window depicting St George killing the dragon.

Although Kingsbury Episcopi is about four miles south of the figure, the church of St Martin is well worth mentioning, being covered from head to foot with dragon gargoyles. There just has to be some significance in finding all these beasts everywhere. Many churches have mythological creatures depicted on their outer fabric but these are usually griffins or yales, etc. Generally not many dragons emerge, and I feel that the medieval masons were trying to keep alive the memory of a serpent, which, on these Somerset moors, was more than just a story to tell children. It could be the vague hint of a UFO visitation or it could be a more racial memory of the huge, geomantic dragon on the hills.

To the east of the dragon's head which looks towards Glastonbury and the Zodiac, there is situated the historic town of Langport. Its church, All Saints, is perched right on the top of the hill that overlooks the quaint dwellings of the area. The views from the church-yard are really very inspiring. Around the outside are ranged several unusual effigies that caught my eye. On the northern side of the church a three-horned dragon with leathery wings gazes downwards with wide open mouth and at the east end there is a good representation of Hermes, the messenger of the gods who also signifies the 'serpent power' of the earth spirit. One other item of importance is the unusual gargoyle of a three-headed man. In Greek mythology Guyon was a three-headed giant who inhabited a sacred island in the west. Whilst Hercules was busily performing his labours in the west, Guyon set his huge hound on him. This is interesting in the light of the nearby hound effigy, to be discussed later, and the well-known Girt Dog of Langport.

The interior of All Saints revealed many clues in the search for dragon memories. The area behind the altar was devoted to a large, carved stone scene with St Michael killing the dragon and upon the cross standing on the altar I found a serpent slithering its way down the richly carved stem. The two candlesticks either side of the cross are worth mentioning, being exquisitely covered in lapis and turquoise enamel with each stem supporting two fishes (the sign of Christianity, but also the zodiacal sign of Pisces), the sacred fertilizing vesica. An unusual stained glass window shows a meteorite hurtling past the head of the prophet Job, whilst Abraham has ten stars twinkling about his head. Quite an astronomical scene. There is also a window showing Joseph of Arimathea, which is quite rare.

Out into the open air again and back onto the road, there stands opposite the Catholic church of St Gildas. It seems everyone wanted to get a place on the hill! The dedication of this church is interesting as St Gildas was busily (and acrimoniously) writing the history of the area at the time when King Arthur was about his business, and he was responsible for conveniently leaving out all details pertaining to the activities and existence of Britain's greatest hero.

Travelling down the other side of the hill, there is an ancient archway crossing the road, and the tower of the church at Huish Episcopi can be seen through it. In fact the archway contains a staircase leading to the tiny 'hanging chapel' (similar to the one built over one of the ancient gates to the city of Winchester), which apparently is now run as a Masonic Lodge. With All Saints behind up the hill, the chapel over the road and St Mary's church straight ahead at Huish Episcopi, a general idea of what ley hunting and geomancy is all about begins to emerge, certainly in its Christian context. The only pagan aspect worth mentioning about St Mary's is the entrance. A carved Norman archway contains a very frightening horned face with a pig's nose and lolling tongue. An elemental spirit if ever there was one!

Back at Drayton, one mile south-east of Curry Rivel, in the churchyard of St Catherine (who gave her name to the Catherine Wheel because she was to be martyred on a wheel-type contraption – but miraculously her bonds were broken at the last minute) stands an old cross and in a niche in the shaft is set a beautifully carved St George slaying the dragon. The glass inside the church is again connected with the sky but in a more meteorological way than the glass at Langport. Stars are featured, but the aspect predominating here is lightning and the heavens opening. Memories of great cataclysms perhaps? The altar window consists of Solomon's seal, the wheel or disc, a sheaf of corn (ancient fertility symbol), a golden dragon, a phoenix rising from its ashes, and last but not least the sephiroth (tree of life) growing out of the head of a prophet. Quite a mixed bag of important mystical symbols.

North Curry is located to the north of the serpentine figure and looks out across West Sedgemoor where the effigy lies about two miles away. There is a most remarkable network of lanes all converging on the market cross in this village. The whole area seems to have been designed for a special purpose – it certainly wasn't built for easy driving. Now this market cross, a triangular structure made out of yellow Ham stone, was erected in the reign of Queen Victoria, but the odd thing about it is that on one of the sides there is a beautiful carving of St Michael slaying the dragon. This seemed strange as the other two sides were more conventionally adorned with star and garter type decorations.

After this good start I came across the church precinct and was met by a wide, straight pathway lined with old beech trees on either side, which alas, now no longer exist owing to a recent blight. The church, standing majestically at the other end of the avenue, was slightly raised up from the rest of the village. Approaching this huge building I discovered that the whole of the outer fabric was covered with serpent-like gargoyles and some very definite dragons. One particular carving caught my eye. It was that of the Devil himself, giving a sly smile to anyone walking his way. Approaching His Satanic Majesty to get a closer look, a large black cat jumped out from behind a grave stone and flopped down in front of me and began rolling about. It gave me quite a start, what with dragons, devils and now 'familiar' black cats! Past Old Nick, the church yard suddenly ended. The ground dropped away abruptly, placing this church on a most outstanding promontory which can be seen for miles around.

Inside, the church of Saints Peter and Paul proved to be every bit as interesting and spectacular as the outside. The ceiling seemed to soar away and the alternate layers of blue lias and Ham stone give a pleasing effect to the onlooker. This church had obviously been restored and enlarged many times in its long and colourful history and yet the essence of the place still remained. There were serpents everywhere. In the north aisle a large window was dedicated to the two most famous dragon saints, George and Michael, and over by the latter, another area of stained glass depicted Adam and Eve with a hideous blue serpent coiling about in the Garden of Eden. Just to the left of the central aisle I found an interesting statuette about two feet high depicting the archangel Michael complete with lance and huge set of silvery wings standing triumphant over the slain dragon, whose gory remains were slumped at his feet. All this pagan imagery in a House of God! This was by no means an ancient relic of the church, however. In fact it was in memory of someone who died back in the fifties, but everything in North Curry seemed to be St Michael-orientated.

There has been a terrific struggle between the Old Religion and the incoming Christians around this area. Although Christianized, it still retains a feeling of earthy power. Mother Church obviously had a job bringing the locals round to her new and rigid ideas of worship; perhaps St Michael was used as a king or intermediary to get the people to take more seriously the slowly growing/engulfing Catholic way of life. Whatever happened, North Curry has been a very important place of long ritual significance. It was held by Harold at the time of the Battle of Hastings and then passed to William the Conqueror. Saxon Kings lived and worshipped here, and who knows what went on before that?

The dragon carved out of the hills above Aller is not alone. Somerset boasts of many serpentine activities such as the Dragon of Dinder near *Worm*inster where the church has a marvellous ancient carving of a dragon with 'port-holes' all over its body. Two other dragon-infested villages are at Crowcombe and Trull.

One controversial theory put forward as the reason why dragon memories exist is that there is a connection with UFOs; that dragon myths are a primitive way of describing actual sightings and landings of craft from another world – another galaxy, another dimension? The fiery breath and huge bulbous eyes with which dragons are associated *could* be the exhaust system and the large illuminated window areas of an extra-terrestrial vehicle *á la* Adamski. But in no way would our ancestors have had a yardstick to measure this kind of vision, so they turned to romantic description and passed down the fiery serpent that flies through the heavens. This is all very well, but what if you take the view that our ancestors were far from primitive, and could probably grasp the real secrets of the universe far more easily than we can today (as is constantly being confirmed by Professor Alexander Thom and other notable researchers)? In the ancient philosophies the dragon represents a fusion of the subtle forces within the earth and the heavens, the microcosm and macrocosm – in a word geomancy, the patterns and mysteries of the etheric currents themselves.

THE POLDEN HOUND

The other guardian effigy I have discovered is of considerable importance in the study of the Glastonbury Zodiac. It takes the form of a huge dog, over six miles long, that runs its course along the Polden Hills – well out of reach of the sea that once covered the flat marsh land below. I found the outline of this hound whilst looking at the two-and-a-half-inch OS map checking some ley alignments. I make this point to show that I was not 'thinking dog' or any other figure at that time. The creature seems to be running directly from the Zodiac which lies just over a mile away to the east.* Unfortunately there is a lack of corroborative place names to give those extra clues, but about a mile eastwards from the tail is a place called Houndwood and certain streets and avenues in local villages have 'hound' prominent in their names.

I toured all over this mighty effigy and found that the shape on the map and the terrain that delineates the lines are both highly significant. I started off from Glastonbury on the A361, this being the main road to Taunton. The road as such clearly defines the line of the animal's under-belly. Not far along this road there is a small village called Pedwell, and according to the OS Map there is a well situated where the animal's genitalia should be.† John Michell has suggested that the village was once called Piddle and that the name was changed later for prudish reasons. Unfortunately, when I investigated the site, the well was completely hidden by earth and weeds. The lady who owned this piece of ground came out to see what was going on and I asked her if there was anything unusual about the well. She told me that her husband one day intended to uncover it, but it would be difficult as there was a huge stone slab right across the well head. Naturally I wanted to know more. She informed me that it had been closed up for many years and the stone had been the nearest and largest object to do the job. The stone must have been close by as nobody had the means to transport such a heavy object far. This *could* have been a single standing-stone, a mark-point, or even part of a stone circle destroyed many centuries before.

Continuing along the A361 in a westerly direction, my next stop was the small village of Greinton. The church is situated on a significant mound on the edge of King's Sedge-moor and is dedicated to St Michael. The windows inside the church, although Victorian, seemed to retain part of the original display, having an area of glass dedicated to

*The Great Dog of Langport also runs towards the west. (*Ed.*)

†The name Pedwell is a corrupt form of St Peter's Well, showing a definite holy well tradition for this specific spot. (*Ed.*)

St Michael and St Andrew, together with a phoenix rising from the flames. Vesica Piscis were everywhere portrayed. Outside St Michael's in the churchyard was a curious grave-stone. Approximately six feet long and four feet wide, the slab was rough-hewn with three poorly carved medieval crosses covering the surface. By its appearance I believe it was once a huge standing-stone that stood on the lonely mound long before the church was built, and through the ages had been re-shaped and used as a grave stone. It was far too large for builders of the Middle Ages to hump around. The church's guide book is very cautious about the whole business but does hint at a strong megalithic possibility.

On the way to Moorlinch, on the left, is Red Hill Lane. This marks the hound's foreleg and covers an area of nearly one mile. A large protuberance at the knee incorporates Sharpenton Hill and the foot is lifted painfully, as though the animal finds running difficult. During the course of my researching I found out that this part of Somerset was once under the jurisdiction of the Crown Forests and game was strictly preserved. All the dogs had to be mutilated about the legs to prevent them from chasing game. This was just the sort of thing I had been looking for, at last an undeniable piece of evidence. Of course this terrestrial hound must have existed long before Crown Estates were established. One may surmise here that the dogs were mutilated not just to stop them hunting game, but as a result of a memory of some long lost ritual which led to the carving of a huge dog in the earth with a broken or mutilated front leg.

The throat of the animal is found near the village of Moorlinch. The church, just off the effigy, stands high up overlooking Sedgemoor. All around the hills are covered with ridged lynches and obviously one would think the name derivation implies lynches seen from the moor, but this is not so. 'Moor' comes from the word *mirie* (merry) which can mean 'magic' – so the name could mean in this instance 'magic hillside'. Nearby rises a very carefully designed Knoll Hill. I would say that this hill represents the hound's heart, although it is perhaps a little high up for complete anatomical accuracy. The Tapmoor Road defines the lower jaw, and around the mouth area there lies Fursland Farm and an orchard. There is a similarity here to the Geminian effigy at Dundon where, at the mouth of the figure there stands a medieval tithe barn. There is nothing quite so accommodating here, but nevertheless, a farm with plenty of barns chock-a-block with food is not out of context. The nose is again marked by a large farm (Sutton's Farm). Travelling on up the face of the creature, there is a cross-roads with an irregularly raised piece of land along-side called Righton's Grave. Historically this alludes to the place where Alfred buried the Danes after his great victory in 878. But why pick a name like Righton? Who was he and did he once have a faithful hound?

The road climbs and bends round to the right marking the sloping forehead, finally reaching Slocombe Hill (over 300 feet). Again the hand of man can be seen around this area, everything being carefully arranged to fit some kind of topographical pattern. On the map, contour lines show an ear falling backwards from the top of the head as if the wind was blowing in the dog's face. At this juncture the minor road picks up the A39 forming the back of the neck and then the back of the hound. It is interesting to note that part of this highway is dead straight, having been used constantly over the centuries. The Romans adapted it from an original ancient trackway, which incidentally forms

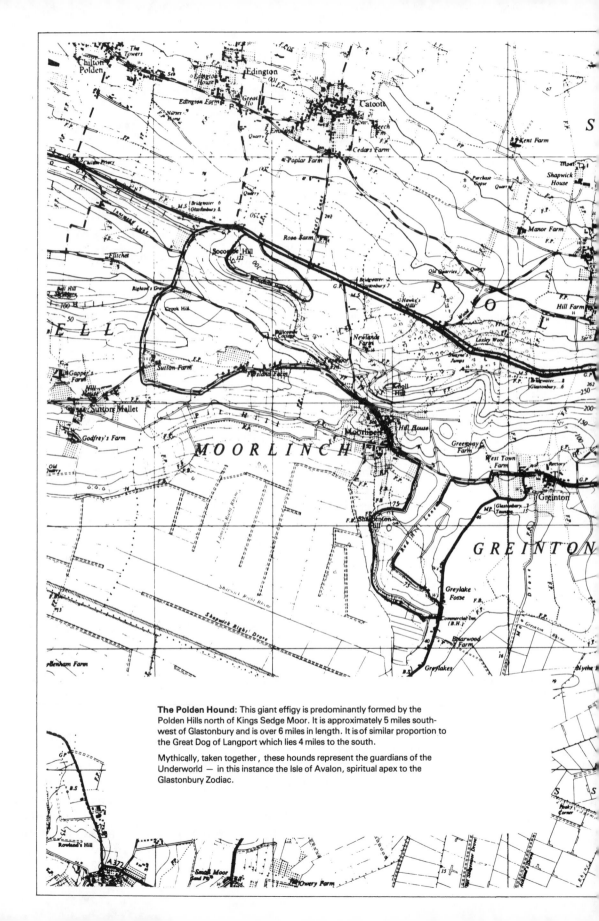

The Polden Hound: This giant effigy is predominantly formed by the Polden Hills north of Kings Sedge Moor. It is approximately 5 miles south-west of Glastonbury and is over 6 miles in length. It is of similar proportion to the Great Dog of Langport which lies 4 miles to the south.

Mythically, taken together, these hounds represent the guardians of the Underworld — in this instance the Isle of Avalon, spiritual apex to the Glastonbury Zodiac.

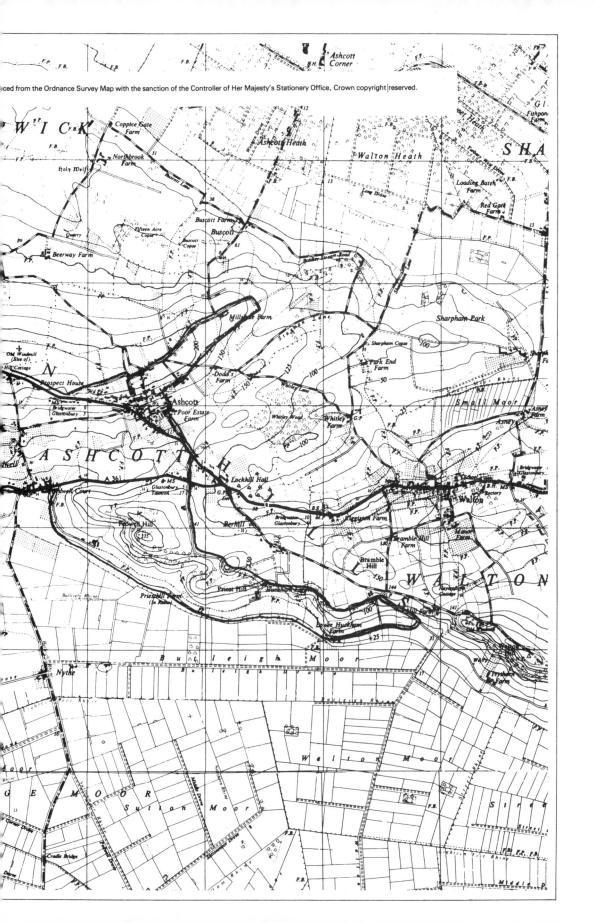

part of a major Somerset ley alignment. About one mile down the road – just where it bends slightly to mark the ending of the neck and beginning of the back – there is a place called Swayne's Jumps. Four stones were erected here after the Civil War to mark the spot where a local man, Jan Swayne, took three mighty leaps for freedom from his captors. The stones now in place are not the originals, leading one to believe that many stones throughout the ages have been placed here, usually marking some local feat of endurance, with the real reason for marking a certain spot by stones, trees or tumuli long forgotten. About twelve miles to the north on the Mendip Hills, there stand the Deerleap Stones which have a similar tale attached to them and which are known to be genuine prehistoric artifacts.

Continuing along the A39 towards Ashcott, the road rarely bends or curves; where it does, it enhances the shape of this mighty beast to perfection. Ashcott is where the dog's docked tail and his behind are situated. Perhaps this village has gone through some name – changing throughout the ages. *Arse,* an old Cornish name would have been very appropriate here, making the name of the village 'Arse-cott'. Country people were more prepared to call a spade a spade! Up a steep hill stands All Saints Church, Ashcott, its marvellous position giving the visitor wonderful vistas of the Somerset countryside rolling away towards Cadbury Castle. There were several Scots pines (*Pinus sylvestris*) in the circular, ancient churchyard, and whilst walking around checking the outer fabric I found many sculpted representations of the old Celtic religion. There were two outstanding gargoyles that took my interest, the first being a huge mouth held open by two tiny figures on either side. This was the *Maw,* the mouth of hell, the entrance to the underworld. The other was a large pagan face with bulging eyes, whose wild hair was entwined with oak leaves. This *Woodwose* or 'wild man of the woods' represents the old religious symbol of earth regeneration and fertilization. The *Maw* has obvious connections with birth, death and the transition between worlds.

Throughout history different people for different reasons have always felt the need to deface and eradicate all hints of the religion that Christianity superseded. That is why these two carvings are so remarkable. They are a direct link with the people who incorporated into their design and craftsmanship a visual representation of the old power and wisdom that was practised millennia ago. Unfortunately a big disappointment came when I entered the church itself. The Victorians had gutted the place and not a hint of the wonderful old building had been allowed to remain. One can't help speculating upon the wealth of clues that might have been hovering here before modernization took place. The Victorians were obviously so busy with the inside, they missed the outside altogether – or just didn't have the time to deface All Saints even more than they did.

The last part of the Polden Hound to be examined was the hind leg. This is outlined by a minor road which, within its perimeter, houses Pedwell Hill and Priest's Hill. If you travel down one of the nearby drove roads out onto the moor and look towards the two hills, you can discern both the shape of the leg and the rest of the dog's body which is running away to the west.

This gigantic creature, as mentioned before, covers a distance of approximately six miles from head to paw and is without doubt a most incredible feat of earth-sculptured

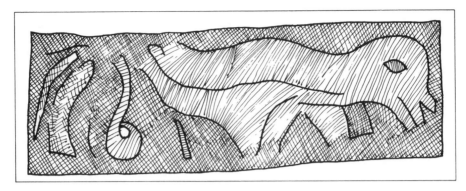

Dragon.

Woodwose. ▬

Maw.

engineering. But what does it all mean?

Glastonbury is a very important area where all sorts of mythological characters converge. It is the place where two worlds meet – the land of the living and the land of the dead. In short it is the British gateway to the underworld, the unknown. Throughout world myth it is recognized that these gateways are guarded by animals – invariably dogs. Cerberus with his two heads is the gigantic beast watching over the Greek entrance, and the two canine effigies in Somerset are the likely guardians of the British gateway to the underworld, the realm of Annwn or Isle of Avalon.

The Langport figure is near the Isle of Athelney where King Alfred threw his burnt cakes into the River Tone, the mouth of the Girt Dog; there is a curious analogy to his act in Greek mythology, where Hercules ritually feeds drugged cakes to Cerberus. Here is another hint that Alfred may have been an Initiate King. Also in ancient Greece, Aesculapius is represented with a dog beside him and a staff in his hand around which twined oracular snakes. This could link up with the double-headed dragon/snake as detailed earlier.

Similar clues are found in Egyptian mythology. Anubis, originally a jackal who turned into a dog, probably so that he could guard the entrance to the Egyptian underworld, accompanies Thoth, the master magician and god of gods. It is documented that dogs in myth are there for a specific reason, namely to guard a secret, and the secret is usually 'that on which the sovereignty of a sacred King depends'.* Within the Glastonbury Zodiac lie two sacred kings: Arthur, depicted as Sagittarius; and the maimed god within the Gemini effigy as discovered by Mary Caine. Perhaps the two animals are guarding the kings or alternatively they may be guarding not only the entrance to the underworld but the terrestrial Zodiac itself (Avalon). They may even be guarding the secret resting place of Merlin which is supposed to lie within Park Wood, the very centre of the Zodiac.

There is a story that a strain of Egyptian hunting dogs was introduced to Britain *c*. 2000 BC to pursue unbaptized souls (hints of the Wild Hunt). Again this links up with Glastonbury, where the souls of the departed start their voyage to what the Egyptians termed the Land of Amenti, the lost Land of the West. Anubis also crops up, being responsible for ferrying the soul of Osiris to the underworld.

Professor Max Müller found that the Indian Vedic poets

have imagined two dogs belonging to Yama, the lord of the departed spirits. They are called the messengers of Yama, bloodthirsty and broad-snouted, brown, four-eyes, and pale – the 'dawn children'. The departed is told to pass by them on his way to the fathers, who are rejoicing with Yama. Yama is asked to protect the departed from these dogs; and finally the dogs themselves are implored to grant life to the living, and to let them see the sun again . . . These two dogs represent one of the lowest of the many conceptions of morning and evening . . . Greece, though she recognized Hermes as guide to the souls of the departed, did not degrade him to the rank of the watch-dog of Hades. These watch-dogs, Kerberos and Orthros, represent however, the two dogs of Yama – the gloom of morning and evening, here conceived as hostile and demoniacal powers. One of them was black and the other was spotted.

Another 'coincidence' is that Glastonbury is the extreme western boundary for the Wild Hunt, and two great leaders of this frightening apparition both have Glastonbury and dog connections. King Arthur's dog Cabal was always by his side and Gwyn ap Nudd, king of the Fairies who lived on the Tor, had a dog called Dormath. It seems that where there's hunting there are always dogs, be they physical or metaphysical.

The need to carve out these giant effigies on the surface of the land was not engendered by the fantasies of primitive idiots who thought they would go and hack out a few dogs here and there on a whim. These beasts were *grown* here through natural prominences of land, through the interaction of yin and yang, which the wise geomancers of long ago recognized. They were then able alchemically to enhance the figures through physically realized geomancy and make them more perfect over the ages. Whatever you choose to believe, these facts do interconnect and what's more, on a world-wide scale – pointing to a vast antiquity.

I hope that some light has been thrown on the great terrestrial sculptures that lie around the Glastonbury countryside. Even if you're not convinced, the beautiful churches with their more than fair share of pagan offerings and the quiet lanes that lead

*See Robert Graves's *The White Goddess* and William Lethaby's *Architecture, Mysticism and Myth*. (*Ed.*)

you safely over the moors are well worth visiting. Perhaps after touring around this very special area you will understand the reason why Glastonbury and its environs have been called 'the holyest earthe in England'.

Recommended Books

Burton, S. H. *The West Country*. Robert Hale, 1972.
Eitel, E. J. *Feng Shui*. Cokaygne, 1973.
Graves, Robert. *The White Goddess*. Faber, 1952.
Holiday, F. W. *The Dragon and the Disc*. Futura, 1974.
Lethaby, William. *Architecture, Mysticism and Myth*. Architectural Press, 1975.
Maltwood, K. E. *A Guide to Glastonbury's Temple of the Stars*. James Clarke, 1964.
Michell, John. *The Flying Saucer Vision*. Sidgwick & Jackson, 1967.
 The View Over Atlantis. Abacus, 1969.

CHAPTER FOUR

Caer Sidi:

The Zodiac Temples of South Britain

JOHN MICHAEL

About the same time that Alfred Watkins was in the process of rediscovering the phenomenon of ley lines among the hills of Herefordshire, Katharine Maltwood was rediscovering the phenomenon of zodiac temples, in and around the ancient sea moors of Somerset.

Although their discoveries have been disregarded by orthodox archaeologists, the publication of their respective books in the late 1920s heralded an era which is giving us a clear and more accurate view of prehistoric society in these islands. The academics would have had us believe that during this period, Britain was peopled only by painted savages. Yet these people have left us such geometrically perfect, astronomically oriented instruments of their complex earth-science as the Stonehenge and Callanish stone circles, the ley line phenomena, and the enormous star charts called zodiac temples.

Since the 1920s, interested groups like the Straight Track Club and the Avalon Society have come and gone, but many of their members have left to the present generation the fruits of their researches in books, and in the journals of many learned bodies. One such man was Lewis Edwards, a member of the Avalon Society, who wrote in their journal *Atlantis Research* (1948–52) a series of articles about a zodiac temple in northern Carmarthenshire centred on the village of Pumpsaint. Accompanying the articles was a map detailing the outlines of zodiacal figures bearing a great resemblance to, and covering an area approximately the same size as the zodiac temple discovered in Somerset twenty-five years earlier. Excepting members of the Avalon Society, few people learned of Mr Edwards's discovery in Wales, and from then till about 1970 most interested people believed that the Somerset zodiac temple was unique. From about 1970 onwards there have been many claims of zodiac temples being discovered all over the country, but little or no proof of these has been forthcoming, with the possible exceptions of the Nuthampstead zodiac temple discovered by Nigel Pennick, and the Kingston zodiac temple, discovered by Mary Caine.

In the summer of 1972 the Pendragon Society organized an expedition to the Pumpsaint area to check out the claims of Mr Edwards. The results of that week's preliminary investigation were obviously inconclusive, but one or two members carried on there the next year, encouraged by the evidence shown on large-scale maps and aerial photographs of the area. While the work in the Pumpsaint area was in progress, it was felt necessary to survey the adjoining areas of Cardiganshire and Pembrokeshire. In the course of this survey it became apparent that the landscape patterns of both the Glastonbury area of Somerset and the Pumpsaint area of Carmarthenshire were repeated on a much larger scale in and around the Prescelly Mountains of Dyfed. The northernmost area of the Prescelly zodiac temple is cut by the fifty-second parallel, the same line of latitude that cuts through areas of both the Pumpsaint Zodiac and the Nuthampstead Zodiac. It was no surprise, therefore, to find a few months later, much speculation about zodiac temples in Herefordshire and Oxfordshire, along the same latitude. Little evidence has emerged since then about these two temples, but the initial discoveries in those areas showed good possibilities for further research.

Like the Nuthampstead zodiac temple, the one in the Prescelly Mountains is oval- or vesica-shaped, both the Glastonbury and Pumpsaint temples are definitely circular, and each covers an area of approximately one hundred square miles. The objections to these temples covering such a large area have not always been constructive, although many have asked why anyone should want to build something that can only be really appreciated from about five miles up in the air. Hopefully future researchers will one day be able to answer this question, but at present there are still considerable differences of opinion as to exactly which criteria should be accepted for the outlines of these figures.*

Mrs Maltwood used the roads, tracks and paths, rivers, streams and, in some cases, field boundaries in Somerset, while Mr Edwards used all of these except field boundaries, but introduced the use of contours in the outlines of two or three of his figures at Pumpsaint. In the absence of all other evidence on the maps, he utilized the 100 foot contour to complete the outlines of the horns of both the goat-fish of Capricorn and the bull of Taurus, and for almost the whole of the outline of his figure for Sagittarius.

Unlike the 'mounted archer' that Mrs Maltwood found to represent Sagittarius in the Somerset temple, the map produced along with his articles showed what he called a 'mounted lancer'. The outline is rather unconvincing, as no legs can be discerned at all. Only the heads of the horse and rider and the bushy tail of the horse, very similar to the horse's tail in the Somerset temple, are acceptably clear. In his notes he says '. . . between the body of the rider and the horse's ear there is a double track, joined at both ends. The two tracks seem unnecessary but the whole outline, with its southern boundary of Afon Fanaffas gives the distinct figure of a lance . . .', which, he goes on to say, '. . . is a very unusual feature in a Zodiac'. If this figure was meant to represent a mounted knight with jousting lance, then it would be no surprise to find the legs hidden, due to the manner in which the horses were draped for a tournament.

But a mounted knight/lancer has never been known as a symbol for the constellation of Sagittarius. One of the earliest known symbols for this group of stars was the centaur,

---

*Some researchers are coming to the conclusion that terrestrial zodiacs are essentially natural; that they are the divine extrusions of a metaphysical power immanent throughout the fields of nature. It is thought that they are recognized and adapted by various cultures as psychic awareness grows through the cycles of astrological chronology. (*Ed.*)

a mystical creature, half-man and half-horse. In the Prescelly temple the Sagittarius symbol is a beautifully proportioned centaur; one arm is outstretched, as if holding a bow; the other is bent, its elbow most prominent. It seems to be holding an arrow which is about to shoot. In the Somerset temple, Mrs Maltwood shows a 'mounted archer', although the horse's head appears to be protruding from the rider's stomach. This, we are told, is because the rider is falling from his mount: the roads from Ponter's Ball to Parbrook, via Court Farm, outline the buttocks of the rider, seen halfway up the horse's neck and giving the impression that he is indeed falling off. It is possible to draw a horse's head protruding from a similar part of the stomach of the 'half-man' in the Prescelly temple, although after doing so the whole figure takes on the appearance of being not quite right. If the horse's head, along with the roads outlining the buttocks of the rider in the Glastonbury temple are disregarded, then the figure left is almost identical to some of the representations of centaurs executed in classical times. If the Somerset temple is as old as Mrs Maltwood suggested (*c.* 2700 BC), then one would expect to find there a centaur and not a mounted archer (the latter was also a symbol for Sagittarius, but did not come into vogue until a much later date).

Apart from these differences, the Sagittarius symbols in both the Welsh temples and the Somerset temple all have one major factor in common. In each of the three temples the Aquarius symbols are always found due north of the centre, with the lion figures of Leo always to the south, in their correct positions. As above, so below. The Sagittarius symbols in all three temples are to the south-east of the Aquarius symbols, and along with each of the Capricorn figures, are upside-down in comparison with most of the other figures.

The Capricorn effigies are to be found in each case in their correct astronomical positions between the figures for Sagittarius and Aquarius. In ancient times the symbol for Capricorn would have been the sea-goat or goat-fish, the contemporary of the centaur. In the Prescelly zodiac temple the horn of the goat-fish is outlined by the fork and two roads leading north out of the village of Tegryn. It bends slightly, pointing towards the centre of the temple. In the Pumpsaint temple the large-scale maps show a goat-fish of sorts, but unlike the Prescelly figure, the fish tail is grossly out of proportion to the rest of the body. Mr Edwards saw a straight horn on these maps but only a brief study of the aerial photographs of the area shows that the very life-like goat's head also has a horn that is bent and pointing towards the centre of the temple. Even though there has been very little development in this area, and despite the undeniable clarity of the head and horn of this figure, no proportionate body, forelegs or fish-tail can be seen on either maps or aerial photographs. But one remarkable place name in the locality lends support to the existence of at least the goat's head. At almost the tip of the horn of this figure, there is a narrow road that affords the only route from the valley below, up between the two peaks, and on to the next valley with its market town beside the river. The pass is called Bwlch Blaen Corn, and means 'the pass of the tip of the horn'. The road has been used for centuries, and must have been the same route taken by the Romans to and from the Pumpsaint gold mines, as it blends into the old Roman road Sarn Helen, which a little further on outlines the lower jaw of the creature.

The Prescelly goat-fish also has an interesting place name to suggest that at one time

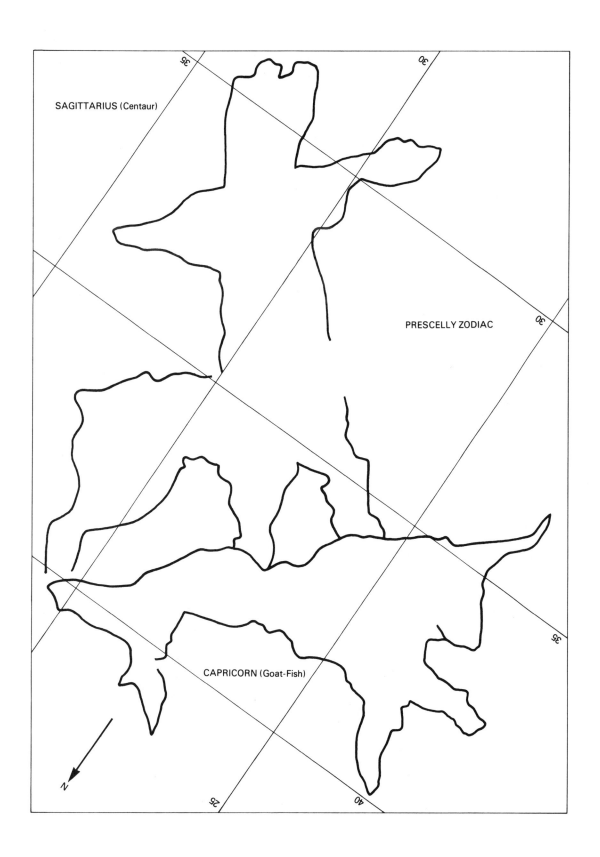

SAGITTARIUS (Centaur)

PRESCELLY ZODIAC

CAPRICORN (Goat-Fish)

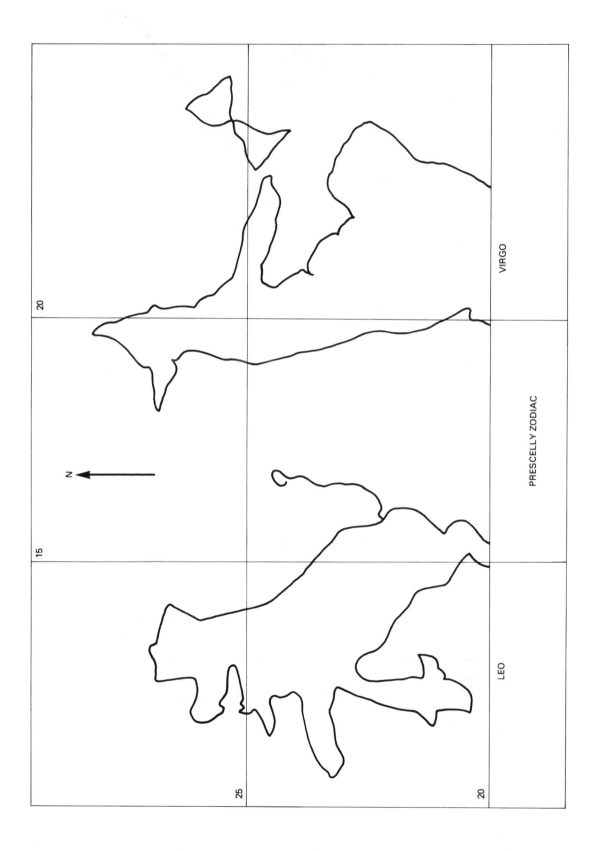

its existence was common knowledge in the locality. About a mile to the south-west of Tegryn is a small stream called Nant-Y-Geifr Fawr, that runs into the river Taf. As it is such a small stream the probable translation of this could only be 'the stream of the great goat'.

In the Somerset temple Mrs Maltwood depicted the Capricorn figure as a one-horned half-goat with forelegs outstretched together, and body tapering away as if to suggest a fish tail. In her version of the Glastonbury temple, Mary Caine, a present-day researcher and contributor to this book, has shown this figure with one foreleg apparently buckling under the belly of what is obviously, by the back legs she has given it, intended to be just a goat. If Mrs Maltwood's figure is completed by using the roads from Pilton to North Wootton and Pilton to Ponter's Ball, a fish tail can be discerned, although like the Pumpsaint fish tail it is out of proportion to the rest of the body.

Both women use Ponter's Ball, an ancient earthwork twelve feet high and five furlongs in length to outline the one horn. In this instance it is dead straight, but like its counterparts in the two Welsh temples, also points towards the centre of its temple. In one part of *A Guide to Glastonbury's Temple of the Stars* Mrs Maltwood described this figure as a goat-fish, displaying her awareness of the symbolism in use around the time that she dated the construction of the temple.

On the opposite side of the Sagittarius figures are the figures representing the constellation of Scorpio. In both the Somerset and the Pumpsaint temples there is fair evidence to suggest the existence of scorpion figures. At Prescelly on the other hand, there is no evidence to suggest anything like the figure of a scorpion. Mrs Maltwood's scorpion in Somerset bears no resemblance to Mary Caine's alternative, which itself is remarkably similar to the scorpion figure that Mr Edwards delineated among the hills east of the village of Pumpsaint. However, Mr Edwards also says that Scorpio is represented by three symbols: the scorpion, the eagle and the serpent. 'The sting of the Scorpion,' he says in *Atlantis Research,* 'points towards the wood that outlines the Eagle'. He shows that further to the south-west is a place called Bwlch Cefn Sarth, meaning 'the pass of the back of the serpent', *sarth* being an anglicized corruption of *sarff,* 'serpent'.

Mr Edwards felt that the proximity of this place to the Virgo figure suggested a connection with the constellation Hydra, the snake, which is outside the ecliptic circle along the backs of Virgo and Leo. This is unlikely as *sarff* is the word used in most Welsh astronomy books for the constellation of Scorpio, suggesting that at one time the zodiac temple builders used the indigenous serpent, and not the foreign scorpion, to symbolize the stars of Scorpio. The roads and rivers south of the Prescelly Mountains appear to hint at a serpent shape, while in the area of the scorpion at Somerset there are similar, very promising possibilities.

The next star-group in the traditional zodiac should be Libra, the scales. Currently it is believed to be represented in the Somerset temple by the dove at Barton St David. At one time it was believed that Libra was represented by the triangular shapes towards which Virgo, in each of these temples, points her hands. Some have said that this is her wheatsheaf, and though it would not be strange to see Virgo, the harvest constellation, in connection with a wheatsheaf, it is highly unlikely that either dove or wheatsheaf represent Libra in any of the temples.

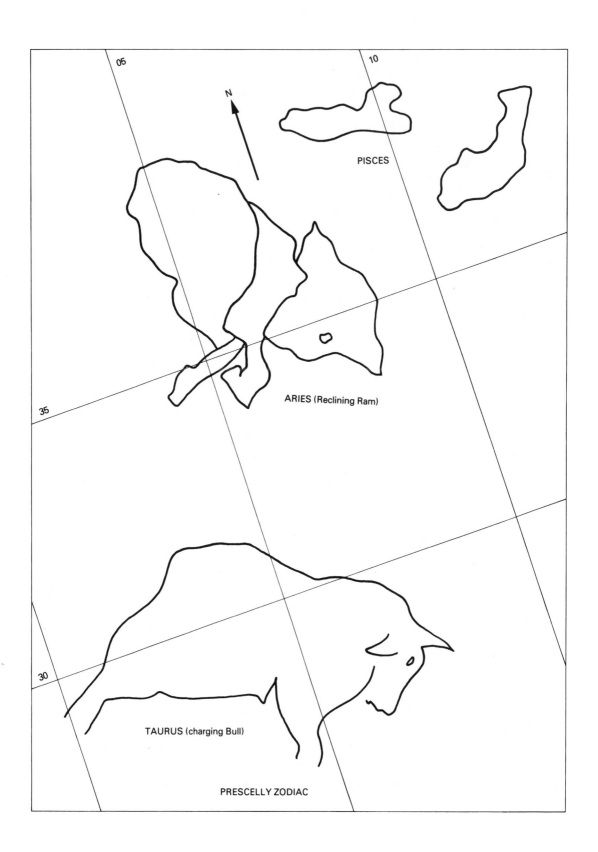

PISCES

ARIES (Reclining Ram)

TAURUS (charging Bull)

PRESCELLY ZODIAC

Peter Lum in his book *The Stars in our Heavens* says that '. . . Libra as a separate star-group was unknown to the Greeks and the Chaldeans, who knew its stars as part of the constellation of Scorpio; the two brightest stars in Libra sometimes still being referred to as the "southern claw" and the "northern claw"'. He goes on to say that '. . . it was the Romans who first used this particular group of stars as one of the signs of the modern Zodiac, and they originally placed there the figure of Julius Caesar, holding a pair of scales as token of his infinite wisdom and justice.' Later on he says that after the figure of Caesar was eliminated, the scales, now shown alone, came to be regarded as those belonging to Virgo or Astrea, the goddess of justice, in whose scales the fate of all mortal men must eventually be weighed. If there is, then, a separate symbol for Libra at all in the Somerset temple, its inclusion may date the temple, at the earliest to Roman times, post-Julius Caesar.

Mrs Caine, in the first edition of this Glastonbury anthology devotes one and a half pages under the heading 'The Dove, Libra'. At the beginning of her article she says '. . . and when the planisphere is placed to scale on the map, the Zodiac stars fall on their earthly counterparts'. Yet the dove at Barton St David is almost at the centre of the circle of figures and therefore nowhere near the zodiacal belt in which the stars lie. A little further on she says '...Libra's Dove . . . begins the last quarter of the year . . . Its shape resembles the Scales; Cancer's ship is crab-shaped; the shapes are the same, but the original Glastonbury symbols are richer and much more profound than their supplanters.' Mrs Maltwood would have agreed whole-heartedly with the last statement. The original Glastonbury symbols were, after all, the ones she discovered, and of Libra she says, 'Zubeneschamali and Zubenel-genubi from Libra fall on the right claw (of the Scorpion) which here takes the place of the Scales.'

Virgo comes next in the traditional zodiac, and is present in all three temples, depicted as the figure of a woman. In the Somerset temple she is shown lying on her back while at Prescelly and Pumpsaint she is upright. In each case her hands are outstretched, at Pumpsaint apparently holding a sickle, and at both Prescelly and Somerset either holding or pointing to the triangular shapes that many consider to be wheatsheaves.* At Babcary

---

*The problem of Virgo's 'triangular object' is intriguing, and the editor would like to suggest an explanation of his own. It is generally recognized that the Virgo effigy at Glastonbury represents the Great Goddess in her triple mystical guise; this would make her the second polarizing force, or moon, to the Sagittarian sun-god who hangs above her. The Great Goddess was at the centre of earliest prehistoric religion – a symbol of the maternal earth affected by the cyclic rhythms of lunar energies. Many scholars (orthodox and unorthodox) now accept that the matriarchal, feminine principle was the predominant religious force up to about 3000 BC when, with the growth of urbanization, the partriarchal concept permanently ousted the matriarchal. The results of this unharmonious historical catastrophe still reverberate today, especially for women!

In the immediate vicinity of the Glastonbury Zodiac a vast complex of neolithic wooden trackways have been uncovered and dated to between 2700 BC and 3500 BC. Many are ruler-straight and run parallel across the sea-moors; it is thought their purpose was as much ritual as practical. Carefully placed in the centre of one (near Westhay), a figurine of exaggerated feminine porportions was found, indicating that the cult of the Goddess existed there around 2900 BC (the date of the figurine). Another trackway, known as the 'Sweet trackway' (near Shapwick, *wick* being a name intimately connected with ley lines), has yielded another (the predominant) symbol of the Goddess, an axe-head pendant. The symbol of the axe (sometimes double-headed as in the Cretan Labrys) is often portrayed in the hands of the Goddess, particularly in the earliest forms of prehistoric art. The beautifully made axe pendant, carefully buried in the centre of the 'Sweet trackway', is dated to 3200 BC. The presence of it and the figurine firmly establishes the religion of the Goddess at Glastonbury. The trackways are preserved in the peat bogs of the Somerset levels, and their excavation has puzzled archaeologists because so many are placed quite close together and run towards the Tor.

[*Footnote continues overleaf*]

in the Somerset temple, the Virgin has a pointed hat, slightly flattened on top and reminiscent of those meant to have been worn by witches. In Pumpsaint she wears an unmistakable bonnet, while in the Prescelly temple she is shown bending on one knee and with a double-pointed hat, typical of those worn by maidens of the Dark Ages and early medieval era.

The ancient Britons personified the earth as a maiden in the early part of the year, when she was called *Morwyn Ddu,* the Black Virgin. It took from the winter solstice to the spring equinox for her to reach puberty, at which time she was wedded to the sun. The result of their union was the fertilizing of the seeds in the earth mother's womb. As proof of their joint creative powers, the flowers bloomed from the spring equinox onwards and from which time she was called by the aptly descriptive name of *Blodwen,* Holy Flora. At the autumn equinox, about the time of the heliacal rising of the stars of Virgo, as the harvest goddess she bore her fruits, and from then she was given the seasonally descriptive name *Tynghedwen Dyrriath. Tynghedwen* means 'holy fortune', in respect of the fruits of the earth, the first of which she bore as early as Lammas. *Dyrriath* has the double meaning 'barrenness' and 'furiousness'. The barrenness refers to the infertility of the 'old hag' as she began to be regarded from the autumn equinox to the winter solstice; the furiousness was meant to typify the attitude of a mother in the protection of her children, in this case the fruits of the earth.

Mrs Caine has rightly pointed out that at Somerset she is the only female figure, and must therefore embody all aspects of the earth goddess at every season. The female human figure would in many ways seem an obvious choice by anyone in any age to symbolize the constellation of Virgo, and quite possibly the small differences in each of these figures may help to date the respective temples.

The next figure, Leo the lion, is the one that has been criticized the most in all three of these temples. The more dog-like shape of the lion figure in the Somerton area of the West Country has led to much criticism, not only of the dedication to Leo, but even of the existence of any such figure. The almost headless lion at Pumpsaint has been explained as having his head turned in the direction of Aquarius, yet the overall figure still leaves a lot to the imagination. The head of the Prescelly lion cannot be completed unless the outline gives the impression that he is wearing a crown. Nevertheless, there are common features in each of these figures that suggest the existence of some design principles known to the builders of all three. Each lion has a prominent river outlining the back legs, under-belly and part of the front legs. Each lion is depicted as 'rampant', with one paw upraised and mouth open wide. The Prescelly lion with its unmistakable crowned head is the most majestic of the three, looking as though it once belonged to some long lost heraldic crest.

[*Footnote continued*]

According to Mrs Maltwood, major constructions within the Zodiac were taking place around the third millennium BC, and this leads to the mystery of what the Virgo (Goddess) effigy is holding in her hands. The pronounced triangular field shape with curving blade-like end looks much more like a ritual axe than a wheatsheaf! It seems likely that this is indeed an image of the Goddess holding out her foremost sacred symbol in a gesture of power and authority. The shape of Virgo's axe is definitely reminiscent of the Cretan Labrys, a motif dating to around 3200 BC (see page 147 for illustration). On a recent drive around the triangular roads outlining the Virgo axe-head, a small church was located at Keinton Mandeville, dedicated of course to the Virgin Mary, the classic Christian adaptation of the Goddess. (*Ed.*)

In the traditional zodiac the next two signs should be Cancer, the crab, and Gemini, the twins. All indications are that these symbols, the contemporaries of the goat, the mounted archer and the water-bearer, were not in use at the time that these temples are believed to have been built. It is no surprise therefore to find that these symbols have not been included in any of the three temples under consideration here.

Instead there is evidence of two other figures. A sort of boat or ship, which Mrs Maltwood and others have felt to represent the constellation Argo Navis; and a human figure with one arm raised above his head, meant to represent either one of the Gemini twins or the giant Orion. Mr Edwards found two very similar figures between Leo and Taurus at Pumpsaint, although the ship was more of a small boat, with no masts or sails. Something similar can be discerned in the Prescelly area also, but they are not of the definite style of the rest of the figures in that temple.

Besides the highly developed star-science discovered in recent years, it is well known that the ancient Britons in general, and the Druids in particular, studied astronomy and were very learned regarding the stars and their courses. A list of star-groups known to the ancient Cymru has been given by Rev. ab ithel Williams in two books. The best known of these books, *The Barddas: The Bardo-Druidic System of Knowledge,* lists twenty-five to thirty astronomical terms, which Rev. Williams translates into English, giving the names of the corresponding stars where known.

Almost without exception, the boat/ship figures found by people researching this phenomenon have been regarded as symbolic of Argo Navis. This is a constellation seen only near to, and south of the equator, and not seen in British latitudes at all. The star lists in *The Barddas* contain a constellation once known as Llong Foel, 'the bald ship'. Llong Foel in tradition is said to be the mastless ship in which the dying sun, at the winter solstice sunset, is taken across the sea to Annwn. Annwn was the Celtic under-world whose physical counterpart, tradition has it, was in the Prescelly Mountains. From Annwn the sun was reborn hours later at the sunrise; the new-born son of the old sun. He was the mabyn of the 'Mabinogion': *mabyn* being the old Welsh for 'young' or 'new-born son [sun]', the whole word *Mabynogion* meaning 'the adherents to' or 'the worshippers of' the young, or new-born son (sun).

From Glastonbury Tor, which has been described as the most sacred of all the areas in that zodiac temple, the midwinter sun sets in the direction of this ship. As the Somerset ship covers quite a large area, it is possible that this could be just a coincidence. However, after viewing from similar sacred centres in the Prescelly and Pumpsaint temples, the midwinter sun setting over the areas covered by similar but much smaller boat/ship figures, it would appear that at one time the zodiacal belt was split up much differently than it is today. Possibly there was a small mastless boat called Llong Foel imagined in the heavens, where today we look for the Crab.

Orion is a most prominent constellation in British latitudes, and although it is just outside the ecliptic circle, it would seem strange if the ancient Britons attached no importance to it in their cosmology. Mrs Maltwood has shown how the stars of Orion fall on the figure of the giant 'man with upraised arm', when the planisphere is placed to scale over it. Mr Edwards was convinced that it was the constellation of Orion that the similar figure in the Pumpsaint temple was meant to represent. Even so, it was suggested

The two superimposed bulls. The long horned (Uchen Bannog) and the Aurox. (Pumpsaint Zodiac).

The Goat's head at Bwlch Blaen Corn (the pass of the front of the horn) Pumpsaint Zodiac.

by Mrs Maltwood that the Somerset figure may have represented one of the twins, as she says, '. . . two stars from Gemini fall on his uplifted right hand'. She was also of the opinion that the second twin was represented by the 'hawk' or 'griffin' that stands next to what she refers to as 'Orion's Ship'. Mary Caine has claimed to have found the real second twin in the shape of a monk, sitting in yogic meditation between the lion and the ship. Possibly it was Mrs Maltwood's own doubts about her own second twin, which she felt was '. . . not contemporary with the other figures', that encouraged Mrs Caine to look for a true second twin. But, if the star-groups in *The Barddas* are correct, the ancient Cymru at least never made the twins a symbol for the stars we now call Gemini. One of the listed constellations is Yr Ychen Bannog, translated as 'the long-horned Oxen', and which, Rev. Williams says, was their symbol for the twins. It is believed they symbolized the stars of Taurus by the head, body and fore-legs of the bull, which were joined in the same constellation to the stars of the now separate Gemini by its long horns. Mrs Maltwood says that '. . . Nath and the other horn star fall on his [the giant's] elbow and head'. Orion occupies a place outside the ecliptic although its stars are still nearest stars to those of Gemini and Taurus. Possibly the Dundon Giant represents Orion in his own right, it may be that at the time of construction, the temple was designed without any figure representing Gemini as a separate star-group.

Utilizing the 100-foot contour, Mr Edwards's original Taurus figure had small horns compared to the size of the head. Only the head was shown on his map as he felt the body was not used in ancient times. Yet aerial photographs of the area show two distinct possibilities for the Taurus figure, both much different from the one drawn by Mr Edwards. One is a side view of what appears to be a remarkable representation of an aurochs,* the ancient creature from which modern cattle are believed to have evolved. The other is an exact likeness of what we today refer to as a Scottish Highland bull, and well suited to the descriptive name Yr Ychen Bannog, the long-horned oxen. Almost all of the body of the bull is shown on the aerial photographs, although the back legs are unclear. Inside the outline of the figure is a farm called Cil-yr-Ychain, meaning the 'shelter of the oxen'.

At Prescelly, also, the whole body of the bull is shown, but it has only small horns, similar to the Somerset bull, which has only head, small horns and foreleg visible. The Prescelly bull has both front and back legs, with one of its horns inside the outline of the head. It is represented by a forked road, splitting to form the horn at Corn Ochre, meaning the 'side horn'. The bulls at Prescelly and Somerset are depicted the same way up, as are most of the other figures in the temples. But the Pumpsaint bull is shown upside down, like the Sagittarius and Capricorn figures in all three temples. This is not the only major difference in the Pumpsaint temple. At both Prescelly and Somerset, the Aries figures are shown as rams, reclining in typical sheep pose, with heads turned towards the west. The Pumpsaint Aries figure however, is a young, bouncing lamb-ram looking due east, and typical of the young lambs seen everywhere each spring. On the head of

---

*The long-horned aurochs (*Bos primogenius*) was the wild ox native to Europe from Pleistocene times until as recently as 1627. The British black Pembroke breed of ox is said to resemble aurochs most closely, for they are thought to have been black in colour. Skulls and bones of aurochs standing six feet at the shoulder have been uncovered from Pleistocene gravels in the Thames Valley. (*Ed.*)

this figure is an area called Ram, which being in English suggests a modern origin, but demonstrates a most odd coincidence.

For Pisces, in each of these three temples there are two well-defined fish, with a third much larger fish meant to symbolize Cetus the whale, this being included at Glastonbury. This figure is not as clear as the outlines of the other two fish representing Pisces, and is shown on the other side of the ecliptic from where its stars are actually in the sky. There is a Mynydd Morvil, 'the mountain of the whale', in the Prescelly area, although it is nearer to the Taurus figure than it is to the Piscean fish. Undoubtedly the Glastonbury shape suggests a whale, but would the temple builders have put it where it is if they had the astronomical knowledge we are detecting in their temples?

The Pumpsaint zodiac, with 'hawk' or 'falcon-shaped' figure outlined by the roads around the village of Falcondale, is quite different from the other temples. The figure is one of the most well-defined in the area, according to the maps; so is the fish figure that its claw appears to be clutching. Here again the English place name, obviously of comparatively recent origin, demonstrates an odd coincidence. The quote by Mrs Malt-wood from Waddell's *British Edda* was given in reference to the phoenix (Aquarius) and the fish in the Glastonbury Temple. But if this refers to a zodiac temple at all, it would seem more suitably attached to the one at Pumpsaint. The quote is: '. . . the Sun Eagle flies o'er it, there Fialla (the Falcon) hunts for fishes.'

When Mrs Maltwood discovered the temple in Somerset, it was at Glastonbury itself that the Aquarius symbol was located. There, a little to the north of the town, and including the magnificent Tor, she found the shape of a bird, which she called the Phoenix of Aquarius. In the area of Bryn Cyssegr Fan, the 'hill of the sacred place', Mr Edwards found the shape of a squirrel, which he felt represented Aquarius in the Pumpsaint zodiac. Neither the phoenix nor the squirrel are known to have been symbolic of Aquarius in ancient or any other times. At Prescelly also, there is a very definite bird-shape where the figure for Aquarius should be. Its well-defined outspread wings give it the appearance of a buzzard in flight. A similar shape is evident in the Pumpsaint squirrel area also.

There are many buzzards to be seen in these areas today, and no doubt it was the same in ancient times. On the tip of one of its wings is the village of Boncath, a quiet place to the north-east of the Prescelly Mountains. Boncath is a corruption, we are told locally, of the word *bwncath*, meaning 'buzzard'. Possibly this is what the Glastonbury and Pumpsaint bird shapes were meant to be, as there is a star-group mentioned in *The Barddas* called Yr Hebog, 'the hawk'. Rev. Williams however, ventures no opinion as to which modern constellation this name once referred.

Many interested people have suggested that these zodiacal temples of the stars were built with the help of Phoenician star wisdom, presumably to help explain the inclusion of Middle Eastern symbols like the scorpion and Argo Navis, which they have felt *must* be there. Mr Edwards had similar feelings about the Pumpsaint zodiac, and especially about the boat/ship figure, which he felt was of an unmistakable Phoenician design. But research in the past two decades has shown that the ancient Britons were far more knowledgeable in astronomy than was at first thought. The megalithic stone monuments, almost all that is left of their ancient times, on analysis have shown achievements in astronomical knowledge in these islands unsurpassed by anyone in history. If Mrs Maltwood and Mr Edwards had had access to this new evidence, they too may have concluded that the zodiac temple builders needed to borrow from no one in this science; their own ancient traditions, steeped in star lore and star science, were the guidelines by which the temples were constructed.

Beyond all doubt sun-worship was the essence of the old Druidic religion, with due homage paid to the moon, planets and stars, although it was the Earth Mother who occupied the central position. It was the polar motions of the earth, after all, that caused the Sun to appear in a state of birth, growth, maturity, decay and death in the course of the year, producing the seasons. The ancient British astronomer-priests, who, towards the decline of their power became known as Druids, poetically allegorized these rhythmically changing appearances of the Sun. At midwinter the old sun died, only to be reborn again some hours later. At the vernal (spring) equinox he was married to the Earth, personified as Cariadwen, meaning 'holy love', his pet name for his divine spouse. Their union was an important aspect of the Druidic religion, as it was at this time that the 'seminal word' of the sun fertilized the seeds in the Earth Mother's womb, ensuring flowers and fruits for another year. After the Earth Mother's fruits had been born, the autumnal equinox would herald the decay and impending death of the now aging Sun, called Tegid Foel. Tegid Foel means 'bald and all beautiful', the hair of a man's head being likened to the rays of the sun; as a man often goes bald towards the close of his life, so the rays of the sun lessen in time and strength towards the close of the natural year.

In these ancient times there was no difference between the science and the religion of the people. Everything they believed in was part of their everyday lives, and became manifest in the course of each year. Great importance was attached to the stars that were in the background of the sun's apparent path. Within a band almost ten degrees either side of the actual ecliptic, they were grouped together into constellations, each having its own symbol, known collectively as the signs of the zodiac. The very first principles of religion consisted of a scientific record of the sun's annual path through the signs of the zodiac. The very first temples perceived in the imagination of the astronomer-priests were temples in the heavens, observed from the sacred high places, the celestial city/castle/temple known as Caer Sidi. In the star lists in *The Barddas,* Rev. Williams says that Caer Sidi represents the ecliptic, or band, of the zodiac; yet many have translated it as the 'revolving castle'. The zodiacal constellations do revolve relative to the sun's annual journey through them, taking approximately 25 920 years for the same stars to rise again with the sun on the vernal equinox. It was not the vernal point but the background constellation which decided the sacred symbol of the astrological age, each lasting 2000 years or more.

During the age of Taurus the sun was symbolized generally as a bull, while in the age of Aries it was symbolized by the ram. Some of the early Mediterranean area star charts have been dated not only by the configurations of planets on them, but also by the poses of the zodiacal star symbols. For instance, some charts dated between 4000 BC and 2000 BC show the bull as 'charging', with some only depicting its head and forelegs. In these same charts the ram is shown 'reclining' as it was the last sign of the zodiac; the year in those times being opened by the charging bull whose stars between these dates rose with the sun at the vernal point. However, from around 2000 BC onwards, when the vernal point had retrograded into the constellation Aries, it was the ram that led the yearly procession.

In both the Prescelly and the Glastonbury temples the bulls are shown as if charging, while the almost identical rams are shown reclining. The Pumpsaint temple, on the other hand, has its bull lying on its back, while for Aries there is a 'bouncy young Lamb-Ram'. The temple at Pumpsaint has many peculiarities which suggest it was built at a different time from the other two. Possibly the very definite style and vesica shape of the Prescelly temple could date its construction at a later, or earlier period of the Taurean age, than the Glastonbury temple; though they both have almost the same symbols with almost the same poses. Both these temples, with their charging bulls and reclining rams, can perhaps be regarded as having been constructed somewhere between 4000 and 2000 BC, during the age of Taurus.

The Pumpsaint temple could have been built from 2000 BC onwards, if the symbolism used there accurately reflects the position of the stars at the time of its construction. It would appear that quite probably the vernal point had not long retrograded into the constellation Aries when the Pumpsaint temple was built. Although the example here is taken from Middle Eastern star charts, the Aries symbol of the newborn lamb-ram, new leader of the zodiacal herd, would fit perfectly the Druidic philosophies regarding new-ages and new-born deities.

In the Prescelly and Glastonbury temples the early symbols of the centaur and the goat-fish lend support to this idea. In this respect, the Pumpsaint temple shows only the much later 'man on a horse' (whether archer or lancer) and 'goat's head', amplifying the difference. The exact dates of the changeover to the later symbolism are not known, but may be due to the almost continuous migrations from the continent that occurred from around 2000 BC onwards. These necessitated the building of fortifications similar to the two forts, one on each of the fish, at Pumpsaint. That, Mr Edwards felt, was an indication that the entrance of the temple was between the two fish of Pisces. Possibly they also felt that their temple should be guarded on other levels against the uninitiated, or at least Mr Edwards got this impression. 'It was guarded spiritually,' he says, 'by the Falcon,' although he refers to it as an extinct bird. This may well be another indication that the Pumpsaint temple was built at a different, possibly later date than the other two.

Changes in the outlines and the features of the figures themselves have been found to occur at different times of the year. Mrs Caine has shown how the head of the Orion figure in the Dundon area of the Somerset temple appears to point in different directions at different seasons. When newly constructed, each figure in these temples, may have been designed to incorporate even the flora within its boundaries as part of its overall appearance. The various species, flowering at different times and growing only at varying heights above sea-level, and the changing moods of nature were reflected in the figure itself. Some of the plants may even have been purposely put there to emphasize the outlines.

So much work must have gone into the building of these temples that the areas must have been the most sacred in the localities. Would these important sacred centres have been abandoned at the changing of each age, and new temples built in different areas? Or would the new figures, oriented to the new heavenly positions of the stars and celestial spheres, have been superimposed on the old ones, retaining the use of the sacred centre but under a new dedication? There are several examples in the two Welsh temples of second, ghost or shadow figures, superimposed over each other but oriented slightly differently, suggesting that the latter theory is much more probable. The bodies of the two different bulls in the Pumpsaint temple are formed from the same outline, with the very different heads each having its own axis. Possibly one is clearer than the other at different times of the year; or perhaps one is a remnant of an earlier figure, of a temple built, dedicated and oriented in an earlier astrological age.

There are differing suggestions regarding the Virgo figure in this same temple. Mr Edwards saw a figure very much like Mrs Maltwood's Glastonbury Virgo, though it was rather unconvincing. One or two alternatives have been suggested: a virgin with a wheatsheaf, looking much like a statue found in Gaul representing the Black Virgin, and another virgin holding a sickle. Possibly the Virgo figures are all there, but were built at different times. The virgin with the wheatsheaf could have been built at a time when the stars of Virgo coincided with the harvest already being gathered in. Similarly, the virgin with the sickle may be much earlier; perhaps it was built around the time that the stars of Virgo coincided with the harvest actually being cut. There are many slight as well as great differences in almost all the figures in these temples, and maybe, on analysis, they could all help to date each temple's construction more accurately.

At the moment zodiac temples are a long way from being given even a second glance by orthodox archaeologists, but they could prove a bombshell, like the previously supposed insignificant stone circles, with their geometric and astronomical perfection.

One of the main factors of the academics' rejection of the Glastonbury temple, besides its size, was Mrs Maltwood's opinion that its presence in that area of Somerset indicated the true origins of the Grail legends. The local place names, she felt, were, along with the zodiac temple itself, the living proof that in this part of Somerset all the events described in *The High History of the Holy Grail* had actually occurred. The zodiacal symbols were described as the various 'Knights of the Round Table', their exploits supposedly mirrored in the relationships of one figure to another.

As Arthur was one of the many names given to the sun by the ancient Britons, it would appear that the Round Table knights could easily be equated with the signs of the zodiac. In the original Welsh, *Arthur* was 'Arddir', pronounced almost the same but meaning 'gardener', and it was the earth that was his garden. But the connection between Glastonbury and the Isle of Avalon was made as late as 1191 when the monks of the Abbey claimed to have found the grave and bones of both Arthur and Guinevere. At the time this discovery was much to the benefit of the Abbey and those concerned with it, and the whole episode should be seen against the background of political and ecclesiastical uncertainty and intrigue that characterized those times.

If the local place names clinch the theory, as Mrs Maltwood believed, then the same could be said, with more confidence, regarding the Prescelly zodiac temple. Many of the place names in this area suggest a much closer connection with Arthur and the Grail legends and this is supported by much local tradition. There is cairn on top of the Prescellies called Bedd Arthur (the grave of Arthur), while not too far away there are some stones known as Cerrig Marchogion (the stones of the knights of Arthur). At the foot of the ridge on which these stand there are two magnificent standing-stones called Cerrig Meibion Arthur, meaning 'the stones of the sons of Arthur'. Should anyone ever attempt to connect the *High History* with the Prescelly area, then the place called Pen Pelles, to the north of the Capricorn figure, would surely help their argument.

If, as we are finding out today, the astronomer-priests were aware of and could accurately measure wobbles in the moon's orbit, then it would seem obvious that they could also have been aware of the precession of the equinoxes and all its astrological implications, which were really the essence of their beliefs. The ingenuity of the astronomer-priests lay not just in their ability to conceive of and build temples so large, nor in the way that the constructions synthesized their science and their religion. It is only fully appreciated in the realization that these temples, although designed for religious worship, were at the same time 'alive' – reflecting in the annual life/death rhythms of the local flora the annual rhythms of the zodiacal figures and of the sun.

Possibly the initial visions of these temples, brought down out of the heavens to the earth, were similar to those experienced by St John (Revelation) in his sacred high place on Patmos. He too saw the sacred city/castle/temple coming down out of heaven to earth, and made manifest through the same sacred geometrical cosmology that is being rediscovered today in the ground-plans of prehistoric sanctuaries in Britain. Many believe that this vision is available to the initiated at the changing of each astrological age. For St John it came after the chaos of the changeover from the age of Aries to that of Pisces, although it had been anticipated continuously from a few centuries earlier in the expectations of a coming Messiah. Possibly this vision is again available today to the initiated (the aware), as we approach the transition from the present Age of Pisces to the dawning age of Aquarius.

Edward Davies, in his *Mythology and Rites of the British Druids,* wrote almost 170 years ago: 'As the Britons distinguished the Zodiac, and the Temples or Sanctuaries of their Gods, by the same name of Caer Sidi, and as their great Bard Taliesin blends the heavenly and the terrestrial Sidi in one description, we may presume that they regarded the latter, as a type or representation of the former.' Today, with the appreciation of prehistoric science on the ascendant, and since the rediscovery of the zodiacal temples of the stars, his words seem even more appropriate.

Recommended Books

Fagan, Cyril. *Astrological Origins.* Llewellyn Publications, 1971.
Lum, Peter. *Stars in our Heavens.* Thames & Hudson, 1951.
Maltwood, K. E. *A Guide to Glastonbury's Temple of the Stars.* James Clark, 1964.
Reiser, Oliver L. *This Holyest Erthe.* Perennial Books, 1975.

CHAPTER FIVE

The Quest for The Holy Grail

KENNETH KNIGHT

Most contemporary students of Glastonbury lore have heard of the Temple of the Stars existing in the environs of the Isle of Avalon. It is a supposedly prehistoric Zodiac said to be hidden within the countryside and to have been carved out of the living soil over 4000 years ago. This claim was first made by a Canadian lady in 1929 when she published a book of the title above quoted. She tentatively dated the Zodiac to 2700 BC, but how she was able to determine such a date is quite impossible to say. Her claims were received with mixed feelings. Archaeologists generally appear to have been hostile: zodiacs of such a nature were taboo, for one thing, and the site lacked any stone circles suggesting possible astronomical associations. Research has since uncovered that a series of stone circles similar to Stanton Drew may have once stood on St Edmund's Hill and also along the northern slopes of Glastonbury Tor.* Such stones were in place as recently as 1880 but, alas, for the most part they have completely disappeared.

The Zodiac, according to Katharine Maltwood, author of the book in question, was about ten miles in diameter and thirty miles in circumference, with the church of St Leonard at Butleigh marking a centre line with Park Wood. Fountain's Wall to the north of Glastonbury, Queen Camel to the south, Compton Dundon to the west, and Pilton to the east, covering an area of some one hundred square miles, represents the landscape of the Temple of the Stars. Whatever proof is lacking, there is little doubt that the *idea* is interesting. It has opened up a new avenue of thought in the whole question of the Somerset legends associated with King Arthur, his Round Table and his Quest for the Holy Grail.

Parallel with Mrs Maltwood's study, an interesting book on the astronomical alignments of Stonehenge and other prehistoric monuments in Britain was published by the late Sir Norman Lockyer in 1901. It was entitled *Stonehenge and Other Ancient British Monuments Astronomically Considered*. This clearly indicates that all stone circles were orientated to particular points of the horizon, and for the most part, faced

---

*The name Stonedown Hill (a rounded hill lying just beyond the northern axis of the Tor) is probably not without its early megalithic significance. (*Ed.*)

the sunrise at the equinoxes and solstices. Other circles were orientated to the opening of the four seasons when the Pleiades rose or set at the time the sun rose or set. The myth associated with the disappearance of the continent of Atlantis became part of a Christianized version of King Arthur being ferried to the west, to the Isle of Avalon, on his healing voyage to the underworld.

Sir Norman revealed that the siting of many monuments created a regular geometrical pattern in the form of a rhombus. This system of landscape arrangement and orientation as well as linear proportion is common to all temples, whatever time in the history of man they may have been built. The measurements are all found to be solar/lunar in intent. The diameter of Stonehenge in its inner circle corresponds to the length in English feet of the choir at Bristol Cathedral for instance, i.e. 104 feet.

Glastonbury Abbey has long enjoyed the reputation of being the first Christian church in Britain, reputedly being founded as early as 37 AD by Joseph of Arimathea. Not until the eleventh century, however, do we hear anything of King Arthur and his knights emerging as historical personages, and still later, of King Arthur being buried in the choir of the great church. This event was observed by King Edward I in 1278 when he re-buried the earlier excavated bones of 'Arthur' at the high altar amid great pomp and ceremony. There is little doubt that Edward's action was tinged with dynastic and political over-tones.* At this time the ancient Order of the Knights of the Round Table was still in existence but it was not until 1349 that the order was transferred to Windsor Castle by Edward III under the title of the Most Noble Order of the Garter.

There is a span of some 600 years between the historical Arthur and the multifarious Arthur of legend. The Arthur of history is associated with the time of the Roman departure from Britain and the incoming Saxons' eventual victory over the indigenous Celts. But Like other men of great stature in our past history, Arthur then became a heroic god. Similarly, in Bristol there is a mythical memory that the twin gods Belin and Bran established the city. Belin and Bran as historical figures lived in the first century BC, but their earlier personifications as gods flourished about 700 BC. Thus a reversed dual analogy may be drawn.

Bran and Belin, being in the first instance nature gods, had the Druids as their priests. The Druids were well informed in subjects such as astronomy, geometry, mathematics, astrology, etc., and accurately interpreted the motion of the heavens through their rituals. Not until the sixteenth century was any further attempt to interpret architecture and its relevant proportions ever seriously considered. Sacred architecture as an image of the universe presented innumerable mystical propositions, all exceptionally difficult to unravel. It may not have occurred to the layman that far from being haphazardly built on any piece of ground which happened to be handy, temples and the like were care-fully sited and orientated in relation one to another. Local legends and folk-lore became an indirect system of preserving them. Local legends around Wedmore are as relevant to the greater Arthurian cycle as are the legends woven around Wells Cathedral, the Tor, or Glastonbury Abbey. Again, Cadbury Hill, more commonly known as the

---

*The overtones were religious as well, for the fanatical Catholic church was (and is) always ready to engulf the memory of any hero of the people whose charisma challenges its authority. Arthur was never liked by the priests, as Gildas's refusal to name him proves. (*Ed.*)

Glastonbury Abbey.

'MARY CAINE'

'Castle of Camelot', has its quota of myths and legends which are relevantly astronomical in intent, and always in an Arthurian context.

Temples, churches and cathedrals all possess measurements which form careful ratios and are in fact microcosms of the macrocosm. In other words they are by design and proportion a scale of the solar system as well as of solar lunar time-cycles, marking the planets passage through the twelve signs of the zodiac over specified periods of time.

Computations were made as to the regularity of these motions, the conjunctions of some or all the planets and the prediction of eclipses. Capping this there is one particular date which has been the basis of all modern astronomical calculations since, and that is midnight of the autumn equinox, with the full moon resting between the horns of the bull (Taurus) at 4004 BC. This date falls within the zodiacal age of Taurus the Bull and is also of vital importance as a mystical foundation point in Christian chronology.

Although it has been known for a very long time that sacred temples were a miniature copy of the solar system, the measurements of which are to be found in the British metrological system, the means of determining these measures had never been made public knowledge. This was due chiefly to difficulties in communication. Everything had to be written by hand, for one thing, making education on a nation-wide scale impossible. Even if it were possible, knowledge was considered sacred, or secret – not to be divulged to the common man or the unenlightened. Although this attitude is unacceptable nowadays, there is an element of wisdom in the opinion, 'a *little* knowledge is a dangerous thing'.* Not everyone is qualified mentally or intellectually to cope with the mysteries of higher mathematics which are necessary to understand the science of flights into outer (or inner) space. That is really what the Quest for the Holy Grail is all about!

A book published in 1897 by an anonymous author was probably the first architectural study of modern times to attempt an understanding of the involved writings of a famous Roman architect, Vitruvius, who lived in the first century. An attempt had been made in the sixteenth century by an Italian architect, Caesariano, who translated his predecessor's book into Latin, but Vitruvius's writings still remained obscure. The original book has apparently long-since disappeared.

In the nineteenth century, William Stirling, a friend and patron of William Morris, spent a great deal of time on architectural research, having to undertake mountains of calculations in order to prove his point. In essence, he showed that there was a link between the seasons, the motion of the heavens, the distances of the planets from the sun, earth and moon, and that their respective cycles around the sun had some significance in all architectural proportion and measurement. Furthermore, he also showed that myths and legends often concealed important celestial events, such as the end of a major eclipse, or a conjunction of planets in a particular part of the heavens. The birth of Christ was heralded and recorded in the temple at Jerusalem in this manner. Moreover he discovered that the finger width, palm width, length from finger-tip to elbow, as well as length of arm from finger-tip to arm-pit, all had some source of sacred measure. The length of the pace and step also had some bearing on calculating the length of the lunar and solar months in days, the average pace being slightly more than twenty-nine inches, corresponding in this instance to a lunar month.

The rhombus was discovered to be the key to the mysterious medieval sign of the Vesica Piscis, the sign of the fish. This was found to be derived from the cube unfolded, producing the sign of the Cross with the three horizontal and four vertical bars, which when cubed, produce twenty-seven and sixty-four. All other numbers in ratio are found

---

Total knowledge, acquired through following the cosmic archetypes through the Earth Spirit, is of course dangerous, but is equally liberating, both of spirit and intellect. (*Ed.*)

in the square of seventy-four, the circle of 231, and a rectangle of 37 × 64. Such is the external measure of the Lady Chapel at Glastonbury Abbey – 37 feet by 64 feet. This was the site of the first ecclesiastical building to be erected there.

Architecture down the ages, in all climes, through all races and civilizations, conforms to *one set of rules only,* and indicates the basic Unity of God and therefore of all religions. It is canonical and eternal and its interpretation has always been recognized in a metaphysical context.

We have now to consider two important facts:

a) Architectural proportions are the same throughout all civilizations.

b) These proportions are to be understood as the means of interpreting astronomy and astrology through various myths.

It is interesting to note that the knowledge which the ancients possessed coincides with the knowledge of the solar system and universe we have today. This knowledge has been gained through use of the most scientific instruments and is of such a complex nature that even now it has not been fully interpreted. How this knowledge was obtained before is a mystery, but the ancient astronomers knew the distances of the planets from the earth and sun and also the time it took them to move round the sun. They computed the planet Pluto (apparently) even though it was not visible to them. They also computed Saturn and Jupiter as well as how often they conjoined and in which sign of the zodiac they lay.

It takes Pluto 248 years to move through the twelve signs of the zodiac. The length of the nave to the high altar in Bristol Cathedral is 248 feet. The height of the central tower of Wells Cathedral is given at about 164 feet. It takes Neptune some 164 years to pass through the twelve signs. There are eighteen periods of thirty-seven lunar eclipses which total 666 years and are called a 'saros'. The overall length of Glastonbury Abbey was 666 feet. This number is also associated with the 'magic square' of the sun.

Although I have not carried out an on-the-spot survey of the parish church of St Mary at Wedmore, nevertheless a rough estimate may be attempted that the overall length of the church will be in the region of 222 feet. This is also the measure of St Mary Redcliffe, Bristol, whose spire is also about 222 feet in height. The correspondences might appear vague but they *are* correspondences.

The system adopted by the antique architects appears to have been called the 'Canon of Proportion', which relates all the seven sciences of the ancients and interprets them through use of the Hebrew grammar. Hebrew is a very old tongue and was in reality the sacred tongue of the Church until it was removed and Latin adopted in its place. The Hebrew alphabet, like the Latin (and Greek for that matter), has numerical values for each of the letters; when a group of letters are placed together they give a total which in turn, when grammatically considered, produce a word or a phrase. Such a system is known as 'gematria'. Only consonants are considered; they give the root-origin to a word or a phrase. When transferring such words and phrases to the heavens it is of some significance to discover that the main star-groups are mentioned in Hebrew and to this day many retain their original Hebrew names. Astrologically of course yet another system or canon develops and this in turn reveals that stars not only changed their names but

'You shall know the truth:
And the truth shall make you free.'

John 8.32

Three symbolisms: The breakthrough into Cosmic Consciousness; the realization of the Quest for the Holy Grail; the reading of the Macrocosm.

their nature, according to the time of year and day in which they moved across the sky. This is where the renewable nuances of myth enter the picture.

The Hebrew root-origin of 'King Arthur' is *MLKARTh* with a gematric value of 691.* Transferring this to the heavens, it corresponds with the number of diameters of the earth in the earth's orbital path round the sun. In the light of the Hebrew Cabbala (upon which the whole basis and system of the seven sciences or arts collectively depends) Arthur becomes an earth-related wanderer across the starry firmament. In Hebrew the word 'cabbala' means 'to receive', in the sense that what can be related by the seven sciences one to another is acceptable in the method of interpretation. Thus we find that King Arthur, by veiled allusion, is, in the cabbalistic sense, a figure symbolizing the sun as well as in some instances the king of the earth. The tenth Sephiroth on the cabbalistic Tree of Life is called 'Malkuth' (which is a derivative of 'Malkurth').

It is to Glastonbury and the Isle of Avalon that the wounded king is taken, and long before the Christian era the area was known to the Celts as the Isle of the Dead (or Blessed). A book written about 1200 at the library of the Abbey was presented to King Edward I on his visit there in 1278. This book has been preserved and was popularized in the early part of this century when it was published under the title of *The High History of the Holy Grail.* It is so obscure and full of symbolism that only one acquainted with subjects such as astronomy, astrology, grammar, architecture, etc., could hope to get even a glimmer of its inner meaning. However, this glimmer reveals a series of ancient initiation rites always in a cyclical, zodiacal context.

There is an indirect reference to an actual zodiac which is only seen through the mind's eye, in other words through the power of inner perception. The legends associated with Cadbury Castle, not far from Glastonbury, also suggest that there is a zodiac in the immediate vicinity. There is reference to buried treasure and anyone who tries to dig for it will never find it because it will only sink deeper into the ground the deeper they dig. The celestial inference is obvious. Although there is visible evidence of what the Round Table looked like at Winchester, yet, in its deeper aspects at Cadbury, the table, being also a pattern of the heavens, sinks from view. One does not have to look to tangible evidence in order to understand its purpose and function. Thus it is with the legends as a whole: the real understanding comes on the mental plane. The late Carl Gustav Jung, the famous Swiss psychiatrist, appreciated the true sense of the Cabbala and the psychic function of the Arthurian legends, for he had divined their intimate interrelation as symbols.

According to an ancient Egyptian tradition, when the soul of the departed had to undertake its long journey to the Land of the Blessed, a guide book was presented to it so that the journey would be more tolerable. Called *The Book of the Dead,* it was in fact a book of initiation into the mysteries of death, as the *Morte d'Arthur* indicates. As the Great Pyramid in Egypt was the same theme in stone, revealed by its hidden symbolism,

*All mythologies contain an Arthur-type figure within the framework of their psychic foundations. He is a hero or king who dies for his people and is usually a fusion of earthly and celestial influences. He is always involved in a quest, mainly for magical vessels or weapons (cups, lances, swords, etc.), and is a personification of the returning power of the eternal life cycle - fertility is emphasized through sexual symbolism (sword/lance into cup/grail). (*Ed.*)

so too *The High History of the Holy Grail* had its counterpart in the dimensions and proportions of Glastonbury Abbey as a whole. The *High History* is but a copy of the Egyptian *Book of the Dead*. It is a cultural counterpart, bridging the gateway of death.

Despite the apparent circuitry contained in the theme of this writing, it is hoped that the subject as a whole may stimulate a wider interest. Much work has still to be undertaken and this particular approach to archaeology has yet to be accepted as an integral part of future diggings. Careful work needs to be done when noting the site's axial direction and points on the horizon and the distances between different buildings and their respective angles. What is lacking at the moment is the *interpretation* of these ancient buildings and monuments, particularly Glastonbury Abbey and Wells Cathedral. Only when this becomes an accomplished fact will historians be able to present a true picture of the purpose and intention of such sacred buildings. The Quest for the Grail continues.

Recommended Books

Ashe, Geoffry. *Camelot and the Vision of Albion*. Panther, 1975.
Bord, Janet and Colin. *Mysterious Britain*. Paladin, 1974.
Evans, Sebastian, trans. *The High History of the Holy Grail*. Everyman.
Maltwood, K. E. *A Guide to Glastonbury's Temple of the Stars*. James Clarke, 1964.
Stirling, William. *The Canon*. Garnstone Press, 1974.
Treharne, R. F. *The Glastonbury Legends*. Abacus, 1975.

CHAPTER SIX

Glastonbury Abbey

NIGEL PENNICK

Since remotest antiquity Glastonbury has been recognized as one of the most important geomantic sites in Britain. Under its former names of Avalon and Yns-witrin it was sacred to the ancient cosmic religion of Druidism and finally to the nascent but flawed revelations of rampant Christianity. The great cosmic temple of the Zodiac, arguably the earliest and most perfect and the first to be rediscovered this century, was connected to sacred sites in the surrounding countryside by a network of alignments and orientations, each symbolically representing their ritually arcane attributes. These are the ley lines that stamp the area with an indelible imagery of sacred geometrical form.

Overlooking (and part of) the Zodiac is the Tor, a major landmark and a major point in the geomancy of southern Britain. Surmounting this commandingly conical hill is a tower, sole remaining fragment of the church of St Michael, last of a succession of so-named churches on this sacred spot. Its dramatic Christianization is recorded in the legendary *Life of St Collen,* alleged converter of the Greeks. Although abbot of Glastonbury Abbey for five years, Collen became a hermit with a cell on the side of the Tor. Whilst in this austere cell, he heard two men talking about Gwynn ap Nudd (who had an abode on the Tor), remarking that he was King of Annwn and master of the Fairies, an elemental spirit of wide powers. Collen warned them against such heathen talk, but they told him that he would have to answer for such haughty words. Soon the eerie messenger of Gwynn ap Nudd arrived at Collen's cell and summoned him to the top of the Tor, where he saw a fine castle. On entering, he was taken to Gwyn himself and asked to eat a banquet the Fairy Lord spread out before him. Whereupon he angrily refused and threw holy water over them all, who vanished along with the castle, leaving only grassy turf on the hill's flattened summit. This legend points to the Tor having retained its pagan sanctity (and possibly buildings) after the foundation of the first Christian church near the sacred Omphalos, a site now covered by the ruins of the later Benedictine abbey.

The Abbey, once of primary importance in England, was ruthlessly attacked in 1539 and subsequently almost totally demolished in order that the stone might be re-used in local secular buildings. The site can claim to be the most sacred in Christian reckoning, as it is the place where, according to tradition, in 63 AD Joseph of Arimathea founded the first Christian church on land given him by the local King, Arviragus. To this ancient wooden and wattle church, referred to as the *Vetusta Ecclesia,* Faganus and Deruvianus, missionaries sent to Britain by Pope Eleutherius, added in 160 a stone church dedicated to Christ and St Peter. Fragments of quality Romano-British carved stonework, which had subsequently been re-used in a later Romanesque building, dug up in F. Bligh Bond's excavations early this century, probably represent fragments of this edifice.

Joseph of Arimathea's building, though in a sorry state of disrepair, was not replaced or demolished, but was repaired by Faganus and Deruvianus. In effect this was a second foundation, being an extension and restoration rather than a replacement. In turn St David, in about 540, shortly after the death of King Arthur who was allegedly buried there, founded another church on a different site but on the same axis as that of Faganus and Deruvianus.

In 601 Gwrgan Varvtrwch, King of Dumnonia, gave the land of Yns-witrin to the Old Church (i.e. the Celtic Church at Glastonbury) under the auspices of Abbot Worgret. This made the whole island of Yns-witrin into a monastic island. In 633, Paulinus, Bishop of Saxon York, had the *Vetusta Ecclesia* boarded over and covered with lead in order to preserve the sacred but now rapidly decaying fabric.

The Saxons who conquered Yns-witrin were already Christianized and did not destroy the ancient church, although this was the beginning of the end of the independent Celtic church, direct descendant of Druidism. It was at this time that the name Yns-witrin was changed to Glastonbury. When Aethelfrith conquered Chester in 605, the total British population was exterminated, including the Celtic priesthood. In 607, the ancient library of the former Druidic University of Bangor, containing thousands of priceless volumes, was burnt. Because the Saxons were Christian this naturally did not mean they were pacifists. Ceadwalla, King of Wessex from 685 to 688, the predecessor of King Ine, benefactor of Glastonbury Abbey, exterminated the total population of the Isle of Wight with the full backing of St Wilfrid, in that those put to the sword were Jutish pagans and were to be replaced by Christian Saxons. What happened at Glastonbury is not recorded although there is evidence that some people with knowledge of the site survived to transmit it to the Saxon conqueror.

In 704 (or, according to some sources, 708), the Saxon King Ine of Wessex founded a new church, demolishing some stone ruins, possibly the Romano-British church of Faganus and Deruvianus, and erecting a totally new building dedicated to St Peter and St Paul. It was during this period that the establishment was reorganized on Roman monastic lines, the remnants of the British Celtic church having died out since the rigged Synod of Whitby in 664. At this time the *Vetusta Ecclesia* was still standing, as it is recorded that King Ine signed a charter for it in 725. In 794 Offa, king of Mercia, whose name is associated with several major geomantic works (Offa's Dyke, etc.,) donated ten hides of land to Glastonbury Abbey.

In 878 the monastery was ravaged by the Danes but the *Vetusta Ecclesia* was not burnt, almost certainly because of its special sanctity and aura of magical power.

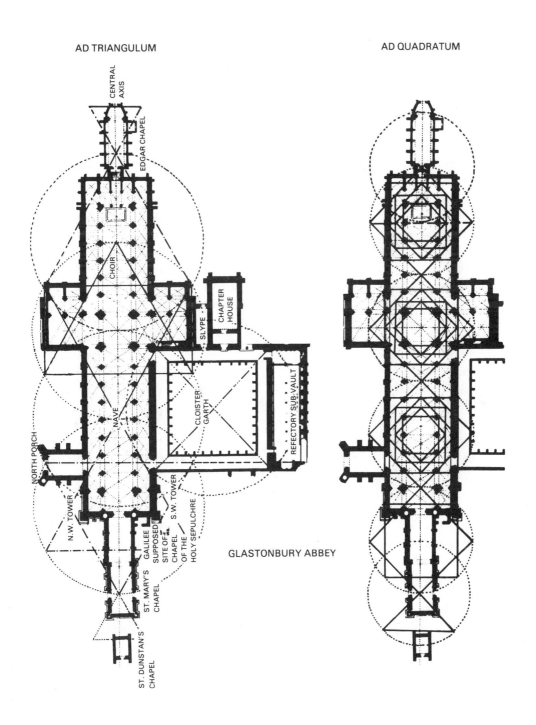

AD TRIANGULUM

AD QUADRATUM

CENTRAL AXIS

EDGAR CHAPEL

CHOIR

CHAPTER HOUSE

SLYPE

NAVE

CLOISTER GARTH

REFECTORY SUB-VAULT

NORTH PORCH

N.W. TOWER

GALILEE

SUPPOSED SITE OF

S.W. TOWER

CHAPEL OF THE HOLY SEPULCHRE

ST. DUNSTAN'S CHAPEL

ST. MARY'S CHAPEL

GLASTONBURY ABBEY

Both masonic systems of sacred geometry are combined at Glastonbury Abbey — Ad Quadratum and Ad Triangulum, fitting for a major Omphalos.

In 943, St Dunstan placed the monastery under the rule of the Benedictines, linking all the old church buildings into a large one in emulation of Continental practice. The big Saxon church extended from what was then St Mary's Chapel (the *Vetusta Ecclesia*) to a point in line with the outer east wall of the north porch of the later church. It had a divergent axis, the westerly in line with the *Vetusta Ecclesia* and the easterly on the axial line of the later abbey. This axis is the ley alignment from St Benedict's (St Benignus' in reality) through the abbey to Dod Lane and on to Stonehenge. Lack of accurate plans hinder geomantic calculations, but, according to V. M. Dallas's plan, the main orientation of the Abbey is about 3½° to the north of east. From the central Omphalos, Stonehenge is 3° 38', so it is probable that the orientation was intended to be 3° 38'. In width the eastern end of the Saxon church was in line with the centre line of the walls of the later church. The monk's graveyard was raised in level by St Dunstan, who had masses of earth imported from the surrounding areas. A memorial cross of this period was found by Bligh Bond although it is not in the Abbey museum. It was dug up at the extreme south-west corner of the nave just outside the foundations of the great tower.

It is possible that the central Omphalos* of Glastonbury, utilized by the Normans for the crossing of the great church, was marked by a stone cross in Saxon times, possibly by a megalith or egg-stone in pagan times. This place may have been considered too holy to be covered by a building, perhaps earlier revered as a powerful pagan cult centre. In the 1912 excavations an egg-stone *was* discovered. Roughly egg-shaped, the huge boulder measured 3 ft × 2 ft × 1 ft 4 in. One side of the egg-stone was artificially flattened and bore a cavity, perhaps a socket for a cross-shaft. In Bligh Bond's writings he mentions an unnamed friend who remarked '...that such a cult-stone must necessarily have existed at any place bearing the name of "Avalon"'. The stone was carved with small circular holes, parallel grooves, convergent grooves like star points, grooves with X-shaped intersections, chisel marks and 'other incised marks of peculiar shape'. Being found in the bank by the east alley of the cloister it was not far from the Omphalos, and it had obviously been shifted about. Possibly this stone originally marked the actual Omphalos, and subsequently, on Christianization, had a cross erected in a socket prepared for the purpose. Part of a cross which may have fitted into the Omphalos stone was found in the rubble core of the Norman walls of the nave. It bears fragments of an interlace pattern with the head of a Wyrm or dragon!

Several other cross fragments have turned up, one of them in the wall of a house in High Street. At present some of them are languishing in a sparsely labelled glass case in the Abbey museum, and the only information available on them is that which can be gained from looking at them.

After the Norman Conquest, most major existing churches and monasteries were demolished and replaced with much larger and more elaborate buildings, erected by Continental masons. These buildings were constructed according to the Romanesque system of sacred geometry, Ad Quadratum. However, at Glastonbury, a supremely

*'Omphalos' means cosmologically perfect ideal; a magical placing in space and time on a geomantically charged site. The Omphalos represented harmonious selection of position, conducive to spiritual power reflected through man, planet and cosmos. It was always marked by a 'gnomon', usually a round stone or upright pillar. (*Ed.*)

Geometry of Glastonbury Abbey.

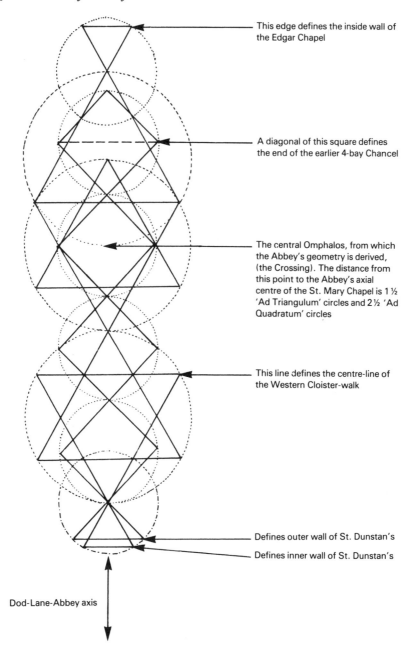

This edge defines the inside wall of the Edgar Chapel

A diagonal of this square defines the end of the earlier 4-bay Chancel

The central Omphalos, from which the Abbey's geometry is derived, (the Crossing). The distance from this point to the Abbey's axial centre of the St. Mary Chapel is 1 ½ 'Ad Triangulum' circles and 2 ½ 'Ad Quadratum' circles

This line defines the centre-line of the Western Cloister-walk

Defines outer wall of St. Dunstan's
Defines inner wall of St. Dunstan's

Dod-Lane-Abbey axis

important site, the geometry shows a more complex system, related to the elaborate landscape geometry of the surrounding areas.

The new abbey, built under the rule of Abbot Turstin about 1082, was demolished in 1110 so that a more imposing edifice might be erected. The internal geometry of the later buildings still reflects this structure, as exemplified by the fact that the line where the foundations of the Norman west wall were excavated is defined by the square centred on the Galilee Chapel, five radii from the Omphalos at the crossing.

In 1184 a major fire destroyed the *Vetusta Ecclesia* and the rest of the building. Reconstruction ensued and the edifice which endured until the Dissolution was finally erected. From the work of antiquaries and archaeologists there has been pieced together the information we have today, including accurate reconstructions of the ground plan from which the metrology and sacred geometry have now been recovered.

Several interesting features emerge, as must be expected for a major Omphalos. The Abbey is extremely noteworthy in that its ground-plan combines *both* the Masonic systems of sacred geometry – Ad Triangulum and Ad Quadratum – into the one pattern, giving effectively a twelve-fold geometry symbolically associated with the zodiac, both celestial and terrestrial.* Numerous important parts, such as the position of all the nave and chancel pillars, are defined by the octagrams generated by the system Ad Quadratum. The outer width of the nave and chancel walls, features of the erstwhile vaulting, the limit of the steps of the Edgar Chapel, the transept pillars' position, the central point of the Galilee Chapel, the outer wall of St Dunstan's Chapel, the original four-bay chancel (not taken into account by previous analysers of the ground-plan), and even the size of the buttressing on the wall of the cloister next to the church, are all defined by Ad Quadratum, based upon the central Omphalos sited beneath the crossing. From this central crossing is also developed the system Ad Triangulum, which defined the north and south transept walls, the position of the north porch, the doorways of St Mary's Chapel, the external corners of the crossing, and, by projection to the points where the lines cross circles of Ad Quadratum radius (see diagram), the internal wall of the apse of the Edgar Chapel and the internal wall of St Dunstan's Chapel. The geometry which defines the positions of several important features around the town of Glastonbury is derived from the Abbey's geometry.

It is interesting to note that all work done to date has used the unmodified plan prepared by Bligh Bond in 1912. This showed a western aisle to the north transept which Bond believed to have formerly existed at that site contrary to normal Benedictine practice. Subsequent work by 1919 disproved this theory, and Bond published at length the steps which led to the disproof. However, guides on sale at the Abbey today still show the aisle which was disproved by 1919! The plan drawn by V. M. Dallas in the 1920s is accurate as far as this feature is concerned, but sadly ignores the famous apse of the Edgar Chapel.

The dimensions of the Abbey, as in all such buildings except King's College Chapel, Cambridge (where they were laid down in writing by the founder†), have been subject to controversy. Those who study such matters will know the exasperation of finding three 'authorities' quoting different dimensions for the same building. The St Mary Chapel is subject to so much dimensional conclusion, its dimensions even having been tampered with by some authors so that their pet geometrical theories will fit, that its geometry must be passed over until a proper, unbiased survey can be published. The

---

*The fact that solar and lunar figures are integrally incorporated into the building's numerological structure under-lines this sacred geometry, giving a continuous zodiacal tradition to the Abbey's mystical patterns. (*Ed.*)

†This founder was the celebrated mystical scholar, King Henry VI. (*Ed.*)

plans recovered by F. Bligh Bond showed that a 74-foot constructional grid was used to lay out the edifice. Based on the crossing, it accounted for the positioning of several important features of the Abbey, being comparable with the 50-Norman-foot grid at Archbishop Thomas's church at York. However, Glastonbury Abbey was laid out more than a century before the English foot was legally defined on the orders of King Edward I (1305). Before 1305 this measurement existed as an esoteric constant, but several different 'feet' were in use as well, namely the Welsh foot, Roman foot, Norman foot (of York), French foot and Saxon foot. The 74-foot module of F. Bligh Bond corresponds to the following:

90	Welsh feet	75.7	Norman feet
76.3	Roman feet	69.4	French feet (*pieds du Roi*)
		67.3	Saxon feet

Ninety Welsh feet give the dimensions to Bond's overall grid as 810 × 360 WF; 9 × 4 squares of 90 WF = 1080 Welsh inches; 810 is 10 WF over a furlong in length, the Welsh foot being a logical division of land measure equal to one-twentieth of a rod, giving 6400 WF in a statute mile or 8000 WF in an old (decimal) mile of ten furlongs.

The 1080 Welsh inches in 90 WF correspond to 1080, the mystic number symbolic of the terrestrial and lunar powers of water as opposed to fire, the moon as opposed to the sun, the people as opposed to the king.* The original part of the Abbey, St Mary's Chapel, is lunar, the Virgin Mary being associated with the moon and opposed to the easterly solar hill Glastonbury Tor, which became St Michael's sanctuary. The Tor was a holy place where the seasonal beacon fires were lit. This is comparable with the Holy Hill/Solar Site orientations observed by Heinsch, although the angle of deviation is slightly greater than the 6 degrees observed by Heinsch. The number 1080 represents the Holy Spirit, the fountain of Wisdom in Greek gematria; it is fitting for the centre of terrestrial geometry from which the geomantic Knowledge emanated.

The vexed case of dimensions is somewhat resolved by recourse to ancient manuscripts. The diary of Jon Cannon, schoolmaster of Meare (born 1684), stated that the Abbey ruins, including the chapels of St Joseph and St Dunstan, were at one time 638 feet in length. Translated into Welsh feet, this is 775, virtually double the 386 figure found by Kenneth Knight. F. Bligh Bond gives the internal dimensions as 580 feet (704.3 Welsh feet), and Janette Jackson gives 581 feet (705.53 WF), so it is reasonable to suppose that the length was 705 WF. The actual integral fabric of the Abbey (i.e. nave and choir only) is 80 × 460 WF, giving a width to length ratio of 1 : 5 1/9.

Thus it appears that a module of five WF was used, one-eighteenth of the major grid, in turn one-ninth of the overall rectangle, giving the ratio of module to overall rectangle 1 : 162. Modular construction is not unusual in medieval architecture; a five-Roman-foot module was used at Cluny; a four-English-foot module at King's College Chapel and a twenty-five-Norman-foot module at York. The external dimension of Glastonbury Abbey

---

*John Michell has also proved the existant efficacy of the number 666 in the Abbey's dimensional proportions, thereby giving it the solar accolade as well. By combining the magic numbers, 1080 and 666, the ultimate gematric number 1746 is obtained. This is the supreme number of alchemical fusion, the merging of dynamic opposites, and the fact that Glastonbury Abbey yields mathematical ratios incorporating all these mystical dimensions seals its reputation as the greatest Christian structure in Britain. (*Ed.*)

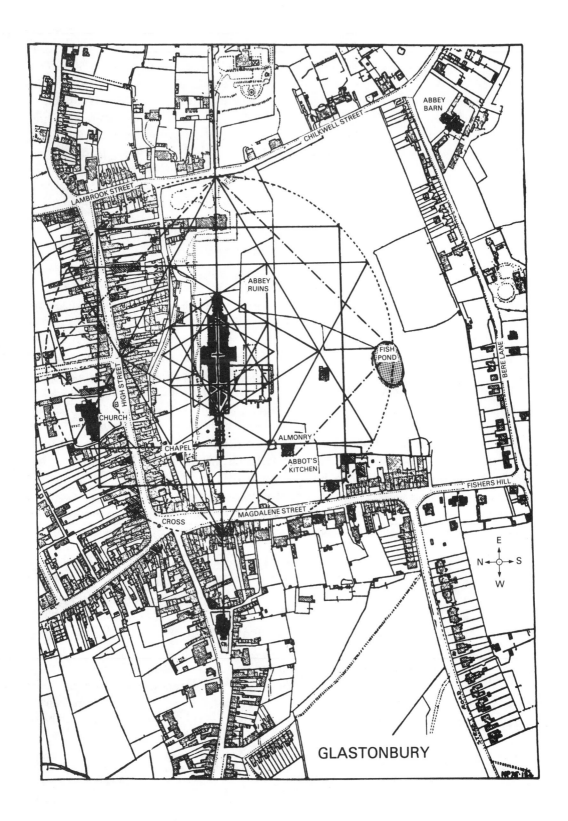

GLASTONBURY

without the St Dunstan Chapel has been given as 594 English feet. This is equivalent to 144 five-WF modules (12 × 12).

The Abbey has been so mutilated since 1539 that many of its subtler constructions will never be recovered. The internal features of the Abbey church included rises in ground level, still traceable by rises in the level of the lawns, originally accommodated by steps. Steps and a screen existed at the eastern end of the nave and further steps raised the altar area, a progressive heightening of the floor in the manner formerly visible at King's College Chapel in Cambridge. This of course was before the purposeless vandalization of the chapel in the last decade in the name of aesthetics. The height of the steps at Glastonbury and their number is not recorded. Their function was doubtless symbolic and representative of telluric energy, as at King's College Chapel, there being no 'orgone'–accumulating crypt at the end of the building.

Combining the systems of Ad Triangulum and Ad Quadratum, the Abbey is also the generative point for an outer sacred geometry based upon a circle whose radius is the distance from the central Omphalos to the site of the erstwhile market cross. The cross is now marked by an innacurate nineteenth-century replica. This distance is also the point at which the central axis of the Abbey cuts the edge of Chilkwell Street, opposite Dod Lane. From this point an equilateral triangle can be drawn, one side of which cuts through the south-east corner and the main fabric of the church of St John the Baptist. The next side of this triangle cuts straight through the old almonry and defines the eastern edge of the wall of the abbot's kitchen. The other triangle, forming the magic Star of David (Seal of Solomon) pattern, also cuts through the old almonry and the northeast corner of the Chapel of St Patrick. The point where the two triangles intersect in line with the transept crossing defines the building line of the High Street. The intersection of the same two triangles on Silver Street defines the building line at that point too. The corner of two inner triangles is also at this point, and the intersection on Silver Street defines the southern side of that street. Also projectable inside the circle are the squares of Ad Quadratum. The square parallel with the Abbey axis defines the edge of St John's church, and the southern edge of the High Street is defined where the square's corner touches it. The other square of the pair marks the fish pond, the transept of St John's church and the southwest corner of the abbot's kitchen. Doubtless the geometry marks other significant points but this has not yet been investigated. Work is now in progress to evaluate the relationship of this geometry to the overall geomantic pattern of the area, incorporating the Zodiac and other sites of proven prehistoric provenance.

Recommended Books

Behrend, Michael. *Landscape Geometry of Southern Britain*. Zodiac House/Fenris Wolf, 1975.
Heinsch, J. *Principles of Prehistoric Sacred Geography*. Zodiac House, 1975.
Maltwood, K. E. *A Guide to Glastonbury's Temple of the Stars* James Clarke, 1964.
Michell, John. *City of Revelation*. Garnstone Press, 1972.
Pennick, Nigel. *European Metrology*. Fenris Wolf, 1975.
    The Mysteries of King's College Chapel. Cokaygne, 1973.
Russell, Geoffrey. 'The Secret of the Grail' in *Glastonbury: A Study in Patterns*. RILKO, 1969.

CHAPTER SEVEN

Gematria in the Hebrew Cabbala:

Its possible Interpretation through the Ley Line System with the Direction of Orientation between Wells Cathedral and Glastonbury Abbey as an example

– KENNETH KNIGHT

If there is any substance of truth in the theory here suggested of the cabbalistic significance of the cathedral of Wells and the abbey at Glastonbury, and of the general direction of the ley lines between these two sacred sites, then it is hoped that it may be of some use to those interested in the magical viability of the Hebrew Cabbala. More specifically the method of *interpretation through the passage of the sun* in its annual course through the twelve signs of the zodiac. So much has been written about the direction of ley lines, multitudinous as they are, that it is necessary to come to some point and commence to interpret such lines.* The horizon differs from place to place as far as distance is concerned due to the general topographical surroundings in any given area, but, like the mythical Round Table, it is only mystically present to those 'who have eyes to see'. The fact that at South Cadbury (Camelot) the legend persists that whoever sets out to search for King Arthur's Treasure will sink, perfectly illustrates this point. A rather fruitless occupation one would think, under the circumstances; the treasure must surely be referring to the more esoteric, magical quality of King Arthur's Round Table. Bearing these points in mind with regard to the Somerset Zodiac, the 'Round Table of the Stars', it will be easier to interpret the following argument in a more scientific and astronomical manner.

It is generally conceded that there were two major astronomical seasons during the course of a year when stone circles, sacred buildings, etc., were laid out and orientated. These were the position of the sun in relation to the earth at the equinoxes and solstices, and the rising and setting of the mythically potent Pleiades stars in the constellation of the bull (Taurus).

As far as the siting of Wells Cathedral is concerned, both the earlier Saxon edifice and the present transitional, Norman–early English building were orientated to particular

*Leys are made up of perfectly aligned, often astronomically oriented arrangements of ancient sites, incorporating such important landmarks as megalithic stones, prehistoric camps, beacon hills, barrows, processional tracks, pre-Reformation churches and chapels and Gothic cathedrals and abbeys. Pioneer work has been executed on leys by numerous antiquarians, foremost among whom were Alfred Watkins of Hereford and Dr Josef Heinsch, the German geomancer. (*Ed.*)

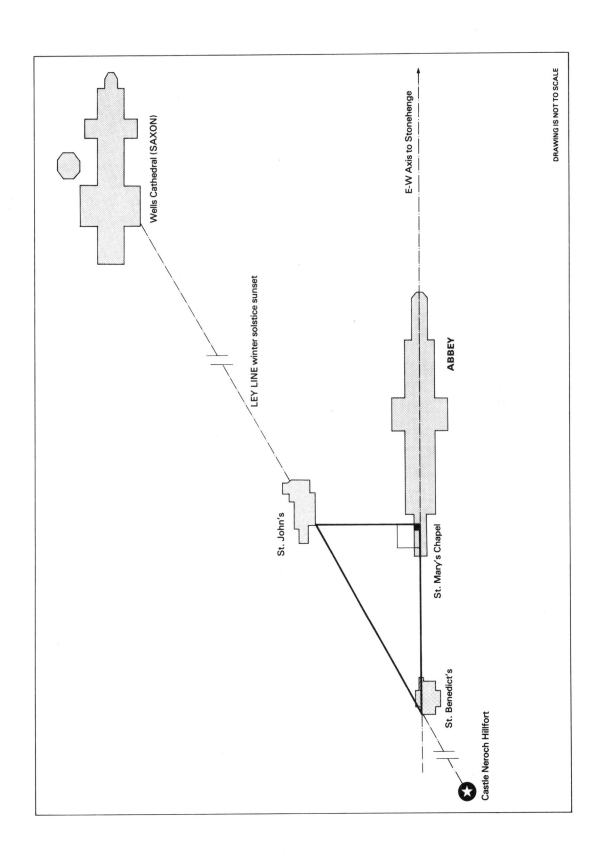

Castle Neroch Hillfort

St. Benedict's

St. Mary's Chapel

St. John's

ABBEY

E-W Axis to Stonehenge

LEY LINE winter solstice sunset

Wells Cathedral (SAXON)

DRAWING IS NOT TO SCALE

points on the horizon. The central axis of each building was designed pointing to the heliacal rising of a particularly bright star almost coincidentally with the sunrise/sunset on a particular day or season. Although it is impossible to prove with any absolute certainty, there is reason to suppose that the Saxon cathedral, lying on a central axis of 14° N of E, would point to the horizon on which would occur, in their due seasons, the sunrise and sunset of the summer and winter solstices. The present building, erected further north, lies on a central axis of only 3° N of E, and faces the general direction of the rising and setting of the Pleiades during the months of May and November. Many argue that some of the earlier prehistoric stone circles were orientated towards this star-group. This is certainly true, and any distortion is due to the precession of the equinoxes and the related motion of the equinoctial and solstitial colures, plus the latitude and longitude of such sites in relation to declination and the Arc of Ascendancy. This distortion would appear to resolve the difficulty with the older orientation. It is of some significance that the present street plan of Wells city was orientated to coincide with the direction that the Saxon cathedral faced, with its west front directly on the present market place. Archaeologists have come across difficulties in discovering the earlier foundations due to the present buildings and the main body of the church lying across the old cloister garth, now a cemetery. A ley line from the assumed west front lying to face the main High Street, follows to a natural point of the sunset at the winter solstice, via the tower of St John's church at Glastonbury and, in a direct north/south line with the present Chapel of St Mary at the Abbey, forms a triangle with the church of St Benedict, due west of the chapel.

Unlike Wells Cathedral, the abbey at Glastonbury has maintained the same line of orientation as well as the system of building from east to west. However, at Glastonbury the process was in reverse, building commencing from west to east.* Has this any direct occult significance? At the time when Wells was rebuilt, between 1180 and 1190 in its earliest stages, the chapel at Glastonbury was also rebuilt. There was much rebuilding activity at this time in the country as a whole, and the central line of orientation varies in different cathedrals, etc. The older Saxon-Norman buildings appear to have maintained a specific measure, namely a ratio of 2:5 :: 1 as observed in the Vesica Piscis, with the linear marked at 385 ft × 153 ft. These measures have within them the kernel of measurements relative to the actual construction of our solar system, based in their elementary form on the unfolded solid cube with three horizontal bars and four vertical bars cubed to the numbers of 27 and 64. These specific cross-measurements are prominent in the actual canonical proportions as a cosmic whole. By ratio, such a cross when placed within the square, circle, and rectangle, produces all relative measures architecturally and astronomically; they not only represent the distances of the planets as viewed from the earth (the Ptolemaic system), but also various time-cycles of these planets in their passages round the sun (the Copernican system). We find these basic measures of 385 and 153 present in the 'Great Churches' of Wells and Glastonbury, as well as in many other buildings of similar dimensions. Guildford cathedral is the latest example where

---

*This refers to the legendary erection of the famous wattle church by Joseph of Arimathea early in the first century. All subsequent building radiated eastwards along a ley-line axis that connects the site of Glastonbury Abbey with Stonehenge. (*Ed.*)

the same measurements are carefully preserved. Liverpool cathedral likewise strictly observes this ruling. We have in our midst, then, a universal solar temple in heavily Christianized form, adapted into the proportions of key ecclesiastical buildings. The proportions are of course found in the more elaborate prehistoric temples such as Avebury, Stonehenge, and Callanish.

Is there any significance in the period when so much rebuilding was undertaken? Recognizing the subtle intention of myths and legends, the myth associated with Bishop Jocelyn de Bohun, who commenced and supervised the rebuilding of the present Wells cathedral about 1180, is of interest. He is reputed to have fought a human-headed dragon outside the cathedral on the site which is now the Bishop's Park to the south, releasing thirty children from its belly. The occasion was re-enacted not so many years ago in a local pageant depicting important historical events associated with the whole county of Somerset. Could the legend be a subtle reference to a necessary change of calendar due to the precession of the equinoxes, and to the possible re-selection of a fixed star relative to the saint to whom the cathedral is dedicated? This martyr is St Andrew, whose feast day is 30 November, on which day incidentally, the constellation of Orion (metaphorized in the Christian calendar on that date) and the Pleiades set at the time the sun rises. When Orion sets in the west it is considered palendromic, in contrast with its upright position when rising in the east. St Andrew, like St Peter, is said to have been crucified upside down.* He also has strong connections with dragons.

According to the medieval cabbalists, the year 1260 was to witness a 'new influx of the Holy Spirit'. Whatever meaning this has, if nothing else events of the time suggest a change not only architecturally, but also in the philosophical arguments of the period. It was then that the mystic Cabbala became externalized in architectural decoration and style. Astronomically considered, the number 1260 is the conjunction of a solar/lunar cycle commencing at a particular point on the ecliptic belt in the sign of Taurus the bull. The *mean* measurement of both Wells Cathedral and Glastonbury Abbey in the 'great church' is 401 feet, whilst the internal length is 386 feet. The number 401 multiplied by 3·1415 is 1260. At Wells, if the Cathedral Green is included in its length, and a circle is drawn in theory to include the circle enclosing the cathedral proper, the number is 2520. This is a number of great importance in biblical lunar cycles associated with certain apocalyptic prophecies. The thirteenth century itself is a period considered important by students of biblical prophecies. It was recognized as 'the Time of the Gentiles', and there was much speculation as to the outcome of its cabbalistic interpretation being fulfilled by the end of the First World War. Astrologers following the cabbalistic system have much to say on this numerically symbolic aspect of interpretation. The year 1260 also saw the Arthurian legends attain the apex of their development, and local history records many bitter disputes between Wells Cathedral and Glastonbury Abbey about the seniority and importance of the two sacred buildings. Glastonbury Abbey won the day because

*Astronomical application of saints' feast days is common throughout Christian hagiography. For instance, St Christopher, a third-century saint, is always associated with roads (i.e. alignments) and travelling. Most legends refer to him as a pagan giant who was 'converted'. His feast day became registered as 25 July and it is remarkable that on this day the star Orion (always associated with a giant) directly crosses the summer solstice line. There are countless other examples. (*Ed.*)

ORION
(the Glorious One)

Symbolic representation of myth in the star patterns. The giant Orion is associated at Glastonbury with the Gemini effigy in the Zodiac Temple of the Stars. Note the Hebrew names of certain of the key stars. Orion in myth was blinded, and followed the quest of the sun, travelling east until his sight was restored by its powers. He then pursued the Pleiades (in Taurus) and was stung to death by Scorpio. He was in fact another 'divine sacrifice' fulfilling the esoteric purpose of zodiacal mythology.

Joseph of Arimathea* founded the first wattle church there, at the site of the present Lady Chapel. This chapel's measurements are thirty-seven feet by sixty-four feet externally, the figures corresponding to the two disputed dates as to when Joseph and his disciples actually arrived on the Isle of Avalon. Avalon, the Isle of the Blessed, the Isle

---

*In many medieval genealogies King Arthur was traced in direct line of descent from Joseph of Arimathea through his son. (*Ed.*)

of the Dead, was the earlier Celtic entrance to the underworld, in other words, to the Chamber of Initiation, and Glastonbury had long enjoyed the reputation of being the great seat of sanctity and learning. Its most famous abbot, Dunstan, was a known cabbalist and the legends associated with this saint are of interest, for he confounded the Devil on more than one occasion. In fact Dunstan first joined the church (about 945) after being accused of practising the Black Arts!

The diagonal cross of St Andrew, when considered in its cabbalistic and astronomical significance, is said to represent a terminal point, or a junction where two lines meet. To the ley hunter this is of particular interest, for it may well be that it provides a definite link-up with other similar lines of orientation (ley power centres, etc.). In medieval zodiacs, St Peter and St Andrew, being brothers according to the gospel records, marked the 'crossing of the waters' from the winter to the summer half of the year at the vernal equinox. At this point, the Pleiades rises heliacally with the sun, whilst Antares in Scorpio sets. These are some of the vital aspects of ancient, particularly Hebrew, zodiacal lore. St Peter and St Andrew were intimately associated with water, being fishermen.

At Wells, the seven springs rising in the garden of the Bishop's Palace seem to have some bearing cabbalistically. In Hebrew cosmology, 'the Well of Seven' (from which the city of Wells derived its name) is *Bathsheba,* which, in the gematria* of numbers has a value of 775, and divided by two is 387.5 feet, or just a fractional number (cabbalistically considered) over the 385–6 measurement. The significance of 2520 becomes more apparent. It was a unifying and interpretative figure, representing prophetic (and numerical) fulfilment.

If the ground plan of Wells Cathedral is placed in theory within the confines of a Vesica Piscis, then the central axis measures 432, where the four points of the building touch the Vesica Piscis sides. Astronomically considered and measured, this number multiplied by 1000 represents the radius of the sun. The same idea prevails at Glastonbury, for the overall length of the Abbey contained in a Vesica Piscis is 666 feet, a number directly related to the Magical Square of the Sun. As well as coinciding with 660, this cosmic length, in scaled-down proportional ratio, is often that of prehistoric barrows at converging lanes where ley lines meet. Examples of this are to be found at various points in Somerset at least. Castle Neroch near Bridgwater is one site which comes instantly to mind, for it is on a line which points to the sunrise and sunset of the solstices, and incidentally, is in direct alignment with certain topographical points that mark the ley line from Wells and Glastonbury.†

It may not be generally known, but all modern planispheres show the main star-groups up to the fourth magnitude, written in their original Hebrew. The more prominent individual stars also have the Hebrew name. In many cases however (the zodiac, for instance), the Latinized names have been preserved, whilst a few are still in Greek, the direct mystical descendant of Hebrew. When the Hebrew is interpreted into English it will

---

*Gematria is the cabbalistic science of substituting numbers for letters of the alphabet. It was a favourite method used by medieval cabbalists to derive mystical insights from the sacred writings. The most favoured language for gematria was Hebrew, but it is applicable in any language. (*Ed.*)

†This typical prehistoric earthwork is traditionally said to be hollow (the standard tale) and full of treasure. When dug in the eighteenth century, legend recounts that no physical treasure was found and that all the spade-wielding vandals died in various horrible ways! Again, the standard story. (*Ed.*)

be found that by diligent correlation of mythology and legend, the story of King Arthur and his Knights in their Quest for the Holy Grail emerges. This has been confirmed by the author's personal analysis through gematria, which will hopefully be published at a later date. It may be that the year 1260 not only marked the perigree of the winter solstice at that time, but also indicated a change of calendar and a new direction in mythological exposition. Others more conversant with this particular aspect will be able to elaborate upon, and if necessary correct, many of the assumptions presented in this article. The subject is so vast, it is obvious that some observations must have been overlooked, but one thing appears to be certain: ley lines play an important part in the geomantic interpretation of the heavens as reflected in topographical and ecclesiastical patterns across the sacred earth.

Recommended Books

Berriman, A. *Historical Metrology*. Dent, 1953.

Heinsch, J. *Principles of Prehistoric Sacred Geography*. Zodiac House, 1975.

Michell, John. *City of Revelation*. Garnstone Press, 1972.

Pennick, Nigel. *Geomancy*. Cokaygne, 1973.

Thom, A. *Megalithic Lunar Observatories*. Oxford University Press, 1971.

Torrens, R. G. *The Golden Dawn*. Neville Spearman, 1969.

CHAPTER EIGHT

Hidden Treasures of Glastonbury

DONALD L. CYR

Most Americans have probably never heard of Glastonbury, although a few of us have heard of the Arthurian legends that are somehow related to the Isle of Avalon. Mostly we consider that the Knights of the Round Table were story-book heroes, charging around on horseback, generally in pursuit of dragons to slay or damsels in distress to rescue. In fact, of all my American acquaintances only two were familiar with the tradition that Joseph of Arimathea may have come to Glastonbury, and only one of these knew anything at all about the Zodiac that is alleged to be stewn about the landscape surrounding Glastonbury Tor. It seems highly unlikely then, that any American could have sufficient understanding to make a serious contribution towards solving Glastonbury's problems.

Yet, in spite of the hazards, the writer of this article will attempt to outline two or three new approaches that might be of interest to those who live much nearer to the site. Admittedly, limited visits to Glastonbury would hardly seem to qualify one to have an opinion, let alone to be the proponent of any new hypotheses. Nevertheless, the mystery of Glastonbury does strike a common chord in the mystical heritage that we all share, whether or not we reside in Britain at the moment.

The three questions to be considered are these: 'How could the Zodiac have been constructed by people who apparently could not have seen it in its entirety?' Next we would ask, 'What important region near Glastonbury has been seemingly overlooked by other investigators?' And finally, 'Where is the "treasure" concealed?' Now if any one of these approaches turns out to be worthwhile the effort of renewed investigation would be valuable. And if we could answer all three questions, despite a bit of tortuous logic, we would consider that we had indeed made a serious contribution to the subject.

Actually, we have arrived at tentative conclusions and await the necessary research to achieve confirmation. To make the journey easy for the reader we will gladly state the answers at the outset:

1. The people who designed the Zodiac did see it in its entirety using a very special kind of mirror that was then available.

2. The region that needs further inspection is located on Pennard Hill due east of Glastonbury Tor.

3. Some of the 'treasure' is cleverly hidden in the fish pond.

Let us now examine these three concepts in some detail.

THE FISH POND

Illogically, but for the sake of brevity, we will try starting with the last item first. Why look in the fish pond? And why look for treasure? There are a lot of reasons not to look. If the treasure turns out to be gold it belongs to the Crown; if it was a base metal it has probably dissolved over the hundreds of years of the fish pond's existence. Besides, the treasure might really not pay the cost of digging for it.

My own interest in the Glastonbury Abbey fish pond was whetted by John Michell's drawing of the Vesica Piscis pattern on a map of the Abbey grounds. This geomantic pattern intersects the market cross in central Glastonbury and also the fish pond. Assuming that the Vesica Piscis pattern does exist as Michell claims, such an important centre as the market cross might understandably be denoted thereby. But why the fish pond? Of course, the word fish itself is included in the name Vesica Piscis, and is also related to Christianity through an acronym that denotes the word 'fish' in Greek, namely:

Hundreds of tourists have taken pictures of the market cross and of the Abbey ruins, but few seem interested in photos of the fish pond. Hence, one objective of my first visit to Glastonbury was to remedy this omission, and I really didn't know what to expect.

A path leading from the Abbey cloister runs through a grove of young trees to the fish pond. The pond itself is lined with a wall of stones to form a reservoir. Water apparently flows in from a point located near Chalice Well, where tunnels drain a part of Chalice Hill next to Glastonbury Tor. In 1974 the pond was virtually full and the lily pads were huge and flourishing; in 1975, a dryer year, the water level had fallen and green algae was making its appearance. Young boys, both years, were attracted to the pond and patiently fished there.

One supposes that at one time the pond actually held fish that were of some benefit to the Brothers of the Abbey, and one might imagine that even in those days, the lads of the village were wont to vault the fence and poach a few fish from the kindly Brothers. We can even imagine that one of these lads grew up to become a Brother in the Order, and continued to work at length in the Abbey, perhaps rising to some position of semi-authority. At any rate, the state of ruin of the Abbey today demonstrates that the past included dangerous as well as peaceful times. It takes little insight to imagine that at least one of the Brothers would have been fearful of impending events.

We can see this worried monk in our mind's eye moving swiftly down the path towards the fish pond, laden with a sack of church treasures which he had responsibly decided to hide during the danger period. We can also imagine that the political events that made this hurried action necessary might have made it impossible for this frightened Brother ever to return for the treasure. Perhaps, imaginatively, it is still possible to hear the footsteps of that frightened Brother echoing down these hundreds of years. But, since, realistically, few would believe in hearing so acute, let us instead describe the probable location of the treasure, for hypothetically it must still be in the fish pond.

Normally one tends to dig for treasure in logical places; for instance, so many paces from a giant oak tree, or at a triangle formed by three inscribed stones. Certainly pirate treasure was generally buried beneath a windswept tree on a high hill, where the moon at night silhouetted an overhanging limb which supported a block and tackle. But in the scenario that we have described, we are dealing not with a pirate . . . but with a frightened monk . . . one whose fear has temporarily suppressed the peaceful philosophy that has been the primary indoctrination of his religion. He would logically conclude that some ultimate good comes from protecting physical treasures – chalices, golden candlesticks, reliquaries, perhaps.

He would also have the philosophical stamina to conceal his knowledge of the whereabouts of the treasure. All this would follow quite naturally if the political winds were violent enough. And certainly the present condition of the Abbey attests to its having suffered severe violence.*

So the Brother might have taken his sack of treasure one dark night and tossed it into the fish pond, fully intending to make recovery when peaceful days returned. An ordinary brown gunny sack would soon have melded into the muds of the pond. Such a ploy of getting rid of certain church treasure just might have been a success, particularly if the Brother thought out his plot alone. Certainly his superiors would have been in no position to reprimand him for his action. Their lives were in jeopardy as well. Thus, it takes no great amount of imagination to think that treasure may still exist in the fish pond at Glastonbury Abbey. If so, why has no one thought of finding it? We can think of several reasons.

One *digs* for treasure . . . Not until the days of archaeological investigation at the sacred pool of Chichen-Itza did it become popular to 'pump' out the mud of pools located near important religious sanctuaries. Besides, archaeologists did not have to seek permission from Mayan priests to explore the pool at Chichen-Itza. One must necessarily seek permission from the Bishop of Wells to make exploratory digs at Glastonbury Abbey. And it's understandable that Bishops are not notably enthusiastic about archaeological digs on their property. Finally, any gold that might be recovered is automatically the Queen's treasure, so why go to the trouble of digging it out at all? Why indeed, when it is perfectly safe where it is?

With probability curves and trajectory analysis, one can almost pinpoint the location of the treasure. It must be on the Abbey side of the fish pond, and its distance from the

*It is quite possible some special treasure was hidden in the fish pond when the Abbey was sacked by the diseased minions of Henry VIII in 1539. It is not inconceivable that the treasure was something of a mystical importance as the pond is a key site in the geomantic plan of the Glastonbury sacred geometry. (*Ed.*)

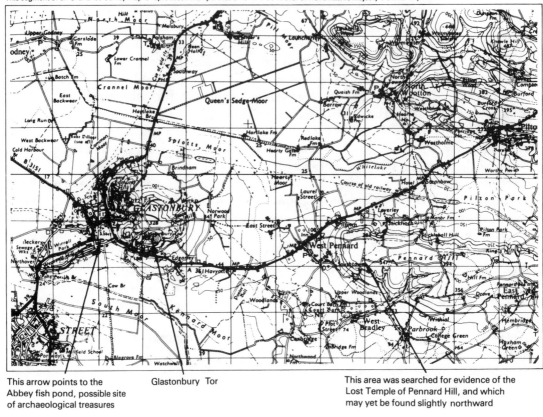

This arrow points to the
Abbey fish pond, possible site
of archaeological treasures

Glastonbury Tor

This area was searched for evidence of the
Lost Temple of Pennard Hill, and which
may yet be found slightly northward

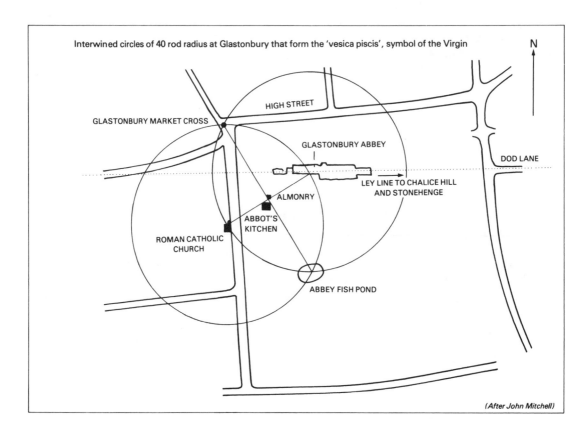

Interwined circles of 40 rod radius at Glastonbury that form the 'vesica piscis', symbol of the Virgin

N

HIGH STREET

GLASTONBURY MARKET CROSS

GLASTONBURY ABBEY

DOD LANE

LEY LINE TO CHALICE HILL
AND STONEHENGE

ALMONRY

ABBOT'S
KITCHEN

ROMAN CATHOLIC
CHURCH

ABBEY FISH POND

(After John Mitchell)

rock-wall shore must be exactly the distance that our good Brother would have been capable of flinging the sack.

Certainly, he would not have scattered the items about. Not if he intended to recover them later. So there it must be, about fifteen to eighteen feet from the edge of the pond, at a point where the path leads to the water's edge. Unbelievable? Of course! But one day, the treasure might be located at a depth consistent with the softness of the mud, overlain by the accumulation of debris of several hundred years. As I visualize this treasure, a triple candlestick of gold will be found pointing towards the Tor, simply because the weight of its base would have caused it to settle that way. Candle holders and other paraphernalia suitable to the period would have been gathered and placed in this perfect vault where it could exist to this day with reasonable equanimity.

An estimate of the amount of labour required to drain the pond and dredge out the mud is moderate given the use of modern techniques. One would hesitate to suggest that the pond simply be pumped out in the fashion of Chichen-Itza. The amount of information to be derived from an inspection of layers of mud, and from analysis of their content of pollen, including perhaps even a layer of charred ash from the great fire at the Abbey, is simply too attractive to let us settle for heavy-handed methods. Of course, the political ramifications are considerable. Permission of church authorities must be granted; the local authorities must be convinced that the stench of the extracted materials and muds from the pond are in their best interest (unless plastic bags full of the material could be transported elsewhere for study). Obviously an organization with personnel, equipment, and a well-thought-out plan would be necessary. Soon the expense would be well in excess of the economic value of any likely treasure.

Was it not Merlin who had a dream about dragons, one white, one red, fighting beneath a pool? Who knows, perhaps in some strange way the pool of Glastonbury will shed light on that esoteric tradition. One thing is certain: one day, when a Glastonbury lad tosses a float repeatedly into the fish pond and you hear the whirring of a recording tape in his nearby lunch basket, you may suspect that he is equipped with a miniaturized device for locating treasure. What could be more fitting than for a present-day son of Glastonbury to fish for treasure, when it was his grown-up counterpart, our hypothetical Brother, who placed it there for safe-keeping?

THE TEMPLE OF PENNARD HILL

Due east of Glastonbury Tor, appearing precisely level on the horizon, lies Pennard Hill. Similarly, a prehistoric sanctuary is located near the road towards Marlborough due east of Silbury Hill, that artificial mound near Avebury. If there is a parallel, should there not be a lost sanctuary on Pennard Hill itself? Why not look for it? In fact, that objective was one of the projects listed for the 1975 visit to Glastonbury. The writer, accompanied by archaeologist Connie Taylor of Washington state, made a cursory site-survey of Pennard Hill. Connie objected that fifteen minutes is not sufficient time to make a proper survey, and indeed she was probably right. At any rate, we drove up Pennard Hill coming from the east and along a series of fertile fields. The road that we traversed seemed to follow an east-west bearing line centred on the maze of Tor Hill and in fact may represent a ley line (as ancient survey lines are sometimes called). Abruptly, the road makes a left turn at a field gate and it was here that we stopped.

Parking the car, we climbed onto a great oak stump, almost on the centre-line of the road, beside the gate leading into a field. Trees along a fence hid the tower on Glastonbury Tor from sight, but by walking into an adjacent field we could spot its pointing finger of stone very clearly.

It was fun to imagine that this stump of a giant oak represented some sacred sapling with an ancestry going back to the time of a long-lost sanctuary on Pennard Hill.* Immediately ahead of the stump, towards the west, stood an abandoned flat-bed lorry; by climbing upon this, we got an inelegant but grand-stand view of the adjacent field. It was difficult to determine if we were quite on the crest of the hill, but we did note a shallow depression containing foliage and plants different from the other grasses in the field. Perhaps this was indeed the site we were looking for, but that would be difficult to say without a further careful look and some preliminary excavation. After all, our survey was limited to what we could photograph and we were not inclined to dig without permission of the farmer and also of the authorities. It will be remembered that the sanctuary eastward of Silbury Hill was originally a structure of wooden posts, so of course we imagined that any similar structure on Pennard Hill would not have a visible arrangement of stones. Nor did we find any stones, above ground that is. To look for post holes from some distant era is not that easy, particularly when we only had fifteen minutes at our disposal!

It is our impression that discovery of an archaeological site within a farmer's field is at best a mixed blessing. For one thing the legalities make it impossible for the farmer to plough through the site ever again, and he must restrict his field usage to simple grazing. So whether or not there is a lost sanctuary on Pennard Hill remains to be seen. If archaeological work is ever carried out the confirmation or denial of our hypothesis will prove to be most interesting and informative. It would help the Zodiac theory no end if such a sanctuary could be verified at such a spot.

GLASTONBURY'S REFLECTIVE CANOPY CLOUD-LAYER

In all the analyses of the mysteries of Glastonbury, as well as analyses of other megalithic sites, there is one contribution made by an obscure American over a hundred years ago that may be pertinent today. The suggestion, made by Isaac N. Vail as early as 1874, explains why megalithic sites appear to have been viewed from the skies by someone. In our own day it is popular to imagine that ancient astronauts could have seen in their entirety such designs as megalithic circles, mazes, or zodiacs and therefore helped in their construction. Vail's mirror-like 'canopy' formation makes it unnecessary to call upon ancient astronauts, for it turns out that even the most humble yeoman in the village could have seen such patterns from any nearby vantage point.

---

*It must be noted here that Pennard Hill forms part of the Sagittarius/Arthur effigy in the Glastonbury Zodiac, and this lends weight to the theory that an ancient shrine may have existed. The area was once famed for its proliferation of oak trees, sacred of course to the Druids. (*Ed.*)

Dragons, sky haloes, earth effigy serpent and cloud canopy all combine to illustrate the mysteries of the heavens and their interpretation through legendary geomancy. Macrocosm through microcosm, as above, so below!

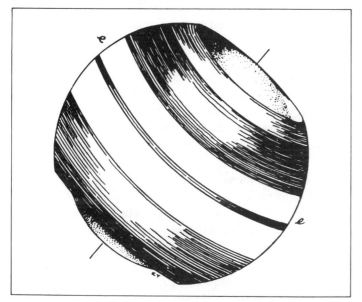

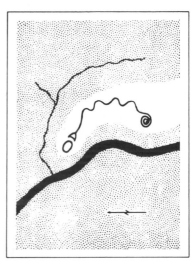

Serpent mound in Adams County, Ohio.

This drawing of the earth's transparent 'canopy' appeared in Vail's book, The Earth's Annular System, *in 1902.*

Han Dynasty dragon halo (100 BC).

One configuration of solar and lunar haloes varies with altitude. Thus, under a canopy of ice crystals, the ancient peoples saw these bodies going through a series of 'signs' or 'houses'.

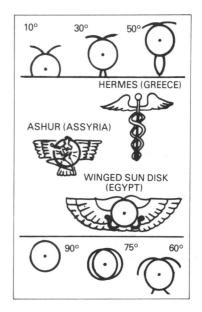

Later, some of these patterns were drawn against the stars as constellations or signs of the zodiac. Others acquired other meanings.

Note that the 75°-intertwined circles suggests the sacred symbol of the Virgin, Vesica Piscis.

Perhaps even the root-word *glas* in Glastonbury can itself be traced back to the days when a canopy-mirror existed over this spot. Of course, some semantic-sleuths point out rightly that *glas* also means 'blue' and might even be related to the woad plant (yielding blue dye) that once flourished in the Glastonbury swamps. In any event, if we can trace out the function of *glas* as related to a blue-tinted looking-glass or mirror, then we are aided by the thoughts of Isaac N. Vail. In his writings, Vail understood and described many of the functions of planetary canopies a hundred years before the swift-moving canopy was discovered on the planet Venus by ultraviolet photography (1974). Space vehicles promise to provide similar information for the planets Jupiter and Saturn, which Vail also believed to have swiftly moving canopy formations. When a space probe dips down below the cloud surface of one of these planets and takes an 'over-the-shoulder' look, the under-cloud surface will be seen to have a mirror-like appearance.

Vail understood that the appearance of the under-surface of a canopy is produced by the swift motion, causing the smoothness, together with the reflective characteristics of ice particles. In ancient literature he read about a 'molten looking glass' and he considered that the under-surface of the canopy would exhibit characteristics expressed by the word 'molten'. If the existence of such a canopy can be established for the prehistoric period, we may be well on our way to understanding the significance of giant effigies of animals, zodiacal and otherwise, strewn about on the several continents.

With a canopy reconstructed, no longer are we required to explain how early man could have built great geometric works that were too extensive for him to see. For with a canopy-mirror of reflective ice crystals, he would be able to see such patterns clearly in their entirety. The patterns would have been at least as clear as those seen in satellite photos taken from 400 or so miles up. Actually, the images viewed by early man would have been seen more clearly because the reflective surface of the canopy may have been only some fifty miles above. The image viewed in a canopy-mirror fifty miles up would appear to be twice this distance, or one hundred miles. Thus, the secret ingredient in our analysis is to run this idea through the computer and see what size the images would appear to be. The secret is this: early man undoubtedly saw images of terrestrial features reflected in the sky before he was inspired to construct his own patterns. Likely, certain features of the landscape suggested images to him that he could modify and thus admire his handiwork as reflected in the heavens. 'As above, so below' was probably a principle in reality long before it gained esoteric connotations. The canopy was the original wide-wide screen!

In a recent issue of *National Geographic* magazine (December 1974) an article appears by David Lewis entitled 'Isles of the Pacific; Wind, Wave, Star, and Bird'. Lewis attempts to rediscover the lost arts of the Polynesian navigators and he finds that the ancient system not only involves a knowledge of ocean swells but also utilizes the colours reflected on clouds from greenish-tinted lagoons in Pacific atolls. We may be sure that the same technique was used during canopy times when the reflections were even more precise and colourful.

What, may we ask, was the ancient appearance of Avalon when the sea level was twenty feet higher than at present? Did this island stand out like an apple tree as reflected from the canopy clouds? Was there then a whole new visual dimension that we now barely suspect? Did people draw gigantic patterns that were clearly visible in this ice-crystal mirror located high overhead in the skies? How much detail could one have seen at this distance? How big would the image appear to be? How big would the pattern on the ground have to be to be seen clearly? Do the effigies of the mounds in North America meet the same size criteria? Do the Nazca lines and drawings? And finally, how much of the world could have been mapped from a single point, say, from the site of the Great Pyramid near Cairo in Egypt? Or, say, from the top of Glastonbury Tor, or from the top of Silbury Hill or even from the centre of Stonehenge?

Actually, all these questions are answerable and the answers are purely a matter of geometry. In fact, the map that results 'appears' to have been drawn from a space ship many miles above the point in question. Taking into account the inverted image of a reflection it turns out that distant points hundreds of miles away may be seen clearly. Navigation on smooth seas under a canopy would have been quite easy in even frail craft. We can imagine that the Sumerians used this navigational aid to select their landing site. The details of each bay, each lagoon, each island, would have shown up quite clearly in the canopy mirror. One can imagine their awe and enthusiasm upon discovery of the 'glass mountain' that we now call Glastonbury Tor.

As Vail noted, the canopy shell was described in the legends and mythologies of a number of peoples, but since legends are looked upon dimly by physical scientists, we will dismiss them from consideration for the moment. Rather, let us pursue the logic of the situation. A canopy of ice particles may be imagined to be superimposed on the E-layer of the ionosphere, acting in some respect as the E-layer does. Arrays of antennae have measured reflected radio waves from the E-layer, showing, by triangulation, that the layer consists of a pattern of 'waves' or billows moving quite swiftly. These characteristics parallel precisely the behaviour of the canopy, with the difference that the canopy was actually observed visually by early man. The E-layer is reflective of radio waves; the canopy was reflective of light waves. Hence if the E-layer shows characteristic billows and flickerings, then at times the under-surface of the canopy must also have shown undulations. According to Vail, who wrote long before the E-layer was discovered, the undulating canopy provided the appearance of a 'molten looking glass'. The specific reference found by Vail in Job 37 : 18 says:

> Hast thou with him spread out the sky,
> which is strong, and as a molten looking glass?

The billowing canopy was 'strong', reflective as a mirror, and certainly spread out across the sky. This mirror in the skies, extending over Glastonbury, would explain how that vantage point would attain legendary fame. Avalon was one of the fair isles of the west, where warmth and happiness and green grass and apple trees were thought about long after the canopy had disappeared. Was this island of Britain really the lost Atlantis? Was the disappearance of the island 'in a single night' really a record of the disappearance of the mirror in the skies? If Britain was indeed Atlantis, then there is perhaps some special purpose in John Michell having chosen his title *The View Over Atlantis* to describe Britain's ley lines and other geomantic configurations.

At any rate, when a friend sent me some excerpts from a book entitled *The Hollow*

Earth, I learned that Admiral Byrd has described a reflective phenomenon in the Antarctic that is pertinent to our discussion. Upon occasion, floating ice crystals in the skies do provide a flat layer that is reflective. In the white-white world of the snow fields any darker object becomes highly visible in this gigantic mirror. Quite naturally it takes a quantum jump to transform this same reflective layer of ice crystals viewed in this century in Antarctica to Glastonbury in Britain some thousands of years ago. But with a little mental gymnastics, the transition can be made. Over that hurdle, it is but a short step to understand that the legends (or even the fiction) of the earth being (or seeming to be) hollow may have once had some basis in fact. That the myth was relegated to the earth's rocky structure must not be allowed to detract from the glorious canopy scene that was really seen in the skies, and that is now only dimly reflected in the form of a myth or a legend or an epic story.

Vail considered that the canopy was originally worshipped by early man as a great enfolding, protective covering. The deified canopy was represented as a serpentine-dragon because of its twisting folds. These same twists can now be observed from time to time on the planet Jupiter. On the earth, another serpentine example unknown to Vail was the 'jet stream' to be discovered in the forties. If one can imagine a sprinkling of ice crystals within the jet stream, immediately all the legendary flying dragons and feathered serpents could be seen to be alive again.

Art forms depicting dragons have preserved many of the features that imply the presence of ice crystals. Some dragons pursue solar emblems with attendant haloes; indeed, some of the geometric curves found on the dragon images are clearly halo configurations. That the form of the dragon was originally seen among wisps of ice crystals in a jet-like stream high in the atmosphere or even higher at the E-layer level, may seem impossible to reduce to a scientific problem. Always however, the basic clues remain to tantalize us.

Always the serpentine maze will wind around the Tor at Glastonbury, like the folds of the dragon that was said to encompass Mount Parnassus. Always there will be the maze, which by the rules is a pattern that defies understanding. And yet, by the rules, there is always a challenger who dares to try to solve the secret of the pattern.

Scientists are concerned with the mysteries of nature but it is inevitable that the mysteries of man are included in the mysteries of nature. Scientists now have the opportunity to put all these concepts together in the proper perspective. Nothing really lies in a realm that is beyond ordinary comprehension. The recent advances of science should have taught us that much. Continued investigation, the inevitable progress of science and the indefatigable courage of mankind confronting a problem, should be sufficient to put all the pieces of the puzzle together. The Glastonbury terrain forms one of the major pieces in this puzzle.

There is a legend that says the influence of Glastonbury will one day again be felt in world affairs. Let us hope that the research and investigation presently being attempted will hasten the arrival of that day.

ADDENDUM

Portions of the preceding article have appeared in the publication *Stonehenge Viewpoint,* a quarterly dedicated to archaeology, astronomy, geology and related arts and sciences. For a sample copy mention this source and write to *Stonehenge Viewpoint,* 51 Charminster Avenue, Bournemouth, Dorset, BH9 1RS.

Reference should also be made to an incredible coincidence related to Glastonbury investigations and published in *This Holyest Erthe* by Oliver L. Reiser in 1974 (Perennial Books, London). Independently, Professor Reiser notes the way that radio waves are reflected from the ionisphere and then continues: 'What we need is a kind of eye in the sky for a kind of global vision of earth-events. Here we have in mind the fact that the Glastonbury Zodiac and Stonehenge were constructed as if they were meant to be viewed from above . . . *as if an architect were looking into a heavenly mirror.*'

Recommended Books

Ashe, Geoffrey. *King Arthur's Avalon.* Collins, 1957.

Cyr, Donald L. *Hidden Halos of Stonehenge.* Annular Publications (Santa Barbara Co.).

Greed, John A. *Glastonbury Tales.* St Trillo Publications, 1975.

Roberts, Anthony. *Atlantean Traditions in Ancient Britain.* Rider, 1977.

Vail, Isaac. *Great Red Dragon.* Annular Publications.

   Heavens and Earth of Prehistoric Man. Annular Publications.

Williams, Mary, ed. *Glastonbury: A Study in Patterns.* RILKO, 1969.

CHAPTER NINE

A Mystery for Ever:
Glastonbury and Arthur

JESS FOSTER

So much has been written and read during the last decade about King Arthur, Cadbury, Glastonbury and the Vale of Avalon generally that it is unlikely anyone reading these words is not fully apprised of the current state of play. It would seem that there is little or nothing left to be said about Arthur as man, king or mystic symbol.

However, an archaeologist who is interested in his work will probably, at close of day, retire to his study to have another look at the items in his 'finds tray': it is always possible that amongst the odd pot shards, bent nails, bits of slag or rusted bits of metal, he may find some item he has overlooked that may provide fresh and interesting evidence. It is important, obviously, that he should not turn them over again with the same glazed, unseeing look that he gave them earlier in the day; after a meal and a rest he may well be able to bring a fresh alertness to his mind.

Not long ago I remarked to a retired architect that a certain new hospital complex was singularly like an air terminal. 'So what?' he retorted. 'All big buildings are designed for the processing of people anyhow.'

Instead of instantly accepting the obvious, let us reconsider this statement as one of the first items in our metaphoric finds tray. Processing people through large buildings is easy because everyone entering such a building is already prepared for processing. Each person enters with the hope or intention of reaching a predestined spot. Each enters through the door marked 'entrance' and then starts to follow the various signs, notices, indicators, offices and staircases until he reaches the spot the designers intended him to reach.

On entering the precincts of Glastonbury Abbey we accept at once the fact that in its heyday it was a bright jewel in the crown of the Roman Catholic church. We then go on from there, along the well-trodden ways, and with the rest of the crowd. But let us turn over this statement and carefully consider it again.

The Roman Catholic church was, further back in time, a break-away branch of the early Christian community. For a long time members of the old Catholic church regarded the break-aways as heretics. Before that again, there had been the Nestorian church and others;* the gospels had been translated from Aramaic to Greek to Latin long before they ever reached Glastonbury at all. The Roman monopoly was only established at the Abbey after a succession of rows, quarrels, meetings, synods and general acrimony; and only after some people – notably Illtydd, said to be the cousin of King Arthur and later the founder of a remarkable esoteric college at Llantwit Major – had flounced out in frustration and protest. What was he so put out about?

Another item in our finds tray is worthy of fresh consideration. At what point did the Roman church achieve its real power and ascendancy? We have a book of reference here. Sir Kenneth Clark, in his television programme and his book *Civilization* said:

> We have grown so used to the idea that the Crucifixion is the supreme symbol of Christianity, that it is a shock to realise how late in the history of Christian art its power was recognised. In the first art of Christianity it hardly appears; and the earliest example, on the doors of Santa Sabine in Rome, is stuck away in a corner, almost out of sight. The simple fact is that the early Church needed converts, and from this point of view the Crucifixion was not an encouraging subject. So, early Christian art is concerned with miracles, healings, and with hopeful aspects of the faith like the Ascension and the Resurrection . . . It was the tenth century, that despised and rejected period of European history, that made the Crucifixion into a moving symbol of the Christian faith . . . The men of the tenth century not only recognised the meaning of Christ's sacrifice in physical terms: they were able fully to sublimate it into ritual. The evidence of book illustrations and ivories show for the first time a consciousness of the symbolic power of the Mass . . . These confident works show that at the end of the tenth century there was a new power in Europe, greater than any king or emperor: the Church.

Granted that Sir Kenneth Clark is just as capable of being processed as the rest of us, consider some of these words again. The early Christian church was concerned with miracles, healings, and with hopeful aspects of the faith like the Ascension and the Resurrection. The Celts, we can remind ourselves, regarded death as a mere change of consciousness and were so aware of Eternity that they were willing to sign and accept IOUs intended to be redeemed in a future life. We can remind ourselves too that archaeology showed us that when Arthur refortified Cadbury after the departure of the Romans, he rebuilt it in Celtic fashion. Maybe he did not dwell overmuch on crucifixion either; maybe his faith was a hopeful, Celtic faith that spoke, as Jesus did, of Eternal Life.

Certainly the *dux bellorum* who rallied the Britons and fought a long resistance campaign against the Saxons was not a favourite with the clerics of his time. The fact that his name was held dear by all the Celtic generations that followed shows that he was a hero of the Celtic peoples. If he was not the church's favourite son there must have been some reason, though it would obviously be difficult to discover that reason now unless fresh evidence comes to light. We can only guess how much of a free-thinker or even 'heretic' he was thought to be.

There is another small item in the finds tray to be reconsidered. Country folk, living close to nature, do not expect dead heroes to return to life. If the country folk were always hopefully awaiting the return of Arthur it could only have been because they were hopefully awaiting a return to those things his name stood for; some kind of faith

---

*During the second century AD the Gnostics (masters of the mystical 'gnosis' or knowledge) maintained much spiritual/magical headway in the environs of the early Christian church. They were later destroyed for heresy. (*Ed.*)

that his name represented. It was evidently a way of life that had been suppressed and finally driven underground after the battle of Camlann, but which could possibly return when or if the suppressing forces were overthrown. The years passed, and the legends began. They grew, and flourished and spread abroad, their main theme the search for the Grail. This Holy Grail was a numinous 'something' that had been raised to higher realms but could return briefly, at certain times, to nourish and re-inspire the faithful. Incidentally, most of the Grail's physical manifestations – Beckery, Pomparles Bridge, etc. – appear around Glastonbury.

If you analyse the qualities that seemed to be required of a Grail-Seeker you find they are the qualities that we have come to associate with Pelagianism and the non-conformist sects generally: self-help, independence, self-discipline, charity and so on. There was huge emphasis on the fact that the great enemy of the Grail was *accidie* – inertia and apathy (sitting around awaiting benediction). The legends also make every Grail-Seeker a knight, whose basic quality has to be courage. Indeed, the Grail was an updated version of the old Celtic Cauldron that would not boil for a coward.* The Grail had been lost or hidden at Glastonbury, yet there was said to be another one in the Pyrenees. Oddly, in the Pyrenees a sect survived for a long time whose members were known as Albigensians and who were finally liquidated by the Inquisition. The Knights Templar were said to be Guardians of the Grail; they too were liquidated by the Inquisition. We all know what happened to the Huguenots, the Puritans, the Quakers. The tale of religious oppression is a long and ugly one.

Yet the legends of a magically based freedom and understanding have survived. Wherever the Celts have gone these same legends have gone with them, as have the belief in a Sleeper, a dormant power for Good. The Grail appears briefly at Pentecost — that moment of illumination and power which comes when a dedicated brotherhood is gathered together. (Oddly, in a book about the Templars by Gerard de Sede, the author throws in a footnote to the effect that at Pentecost the knights feasted on peacocks. One recalls that the peacock was the symbol of Isis. Just how far back does the Grail legend go? That is an odd little feather to flutter into the finds tray.)

So the minstrels wandered from country to country, from castle to castle; from the Grampians to the Black Mountains of Wales, from Brittany to the Pyrenees, keeping alive the faith in a sleeping Arthur who would one day return. It seemed he would never really lie down until . . . In 1190 someone found an answer. Arthur, even at this very late date, could be gathered into the bosom of Holy Mother Church and accepted as one of her finest sons. He could be laid to rest with pomp and ceremony and in the presence of royalty, in the sacred grounds of Glastonbury Abbey. He could never be more dead than that.

Yet Aneiren and Taliesin and the Welsh bards and the Triads are still with us, and they are the accepted recorders of a hero called Arthur and his followers – a supernatural hero

---

*The Celtic Cauldron was also the magic vessel of inspiration and knowledge. Ingestion of its carefully prepared contents was said to bring mystic revelation, a mind expansion that broke down the barriers between subjective and objective consciousness. It was (like the later Grail) a transcendent object that formed a bridging talisman between the worlds of spirituality and corporeality. This is elucidated in detail in Robert Graves's mighty work *The White Goddess*. (*Ed.*)

A mystery for ever. 'And he saith unto them, Follow me and I will make you fishers of men' (Matthew 4:19).

steeped in folkloric magic, whose followers were linked to the eternal pursuit of a magico religious knowledge. Amongst these records is a *Song of the Graves* which lists a company of heroes and describes where their graves are to be found. But there is one striking exception – *Anoeth bid yet y arthur,* which has been translated 'Not wise the thought, a grave for Arthur', or 'A mystery to the world, the grave of Arthur'.

The Resistance Fighter seems to have escaped again, as good Resistance Fighters do, which is why the Quest for Arthur continues. It continues because it is much more than a search for a distinctive historical personage. It continues because it is a quest for enlightenment and spiritual freedom, unhampered by the restrictive shackles of an authoritarian dogmatism. It is really a seeking of the secrets and harmonies of natural magic, linked to the very human presence of a great and mysterious man.

Recommended Books

Alcock, Leslie. *Arthur's Britain.* Pelican, 1973.

Barber, Richard. *Arthur of Albion.* Boydell Press, 1971.

McNeill, John T. *The Celtic Churches.* University of Chicago Press, 1974.

Morris, John. *The Age of Arthur.* Weidenfeld & Nicolson, 1973.

CHAPTER TEN

Underground Tunnels of Glastonbury

ANN PENNICK

Like many other abbeys and cathedrals, Glastonbury Abbey has several lost-tunnel legends associated with it. These were investigated by the psychical archaeologist F. Bligh Bond over sixty years ago, but since then little research has been carried out on what is really a rather important aspect of the overall geomantic mystique.

There are four main tunnel legends attached to the Abbey, three of which have been partially verified.

The first legend is of a tunnel from the medieval Pilgrims' Inn (now the 'George and Pilgrim') to a point within the Abbey walls. As the inn was built by Abbot Selwood about 1470, in the time of Edward IV, the tunnel could have been used for secret access to the Abbey by pilgrims staying at the inn.

The tunnel, discovered by Bligh Bond, starts from the south end of the cellar under the High Street and is clear for twenty feet southward until about the centre of the road, where it is suddenly blocked by a brick sewer. It is assumed that it then continues to the Abbot's Gateway, where there was a porter's lodge, but this again has not been verified by excavation. Mrs Bilbrough in her diary on 21 May 1918 (quoted in Alan Fea's *Rooms of Mystery and Romance*), described a trip into this tunnel:

Off we started on our underground journey down a flight of fearfully steep steps, dark and damp and slippery . . . We groped our way to where the far-famed passage was, which had a great stone step at the entrance, and was only three feet in height, so that those who used it must have crawled on their knees, resting at intervals where ledges are cut in the sides for that purpose. Fancy going for a quarter of a mile like that, when even a few feet of it made my back ache and my limbs quiver all over from the unnatural strained position.

Another legend which is widely believed is that of the long-distance tunnel leading from the crypt of the Lady (or Galilee) Chapel, under the river Brue to a distant point, possibly to the village of Street, where a passage exists from an outlying building in the grounds of the old manor house. A dog is said to have been put into the tunnel at Street and found his way out at the Glastonbury end.* The story of the tunnel passing under

*This tale has quite a few local variants throughout Somerset. Most cogent here is the Mendip story told to the editor by a fine old gentleman, the late James Barnard, who farmed between Wedmore and Wells and who traced his

the river Brue is similar to that of the tunnel which is alleged to connect King's College Chapel to Granchester Manor, Cambridge, passing under the river Cam. Alfred Watkins, in his book *The Old Straight Track,* refers to such legends and states that they might be connected with leys. Michael Behrend in *The Landscape Geometry of Southern Britain* (Zodiac House/Fenris Wolf) has shown that the Kings-to-Granchester Manor tunnel is definitely a ley.

A passage does exist from the Street Manor House grounds but it cannot be explored fully because of an obstruction some distance from its mouth. It is thought to begin in the house and lead straight to the stables. Bligh Bond excavated the reputed site of this tunnel near the Galilee and found the subsoil to be marshy and so probably unsuitable for a tunnel ever to have existed there. A large relieving arch was revealed but this was thought to have been put up to carry the walls of the Galilee over a particularly bad piece of ground. Other explanations are of course still possible.

An old inmate of the women's almshouse remembered seeing in her childhood a passage running from the well chamber on the south side of the Galilee Chapel. This tunnel had to be sealed up by the owner of the Abbey as a lamb fell down the hole in the ground and was never recovered. Bligh Bond decided to cut a trench around the outside of this chamber, starting from the south wall of the chapel and curving round to the east at a radius of twenty to thirty feet. This trench, which was eight to ten feet deep, passed through the monks' graveyard to a point nearly due south of the well chamber, roughly opposite to a bit of free-stone wall bounding the space by the well. The rubble at this point gave way to reveal a filling of clay occupying a trench with vertical sides – which suggests that a tunnel did once exist here. This passage may have run southwards across the graveyard towards the guest hall and Almonry, and would have been connected with the service of the crypt. This would have made a covered way from the monastic buildings to the crypt of the Lady Chapel, thus enabling the monks to gain access to the shrines undetected by the pilgrims and sheltered from the weather or any unwelcome eyes.

The third story is of a large underground passage in the field to the south of the Abbey. There was once a land subsidence in one place and the stone head of a channel had been noticed. An old workman named Thyer remembered having seen a deep-walled passage with flag-stones opened by Mr Austin, owner of the chapel, but when Bligh Bond tried to locate the passage, Thyer was unable to remember the exact position of it.

However, yet another passage was said to have existed to the south of the Abbot's Kitchen. This was a stone-built channel which crossed the orchard to a point in the Abbey's western boundary. As a search was being made for the footings of the Abbot's House, a trench was dug running to the south-east of the refectory. The subsequent passage, which was revealed a little beyond the southern-most boundary of the Abbot's

---

family back hundreds of years. This long-distance tunnel myth is centred around two prehistoric standing stones that lie on the side of the Mendip Hills near the Ebbor Gorge. The megaliths are called the Deerleap Stones and they mark at least one ley line running towards Warminster. Near these stones there is supposedly a tunnel entrance and a dog was said to have been thrust in, to reappear some days later from an exit at Glastonbury Tor. This is a distance of about eight miles as the crow flies. (*Ed.*)

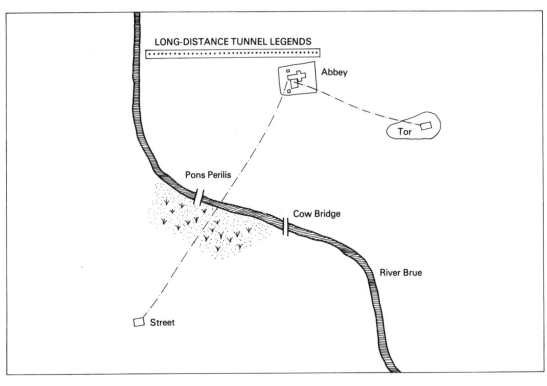

LONG-DISTANCE TUNNEL LEGENDS

Abbey

Tor

Pons Perilis

Cow Bridge

River Brue

Street

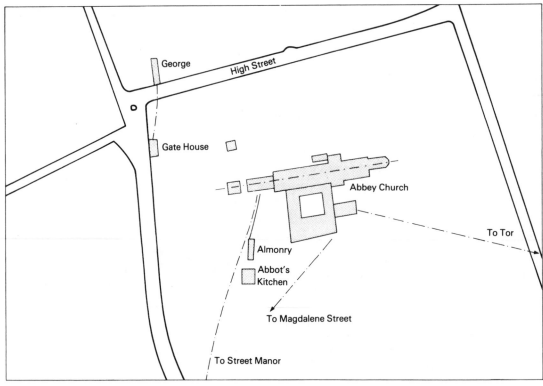

George

High Street

Gate House

Abbey Church

To Tor

Almonry

Abbot's Kitchen

To Magdalene Street

To Street Manor

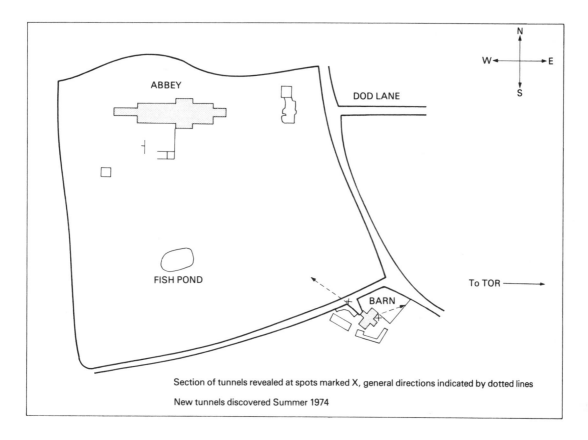

Section of tunnels revealed at spots marked X, general directions indicated by dotted lines

New tunnels discovered Summer 1974

House, was found to be the main drain of the Abbey. One of Bligh Bond's more enter-prising students entered this passage and climbed along it for some sixty feet before encountering any prohibitive obstruction. The tunnel ran in a south-westerly direction to the lowest point of Magdalene Street where there was once a chain bridge and probably a water-gate to the Abbey for the entrance of barges. The Abbey in medieval times relied upon the local canals for its connection with the outside world, and these canals were very active with the Abbot's barges; a highly secular application of religious privilege that was not uncommon at this time.

The fourth and last legend is of a tunnel from the Abbey to the Tor, or to the church of St Michael formerly upon the Tor, and interconnecting with a series of by-tunnels beneath the Tor.* Another large entrance is believed to exist near the waterworks reservoir in Wellhouse Lane. This story is very widely rumoured. Moreover, numerous dowsers have commented upon the supposed 'hollowness' of the Tor and its great variety of underground springs forming a complex network of hidden waterways. But the story has yet to be physically verified.

*Because so many of these tunnel stories discuss passages running for many miles, some current speculative researchers are interpreting them as folk memories of geomantic ley alignments. Although the existence of certain short-line physical tunnels is well proven, the long lines (in some Welsh stories tunnels are said to run under mountains) can be seen as mythologized ley orientations. What helps to confirm this judgement is that tunnels are always con-nected with buildings of proven religic-historical meaning. (*Ed.*)

It is obvious from the above that secret tunnels did and possibly do, exist in the Glastonbury area.* Their exact purpose is obscure, but like their countrywide counterparts, they seem to be reflections of a mystery and sanctity attaching to places of paramount geomantic importance in the topographic interrelation of religious sites.

Recommended Books

Bond, F. Bligh. *The Hill of Vision.*
  The Mystery of Glaston & her Immortal Traditions.
Pennick, Ann. *Dene-Holes and Subterranea.* Megalithic Visions (pamphlet).

*Two new tunnels have recently been uncovered at Glastonbury, both running out from the Abbey barn, a medieval tithe barn situated between the Abbey and the Tor. A correspondent of the editor was working on the film 'Barry Lyndon' in 1974, part of which was shot in the Abbey barn, and he was present when the tunnels were accidentally discovered. First, a heavy vehicle crashed through the road at the corner of the main entrance to the barn. A large tunnel appeared, running towards the refectory area of the Abbey but it was quickly filled in with rubble by the contractors who were then engaged in repairing the barn's fabric. This tunnel most definitely followed a straight course but because of the zeal of the contractors the passage has now been reconsigned to at least a physical oblivion. The second underground trackway was also found by the builders and similarly dealt with. According to the charge-hand on the construction team, this tunnel was behind the barn and was angled directly at the Tor. It too was of considerable size. The existence of these tunnels, midway between and leading towards the two most sacred sites of the area, is good evidence of a vast subterranean complex beneath Glastonbury, as befits a place of such ecumenical and mythological complexity. (*Ed.*)

CHAPTER ELEVEN

Bend Me a Maze

(Here is the Key)

PATRICIA VILLIERS-STUART

The maze on Glastonbury Tor has only recently been discovered; what look like sheep or cattle tracks to the uninitiated, Mr Geoffrey Russell assures us are really its labyrinthine curves. And so they should be. Mazes to the ancient world may have been what atomic stations are to us, power centres.

We are becoming a little chary of our modern power capacity, wondering whether science is not unveiling too much, beginning to suspect that things are getting out of hand, that we may find ourselves launched on a course of self-destruction.

Perhaps we have reached the very stage where we came in, perhaps it's all happened before. Earthquakes, floods, disasters, whole continents swamped, the earth violently changing axis, the planets and stars appearing to alter their courses, the entire universe in a state of shock . . .

But in opposition to this kind of disaster thinking, is the dream of a Golden Age, both in the past and to come, where things will be better ordered, the Kingdom of Heaven really at hand.

Be this as it may, it does seem that past civilizations have left us clues to some kind of unified harmonious system which may have given them great power over their environment. Clues are left in broken, scattered form all over the earth. Temples, pyramids, stone circles, zodiacs, mazes, Tarot cards, the Cabbala, the I ching, myths, cults, fairy tales, philosophical propositions, even political theories, certainly religious faiths, all testify to the belief that it is possible to encompass truth systematically.

The maze has been my own point of departure and I took the squared form as shown on Cretan coins, squared because it is then more readily susceptible to careful geometrical analysis. I found that if the whole maze was on a square of 30 × 30, then the rectangle between the centre of the cross and the centre of the maze was 1 × 7. It was pleasing to find that this rectangle and its diagonal were sacred to the Ancient Egyptians (Schwaller de Lubicz, *Le Temple de l'Homme*). And at Stonehenge, a line from what is generally considered to be the centre to the Heel or Holy Stone forms the diagonal of a 1 × 7 rectangle in relation to the cross of NE–SW and NW–SE, giving added credence to

John Ivimy's contention in *The Sphinx and the Megaliths* that a colony of Egyptians actually built Stonehenge.

After this finding I was convinced that the maze form contained more geometrical and numerical secrets to be uncovered. I tried plotting onto squares the various divisions of a circle, the 1/5, 1/6, 1/7, etc. I was soon in trouble. Nothing fitted perfectly for one reason or another. But I pressed obstinately on, absolutely determined that a harmonious relationship must exist between number and space if only I could detect it. In the end I think I have, with help from ancient Egypt and ancient China.

First, abandon 360 degrees for a circle, as 7 does not go into it. Plato's favourite number, 5040, is far more acceptable as 14 goes into it 360 times. Ideally a circle should be kept as a total unity and its divisions counted as fractions. And above all there must be no dealings with decimals for they introduce false rhythms.

Dividing a circle into 7 and its multiples seems to have been of great importance in the past. Not only are there 56 Aubrey holes at Stonehenge, but other stone circles also respond to sevenfold investigation. Then there is the Medicine Wheel of Wyoming, USA, a stone wheel of undatable antiquity laid out on the ground. It has 28 radiating spokes.

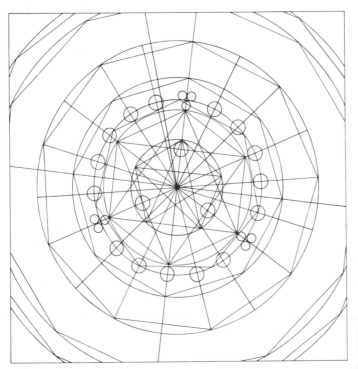

A replica of the Glastonbury Bowl in the local museum, said to be 3000 years old.

Geometry of the Glastonbury Bowl turned upside down. It stands on the three inner circles which are knobs. It bears out the unified geometry of the numbers 3 4 5 6 7 8 9.

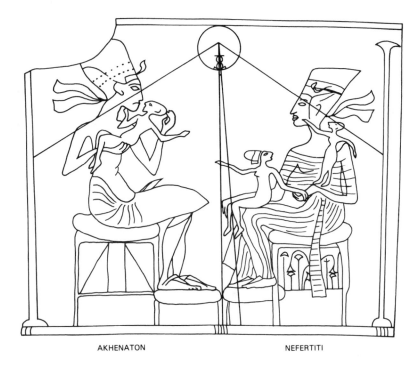

AKHENATON   NEFERTITI

Egyptian rhythmic geometry.

Traced from photograph of a stela from Amarna, Akhenaton's City of the Horizon. Akhenaton, Queen Nefertiti and their three daughters sit beneath the sun's rays.

Angle of rays going towards Akhenaton 1/6th division of circle, angle of Nefertiti's rays 1/7th division. Small angle in between marked by the Royal Cobra and the Ankh equals 1/56. Overall angle equals 55/168.

The whole sun circle is here counted as divided into 168.
168 = 6 × 28 = 7 × 24 = 8 × 21.

Compare with the 56 Aubrey hole divisions at Stonehenge and the 28 divisions of the Medicine Wheel in Wyoming, USA.

It was in studying the geometry of the sun's rays on a stela from Amarna, the Pharaoh Akhenaton's 'City of the Horizon', that I seemed to find the answer, and even more answers may shortly be forthcoming as research progresses. Archaeologists working with the Akhenaton Temple project of the University of Pennsylvania are at present busily engaged in piecing together scenes from this Pharaoh's life which have been found on scattered stones made up into other buildings. Measuring the angles from the sun's disc has helped in the reconstruction, and in my view these angles also have a great wealth of ancient wisdom to reveal.

On the stela under discussion, Akhenaton, Nefertiti and three of their young daughters are seated opposite each other with the sun and its rays ranging between them. Measuring these rays it will be found that the bundle of rays angled towards Akhenaton is a 1/6th division of a circle, while those going towards Nefertiti form a 1/7th division (see illustration). A first ray pierces the centre of her forehead. But most important of all is that between the rays of the royal pair there is a small angle marked with an *ankh* and surmounted by the Royal Cobra. Both Akhenaton and Nefertiti wear this snake sign on their headdresses as if it were emerging from the centre of their foreheads, showing no doubt their connection with the biblical command of being 'wise as

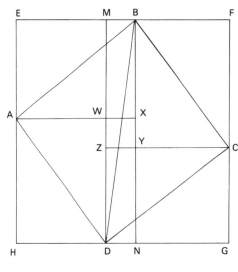

Areas

WXYZ = 1
ABCD = 25
EFGH = 49
MBND = 7
BD divides ABC in half

Basic 1 × 7 pattern

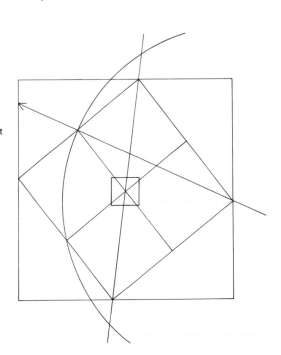

Burning Gold

Bring me my bow
Of burning gold

With my bow brought
The arrows of desire
Flying by night
Steered by thought
Guided by light
Land aright

serpents'. The angle that is marked with such maximum importance I have found to be a 1/56. This is a result of studying much megalithic geometry and discovering apparently a key to it which makes all numbers and angles definable in relation to each other.

The method can be applied to the famous Glastonbury Bowl. When the bowl is turned upside down, the three knobs it stands on can be seen in relation to the knobs on the outside. The whole bears out the unified geometry of the numbers 3 to 9, including 7.

Is this perhaps a small example of what were known as Cauldrons of Inspiration and were attributed to the Mother Goddesses?

It is perhaps relevant here to refer to Dr Aubrey Westlake's recent book *The Pattern of Health*. The author, who worked for many years as a GP in Bermondsey, on retirement interested himself in healing by means of radiesthesia. He worked in co-operation with W. O. Wood and together they explored significant geometrical patterns which they came to find most effective. Some of the patterns illustrated in his book are very reminiscent of my own diagrams. They are called the Diamond, the Celtic Cross and the Star of Bethlehem, and they have two modes of functioning, the static and the dynamic. It seems they were used in metabolic combination with plants, minerals and elements.

Dr Westlake quotes appreciatively from L. L. Whyte's *Accent on Form:* 'To understand anything one must penetrate deeply towards the ultimate form. . . . Only a new scientific doctrine of structure and form i.e. pattern, can suggest the crucial experiments which can lead to the solution of those master problems of matter, life and mind.'

Two men whose researches in the early years of this century went far towards finding this solution were F. Bligh Bond and T. Simcox Lea. For a brief description of Bligh Bond's extensive work on the foundations of Glastonbury Abbey see the article in this book by Nigel Pennick. Their mutual study was gematria, which Bligh Bond applied to his excavations at Glastonbury, while Lea explored the hidden meaning in the Coptic Gnostic Books and the Greek text of the New Testament.

Gematria is a system of correlating words and numbers so that they act upon each other to give deeper meaning to the overt verbal expression. Both in Hebrew and in Greek, letters and numbers can be used in this way. For instance, the Jewish Holy of Holies is $216 = 6 \times 6 \times 6$; New Jerusalem is $961 = 31 \times 31$; and the name Jesus Christ is $2368 = 37 \times 64$. These last proportions, 31×64, are to be found in the Lady Chapel at Glastonbury, so Kenneth Knight tells us. In cabbalistic teaching concerning the Tree of Life, the number 11 signifies the Messiah, so it seems as if in the new dispensation the numbers 11, 31, 37 are extending the old knowledge of 7, 30, 36 in the search for the true relationship between number and form.

I am grateful to our editor Anthony Roberts for drawing my attention to D'Arcy Thompson's seminal work *On Growth and Form* which, when first published in 1917, caused a revolution in the biological sciences. Thompson analyses the whole range of biological function and, stressing the need to do more than document individual cases, begs science to help elucidate the whole grand design of the universe, which he repeatedly points out is founded on rhythm and number.*

It was gratifying to discover in reading this profound book that certain angles, known as Maraldi Angles, which play a vital role in the growth of sixfold form, *appear* to disclose the secret of their proportions when treated in the manner I have indicated.

For the Mexican Indians mazes were certainly an aspect of creative form and Frank Waters, the author of *The Hopi Indians* and *Mexico Mystique,* writes:

Both round and square maze forms are found on the Hopi mesas, and the circular form is found in the ruin of Casa Grande far to the south. A Hopi interpretation of both forms was given according to myth and ritual. The square type, known as T'apu'ut (Mother and Child) symbolizes both the birth

---

*Everything that exists has a basic structural pattern that shapes its energy and gives it meaning. These patterns have certain linking similarities of proportion and design that imply a divine creative spirit or power to the whole morphological emphasis of creation. D'Arcy Thompson's book explores this linking unity of form. During the course of his work he analysed the whole spectrum of biological processes, elucidating the correspondences and organic interconnection and tying them in to the sublime wisdom of ancient doctrines of metaphysical science.

The rhythmic and proportionally increasing *function* implied in creative form is of more importance than the dry cataloguing of mere ancestral progression. There is a designed intelligence and unity behind form that owes absolutely nothing to the emptily random excesses of chance. The rationale is one of a beautifully measured, eternal Control that conforms more to the stabilizing symmetries of a harmonious poem, underwritten by the interaction of certain interlocking scientific facts. As such, this philosophy can be seen as diametrically opposed to the often drily scientific musings of Newton and Darwin, with their empirical theory of a linear, mechanistic evolutionary process. Luckily, this theory is now undergoing a gradual eclipse with the rise of the conception of 'magical physics', eternally cyclic, eternally self-regenerating and eternally governed by a canonical and universal ontology. (*Ed.*)

of a child from the womb and the spiritual rebirth from one world to the succeeding one (the Emergence). The circular form symbolizes the universal plan of Creation.

I find it of great interest that the square maze is designated as being female, and the round maze as male, no doubt. If this opposition of female and male is taken in terms of space and time, the square maze can be seen as producing the angles of space, while the round maze is more suited to the speed of time. These principles, united in some way, could perhaps have been responsible for a form of flight or levitation; alternate coiling, which is an integral part of the production of electricity, forms the essence of the maze. Birds, before migrating appear to make maze-like movements to and fro, and perhaps they are orienting themselves to the power currents of the universe, utilizing a form of genetically 'built-in' energy recognizance!

Legends of human flight are universally distributed and in some rare cases seem to have left their marks, as in the Nasca patterns in Peru which span many miles of desert, or in some Scottish brochs which apparently have been vitrified by intense heat from above, or in England where the zodiacal and geomantic layout around Glastonbury can only be fully appreciated from the air. These important legends are admirably summed up in the works of Anthony Roberts and John Michell.

Just as Arabian stories have their flying carpets so Hindu legend has its flying palace and their deliverer god Vishnu wears on his forehead a threefold sign which is central to the whole design we are discussing.

The integration of form and number, colour and sound to produce a power capable of flight is not merely a science-fiction dream. It may already be a daily occurrence among certain insects, although science will have none of it. I quote from *The Life of Insects* by Dr Maurice Burton: 'It is possible to work out by mathematics whether an aeroplane will fly when it is built. Using the same method, experts say that a bumblebee should not be able to fly. But it can!' Perhaps the bee flies by the fractional, rhythmic, non-decimal method that I have been recommending.

Looking at the complexity of circles, crosses, mazes and diamond shapes when super-imposed on each other, one is almost ready to declare that the blueprint of a flying saucer is about to emerge. And how I wonder would it be powered? By colour and sound perhaps, for there is a law of sound which seems temptingly like the law of diamond shapes. For these, when composed of equilateral triangles it can be said that: the height of triangle A is half the length of dissimilar triangle B, while the length of triangle B is twice the height of triangle A. For sound the encyclopedia states that between octaves it is a case of twice the length and half the frequency or twice the frequency and half the length.

To demonstrate the unsuspected rhythms lying behind such mathematical concepts as square roots and multiplication tables it is necessary to apply digital reduction, or cabbalistic reduction as it is sometimes called.

For example:
$$19 = 1 + 9 = 10 = 1,$$
$$137 = 1 + 3 + 7 = 11 = 1 + 1 = 2$$

Nine is the completing number of the cycle and it seems as if Vedic mathematics were founded on this idea. The Indians also applied it to their astrological system.

As for tenfold decimals introducing false rhythms, which is what I contend, here is a relevant example:

360 divided by 7, fractional method:

$$360 \div 7 = 360 = 51\ 3 = 357 + 3 = 360 = 360 \div 7$$
$$\qquad\qquad\ \ 7 \qquad\ \ 7 \qquad\ \ 7 \qquad\ \ 7$$

There is no change, but no violation of rhythm.

360 divided by 7, decimal method:

$$360 \div 7 = 7\ \ 360.00$$
$$51.428571, 428571, 428\ldots\ldots$$

Note the introduction of an arbitrary sixfold rhythm of 428571.

I now realize, thanks to Robert Cowley's diagrams, that variations of this recurring rhythm are inherent in the divisions of ten by 7, 1/7, 2/7, 3/7 and 6/7. These considerations give rise to the ninefold sign associated with Gurdijeff and others. It is a sign of a stationary triangle with ceaseless movement around it. To symbolize this idea of eternity and passing life, Moslem garden planners liked to plant evergreen trees and flowering trees alternately. It is also a feature of their carpet design in many cases.

Studying this sign of nine at the heart of the decimal system may be the way of liberation from the unrhythmical use of decimals in our mathematical thinking.

If exact proportion between number and space is established in the way indicated, then measurements, whether in yards, megalithic yards, metres, cubits or anything else become quite irrelevant. Proportion is all. The next hurdle is the inter-relationship of proportion and time, which is of course growth.

I would like to draw attention to a recent book, *Nos Ancêtres Venus du Cosmos,* by a French scientist, Maurice Chatelain. The author was attached to nearly all the NASA space programmes, including the Apollo moon space-craft. He decided to feed the details of ancient structures such as the ziggurat of Babylon, the Egyptian pyramids, Mayan temples, Chartres cathedral, etc., into a computer. The results were startling. A number which the Assyrian conqueror, Assurbanipal, had carried off from Sumer seemed to be of cosmic significance. Even in my terms, using ten fingers rather than a computer, its importance is demonstrable.

The number is 195955200000000 and one way of expressing its rhythm is: 9 X 9 X 4 X 7 X 5 X 12 X 12 X 12 X 10 000 000. Each time the number is multiplied, by reduction the new number adds up to 9 because it is on the basis of nine squared.

It is gratifying to relate that two Englishmen, M. W. Saunders and Duncan Lunan, seem to be working along somewhat similar lines. They recently published *Destiny Mars.*

It is interesting to compare Chatelain's number from Nineveh, which he calls the universal constant, because it bears relationship with all the planetary orbits, and my number from Chartres, 164324160, which I say bears relationship to the geometry of dividing a circle into fractions.

In the sequence of numbers 1 2 3 4, etc., the Nineveh number cannot be divided by more than 10 although it can be divided by 14, 28 and 56. The Chartres number can be divided by the sequence of numbers up to 16 and also by 28, 56 and 57. On the other

Bend Me a Maze

Cretan coins in British Museum.

hand it doesn't contain nine squared which the other number does; perhaps they should be multiplied together! But I would suggest that one cannot stop short at any given number because numerical relationships weave endlessly into one another; detecting recurring rhythms is about all one can reasonably do.

In this respect the arrangement of the Tarot pack can be noted. Its Minor Arcana totals 56, so 57 in one way can be seen as the first card of the Major Arcana. There are 22 of these Trump cards, making a total of 78 or 6 × 13. Six is the number of the The Lovers' card and 13 the card of Death, while 57 = 3 × 19, and 19 is the card of the Sun. It is interesting to recall that a Greek writer of the time of Alexander the Great stated that Apollo the Sun God visited the Temple of the Hyperboreans, Stonehenge, every 19 years.* The numerology of the Tarot is highly complex, but has definite links with the gematria of the Hebrew Cabbala. In the cabbalistic Tree of Life, there are 22 paths tracing the journey or quest through the Sephiroth to union with God. Incidentally, there are also 22 letters in the Hebrew alphabet.

The numerical relationships of spatial shape is a study well worth pursuing. For instance, the culminating ninefold rhythm runs all through atomic structure, binding together elements whose relationships have already been established by science, but also suggesting new combinations. About a hundred years ago Mendeliev discovered a seven-fold rhythm in the periodic table of atomic numbers; we may soon find ourselves adding a ninefold one. This would certainly bring us to element 126, of which great things are expected. Could it be orichalcum, the luminous gold that the Atlanteans knew, so it is said, and about which the Dogons of Mali have a legend that their ancestors worked wonders with this metal?

But then the Dogons are a very special tribe: their knowledge, it would seem, came to them from ancient Egypt via extra-terrestrial sources. In *The Sirius Mystery*, Robert Temple explains just how this enigma came about. What he doesn't point out is that one important tribal sign called 'The Spiral of Creation' has angular divisions which fit in

---

*Professor Thom has proved that Stonehenge is also an instrument for working out the major cycles of the moon, which is the sun's mystically polarizing companion. The Greek writer Diodorus, referred to in the article, was emphatic about Apollo's visit every 19 years. This is now seen as a direct reference to the period known as the 'year of Meton', from Meton, a Greek astronomer who practised in the fifth century BC, and who noted that 235 lunar months equal 19 solar years. This means that when 19 years have passed, the phases of the moon (first quarter, full moon, etc.) repeat themselves on the same date. Professor Thom has found all this duly noted at Stonehenge and he has also shown that Glastonbury was an important megalithic lunar observatory. The so-called 'Metonic cycle' of 19 years was a vital part of prehistoric science and was well known to the Babylonians, etc. (*Ed.*)

perfectly with Akhenaton's sun geometry and also with Stonehenge (when the diagram is placed in a reverse direction), and furthermore with the flattened stone circles in the British Isles whose geometry has been demonstrated by Professor Thom. And as if this wasn't enough the same intricate angular divisions appear again, turning up in one of the vast ground drawings of Nasca, in the Peruvian desert. It has been called a flower, but it is the most geometric of specimens. Another 'flower' is almost an exact replica, with its six petals and stalk, of the central design in the maze at Chartres cathedral. And yet another pattern depicts a variation on the path of a maze (see diagram).

To me the most intriguing of these drawings is a kind of geometrical device, weapon or tool, with hooks. This inviting-looking shape positively encourages one to dream up ways of generating cosmic energy. Its twisting form demonstrates the basic principles of a double-image threefold maze. The maze principle can be applied to any number; it doesn't have to be on a fourfold basis, as it usually occurs. However, with uneven numbers the coilings take on the complexity of a cross-section of a cabbage or possibly more like those of a brain.

We may think we are rather forward-looking in trying to find links between all ancient civilizations, but when it comes to reading the works of the nineteenth-century writer and occultist James Churchward, we realize that we are positively latecomers, just filling in a few gaps. It so often happens that official science limps behind the inspired guesses of the pioneers and this case is probably no exception. It seems that wherever we look we find traces of attempts to develop human culture within the framework of universal harmony. Schwaller de Lubicz says of the ancient Egyptians: 'Causal Unity is All and the Universe which results can only be formed of *fractions* of this Unity. Thus all pharaonic arithmetic is founded on Unity and its fractions and then on a return to Unity.'

In the booklet *Chartres Maze*, Keith Critchlow quotes Alain de Lille (twelfth century): 'Number binds all things . . . rules the world, orders the globe, moving the stars, tying together the elements and marrying souls to bodies, earth to heaven, the celestial to the transitory.'

Of Kepler (1571-1630) it is written: 'Because of his firm faith in the order of creation he believed with almost fanatical fervour that there must be some regularity in the relationship between the mathematical concept of "harmony" in the solar system, believing he had thus further extended his search for unification by marrying together intervals in the musical scale with the angular velocities of the planets.'

And our own Dr John Dee, Queen Elizabeth I's scholarly mathematician and astrologer, drew out what he called the 'Hieroglyphic Monad', a geometrical formula founded on the sign for the planet Mercury, which he stated was a diagram of universal synthesis. He further advised those who did not understand to be silent. Perhaps he would allow me to speak one word since I can show why his special number 252 is so important! Glastonbury is a potent magnet. It was Christopher Rudman, a projective geometer living close by at the heart of the Zodiac, who drew my attention to the Monad, and of course Dee himself visited Glastonbury and declared he had found inspiration there. Did he discover the secret of the Tor maze?* But then he was a great traveller; he frequently

---

*The maze on the Tor is of similar design to the famous Cretan labyrinth and is thought to have once had well-shaped earthen walls topped with an interwoven thorn hedge. The detailed researches carried out by Geoffrey Russell

toured the continent and stayed to work in the kingdom of Bohemia, a later hotbed of Rosicrucian enlightenment.

It is very likely that Dee was an influence on Kepler, and through Kepler, on Isaac Newton. Both Dee and Newton were Cambridge men, although of course at different periods. The scientific establishment has greatly played down Newton's interest in astrology, even to the extent of allowing his unpublished papers to leave the country. I like to think that the day we return the Elgin marbles to Greece, Newton's papers may come back to us from Jerusalem!

Tracing this strong desire for wholeness down to our own days, we find it said of Einstein (1879–1955): 'He did not waver from his search to find mathematical relationship between electromagnetism and gravitation. This would be a first step in discovering common laws governing the behaviour of everything in the universe from the electron to the planets.'

So many searchers after unity and harmony. And yet you may ask, particularly you may ask of Einstein, why with this hopeful ambition in his mind did he become the herald of the most destructive splitting of unity, the unity of the atom itself, that human-kind has achieved in the last few thousand years? Perhaps because the very basis of our glorious western mathematics is inharmonious, one-directional, outgoing, infinity-seeking, unreturnable, leaving no room in space–time for destiny, the destiny of the soul's return to earth.

As a woman, dedicated by the processes of the universe to be a more intimate guardian of returning souls than a man, I protest, and how delighted I am to find that these protestations have already been heard, registered and accounted for in a recent book, *The Best Kept Secret in the World*. The author, G. Weston Wells, takes us back through Einstein, Christ, Euclid, Plato and Moses to Egypt, Babylon and beyond, and then forward to the detailed mathematics of the ninth dimension, or 9D. He says:

We have already noted that the three temporal dimensions are additive relative to space, since all are at 'right angles' to space. In the spiritual dimensions we postulated that the first of these, $7D^7$, would be the force of conscience. $7D^7$ Force however will be a very small Force being at right angles to the Forces of Space-Time D^6. We are nine dimensional creatures, created by God though we may not yet be aware of the fact.

---

have convinced him that the imagery of maze and Holy Grail are one and the same, blending in a cosmic harmony of ancient energy invocation and spiritual realization. Mr Russell sees the *whole* Tor as a labyrinth and recognizes that the mound must have been artificially sculpted by expert interpreters of psychological patterns who combined psychic insight with intuitive geomantic sensitivity.

The ancient game of 'troytown' was played for millennia on mazes throughout Europe, and 'Caerdroia' is the 'Welsh' (early British) term for the whole syndrome. There are intimations of fertility, death and resurrection in the maze form, its polarizing spirals creating a balance between the psychic energy that is in constant flux between two poles, sometimes called Heaven and Hell. The resolving of this metaphysical dynamic is crystallized in the physical structure of the maze pattern.

The Glastonbury Tor maze had seven sweeps or circumnavigations flowing around the carefully terraced rings. It would have been entered in the order of (running up from the base) 3.2.1.4.7.6.5) altering direction through a pre-ordained, clockwise/anti-clockwise pattern seven times. According to Russell, a final 5 path would have carried the hierophant to the summit at a very acute angle. The land movement of millennia has gradually blurred the Tor maze and many of the circuits are now hopelessly ruined. However, the spirit of Glastonbury's maze is still sacrosanct, surfacing in the minds of sensitive individuals who can still perceive power through landscape, the true experience of geomancy. (*Ed.*)

And ideas steer
By courses fixed
When Pyramids
Were planned.

It seems as if science and psychic investigation are at last coming together to help plan the future. A steady stream of books treating every aspect of the subject is well under way. But that is not all; there also seems to have arrived on earth many unusually gifted and sensitive young people. I have put out an invitation to them: 'Consider the bumble bee and bend me, yes I mean mentally bend me, a nice, safe, elegant flying machine, so that I can float gently around, looking down by day at Glastonbury's Zodiac and by night looking up, can admire the heavenly counterpart in all its glory'.

One of these children has already made a start, I gave him two pieces of wire in the right proportion and he bent me, yes mentally bent me, a beautiful little maze!

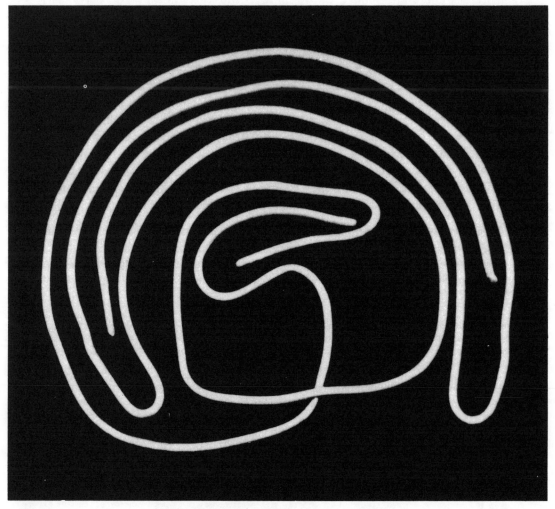

Maze mentally bent by boy of eleven.

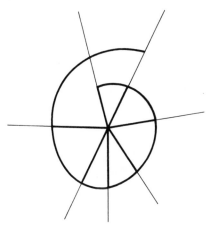

Dogon's 'Spiral of Creation'
Angles 1/3, 1/4, 1/6, 1/9, 3/20, 8/45, 77/360 and 23/72
Cf. Angle 23/72 with Egyptian sun ray angle
$1/6 + 1/7 + 5/504 = 23/72$

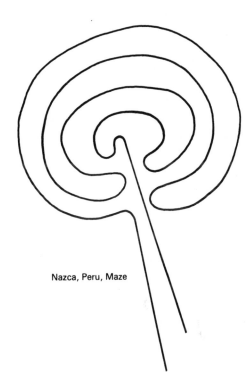

Nazca, Peru, Maze

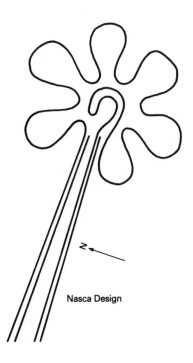

Nasca Design

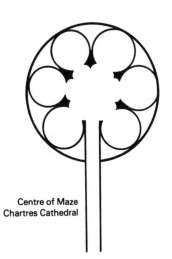

Centre of Maze
Chartres Cathedral

I would like to draw attention to a recent radio programme reporting a conference concerning the structure of matter. The speaker stressed the fact that though physicists liked to be able to reduce all to a few simple building blocks, they were becoming more and more baffled by nature's complexity. He even mentioned Arthur Koestler who has suggested that the next goal of the human mind must be a unified theory of science and mysticism. But what really impressed me was when the overall problem was referred to as an 'Atomic Maze'.

In Greek legend it was Ariadne's thread which saved Theseus after he had slain the Minotaur at the centre of the Labyrinth. Our saving thread may be a better understanding of the coiling geometry of the genetic code, seen both spiritually and physically. As the discoverer of the circulation of the blood said, 'Man is tied to eternity by the strings of the genitalia,' and as the poet, who is more concerned with the circulation of thought replies:

> From harmony, from heavenly harmony
> This universal frame began.

It would seem as if all great world teachers had access to the same cosmic truth. But you may ask, what is truth? Maybe time itself is getting short and we have only so long in which to turn aside for an answer. And this answer, which needs to be global, has to be voiced by parochial men and women.

Speaking for the average Englishwoman I would say: she may not know much about music or art or the destiny of her country, but there is *one* thing beyond jam-making, child-rearing and animal-loving, that every earnest Englishwoman knows. She knows she is fated to build Jerusalem. Her romantic sisters in Wales, Scotland and Ireland may lead their countries in creative crusades of the future; your true Englishwoman is stuck fast with the past. Her duty is to clean up the whole agonizing mess, her hope is almost an impossibility – to reconcile militant men, to set them working willingly, cheerfully, even lovingly. What a hope!

This hope, this millennial ambition, is aimed at a particular earth target, Jerusalem, but can it possibly succeed? Jerusalem, this evocative word of beginning, could it shrink in size as a geographical storm centre while growing in significance and magnificence as a symbol of harmony? It could and it must.

The Jerusalem to be built in England is one of children, colours, sounds, angles, numbers, even words and above all of stars, a remembering of the stars. And where in England have the stars been best remembered? Stonehenge, Avebury and many other circles spring to mind, but they are not the place where William Blake envisaged those walking feet of ancient time. Every country, every language may have its own answer for the Omphalos, the world navel. For us, the New Jerusalem, the New Atlantis, the 'brave new world' begins, began, at Glastonbury. It will grow again.

SEVENTH ANGLE REVEALED

I would like to add the result of my most recent research, which seems to indicate that the ideas I have been suggesting are correct. I owe this almost entirely to one book, *Gematria,* by Bligh Bond and Simcox Lea. I quote from the title page to explain their intentions: 'A Preliminary Investigation of the Cabbala contained in the Coptic Gnostic Books and of a similar Gematria in the Greek text of the New Testament'. Simcox Lea was an inquiring, scholarly, West Country vicar; Bligh Bond was an architect who in the early years of this century was concerned with excavations at Glastonbury Abbey. His findings at the Abbey, he claimed, bore out the numerical formulations of the Cabbala. This book has just recently been republished (1977).

While looking at one of the illustrations – a diagram of a cube showing seven rays descending, said in the text to symbolize the perfect or New Creation – I realized it would demonstrate my findings and bring them to some kind of completion. All it needed was to be put upon squares so that the angles could be precisely determined. The result was far better than I had hoped for: the whole scheme of angle in relation to fractional number seemed to disclose itself and be capable of proof. When I made the central ray descend in a direct vertical (it is a little uncertain in the diagram if this is intended or not) then the other rays fell into place as being the diagonals of 1×7, 1×1, 1×4, 1×2, 3×4, 3×7 and 4×3 rectangles. When I read that the sides of the cube are figured at 100, it was another proof of my being on the right lines, since the sides of my cube, the hypotenuses of 3.4.5 triangles, could be any multiple of five.

The next thing was to find a large enough number to accommodate the proportions of the rays. I started with a modest 5040, but soon found it wasn't adequate. In the end I realized that nothing short of 5765760 would do. This number proved to have very special qualities; not only was it divisible by all numbers up to and including 13, but also all the fractional numbers of the rays were divisible by 13 and by 7 too, for good measure. But the really spectacular part of it is the repetitive number pattern of all the outstanding angles: The smallest is 132132 and the largest is 852852. This pattern exemplifies the 1/8 division of a circle, while for other divisions further diagonals have to be found.

For a 1/7 it needs to be a 1×32 diagonal which is also the hypotenuse of a triangle whose other sides are 16 and 25. Side 25 of this triangle is also the hypotenuse of a 15.20.25 triangle and the third side of the 1/7-angle triangle is the hypotenuse of a 3.4.5 triangle. Madame Blavatsky apparently stated that 'the seventh angle had not yet been revealed'. I think I am revealing it. This I suggest may have been the method by which the builders of the Great Pyramid obtained such accuracy in their use of the seventh angle.

Other divisional angles can be found with a further use of those triangles which so much later came to be called Pythagorean. There is a list of these triangles from Sumeria (c. 3000 BC) known as 'Plimpton tablet 322'. When I tried plotting them on to squared paper, I thought at first that I needed a ballroom to contain it, but then realized the paper would need to be more than a quarter of a mile square.

It seems that linear and angular measurement can be put into each other's terms in two ways: by whole numbers worked through 'Pythagorean' triangles which form a correct but limited expression, or by decimals which are only approximate but limitless. Perhaps we need to apply the two systems together for a more harmonious approach to the release of universal power.

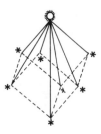

The perfect or New Creation symbolized by the cube. Source: F. Bligh Bond and T. Simcox Lea, Gematria.

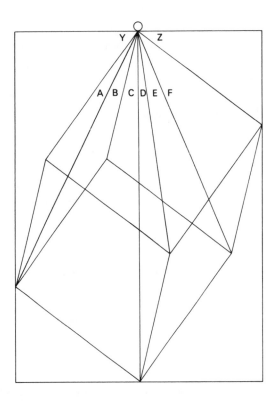

The Cube of Creation has fractional proportions of the number 5765760.

The Seven Rays are diagonals of the rectangles
$3 \times 4 \quad 1 \times 2 \quad 1 \times 4 \quad 1 \times 1 \quad 1 \times 7 \quad 3 \times 7 \quad 4 \times 3.$

All the following numbers are fractions of 5765760, and are divisible by 13 and 7:
$A = 162162 \quad B = 206206 \quad C = 220220 \quad D = 132132 \quad E = 252252 \quad F = 468468$
$Y = 852852 \quad Z = 588588$
$A + B + C = 1/8 \quad E + F = 1/8$
To accord with the precession of the equinoxes, which takes 26 000 years, the total number needs to be 576576000.

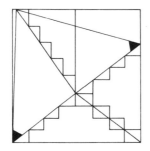

Seventh angle decoded.
Triangle with two 1/7 angles: height 25; base 40.
Triangle with two 49/480 angles: height 12; base 12.
Triangle with two 71/480 angles: height 16; base 12.
Triangle with one 49/480 angle: 15.20.25.

Great pyramid.

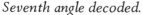

I know I have only made a tentative beginning, but it does seem that I may be working towards what John Michell describes in *City of Revelation:* 'Throughout his work Plato makes guarded reference to a secret canon of numbers that applies universally to every aspect of human life and activity.' And if I am called to book because I am envisaging space to be straight whereas really it is curved, I would reply: perhaps it is both, the way energy is both waves and particles – the union of opposites, the secret of the universe.

GLASTONBURY AND THE AMERICAN PRESIDENTIAL CONNECTION

I would like to end where I began, at the heart of the Glastonbury Zodiac, but to do so I shall first have to cross the Atlantic. An article in an American magazine *East West* by the historian Andrew E. Rothovius was brought to my attention. It had the intriguing title, 'The Adams Family and the Grail Tradition: the Untold Chronicle of the Dragon Persecution'.

To American ears mention of the Adams family rings a bell: John Adams was their second president and he lived to be ninety years old. In 1823, three years before he died, he had a flat, inscribed stone put on the top of the grave of his great-great-grandfather who had come to America as a settler in 1639. It reads, 'In memory of Henry Adams who took his flight from the Dragon persecution in Devonshire in England and alighted with 8 sons near Mount Wollaston'. Later historians have wrongly concluded that he was fleeing from the persecution of Puritans. Not at all, it was just the reverse, for he was not a Puritan. He was a 'Dragon' fleeing from a far more esoteric persecution.

Who were the Dragons then? It seems they were a group of far-sighted people who looked backwards to the ancient megalithic knowledge of the precession of the equinoxes and forward to the hope that a more harmonious way of life could be established in America. In earlier times the pole star had been the head of the constellation Draco or dragon. The Welsh still have the dragon as their symbol, as do the Chinese, and Mary Caine has discovered the Draco stars depicted in the Glastonbury Zodiac.*

At the beginning of the seventeenth century some famous names were connected with this approach. Thomas Hariot the mathematician, his pupil Sir Walter Raleigh, Dr John Dee, Christopher Marlowe, George Chapman, the translator of Homer, and many others. They were sometimes said to belong to the 'School of Night' and were feared for a possible association with witchcraft. Their perhaps slightly unbalanced idealism was gently mocked by Shapespeare in *Love's Labour's Lost*. This combination of extremes is no new thing; our own age has had its 'flower power' and its Manson massacres.

Seen in this context it is fascinating to relate that the Adams family came from a village at the heart of the Glastonbury Zodiac, Barton St David. Ancient wisdom in their blood (and genes) no doubt.

From time to time traces of this wisdom seem to surface in members of the Royal family. Perhaps Henry, Prince of Wales, the son of James I, was a case in point. He was a brilliant youth who many hoped would prove to be another Arthur. Raleigh, who was by now imprisoned in the Tower, wrote his *History of the World* as instruction for the young prince. In return he protected Raleigh's life, but alas Henry died of a fever at eighteen and Raleigh was summarily executed. The Dragons began to lose heart, some lingering on in Devonshire as a persecuted minority, some emigrating to the new colonies that were eventually to become the United States.

(The precession of the equinoxes through the zodiac takes 26 000 years to accomplish. I was trying to see how it fitted into my geometrical working total of 5765760; another two noughts need to be added, I found. Then the answer is 221760, a number into which all numbers up to 12 divide. Whether this has any significance I do not know, perhaps it needs exploring from both sides of the Atlantic.)

ADDENDUM: THE MAZE PUZZLE

Why not rebuild Jerusalem straight away? Silence. Are there any children in the house? There are and that's grand because there's something to be discovered, a secret to solve. Look at these instructions found in an ancient box on Treasure Island. What do they say? 'Start at Point X.' Suppose we can't find 'X'? Anywhere will do for X as long as we all agree on its initial importance.

Start at Point X and go North for 16 steps, East for 4 steps, South 12, East 8, North 20, West 20, South 16. Return to X.

*The dragon is also recognized as a symbol for the planet-wide geodetic earth currents, known as 'dragon lines' and seen esoterically as movements of an energizing 'serpent power'. Arthur is symbolically tied to this power, being a mythical dragon-slayer whose father was Uther Pendragon or 'head dragon'. This could represent a heavily disguised esoteric notation of the age-old cult of the dragon. It is interesting that in Vermont, USA, one of the earliest settled areas (contemporaneous with the exodus of the Dragon sect), there is a town named Glastonbury. This American town has a reputation as a mysterious place; there have been many 'disappearances' over the years and numerous UFO sightings! One US correspondent of the editor has described it as a 'gateway to another dimension', surely an apt description of the British Glastonbury as well. (*Ed.*)

From X go East 16, N. 28, W. 28, S. 24, E. 8, N. 16, E. 12, S. 12. Return to X.

From X go W. 16, N. 32, E. 36, S. 36, W. 16, S. 8, E. 24, N. 52, W. 36, S. 48, E. 16. Return to X.

From X go S. 16, E. 32, N. 60, W. 56, S. 56, E. 24, N. 8, W. 16, N. 40, E. 44, S. 44, W. 16. Return to X.

How to remember what you have done? You know the story of Hansel and Gretel: they wanted to know the way home and so dropped breadcrumbs, but alas, birds ate up the crumbs and the children were lost. Well you must use *stones* if you want the way to last, but you could mark it in chalk on the road or perhaps on the playground or beside the sea on the sands.

What structure will you have found or made? That's the secret, but I'll tell you an old name for what you will be doing if you do it. It was called 'taking a trip to Jerusalem'. What should you do when you get there? Look for a door. Which door? A door with lines written over it. What lines? Well if time hasn't quite rubbed them out, they ought to say:

> Whoever seeks this hidden truth
> Must find it in their earliest youth
> Whoever grasps this secret gold
> Can only use it when they are old.

What should you do in front of the door? Knock and it will open. You're a bit scared to knock. Wait a bit and watch the door, something magical may happen. It does. Letters are there and they are the key. It isn't so much a door as a book; a book that's a door, a door that's a book. It's quite all right – it often happens in dreams. What is the book called? It's a long word. Try spelling it out. L.A.B.Y.R.I.N.T.H.S. Who is it by? A funny name. I don't expect it's funny to him so try saying it. Jorge Luis Borges.

Well done; now you're advanced enough to read and remember. You've read it through and through and it doesn't make any sense at all? Try opening it at random. That's against your principles? Try sacrificing your principles. Sacrifice is an unpleasant, unpopular word? Go on, dare to be a Daniel, open it, it won't bite you. Bravo, what page is it? One hundred and one. It's not any better, it's all a kind of crazy crossword puzzle, it's called a fiction anyway and now you're off. Goodbye. But you, on the other hand, are not. You like unravelling puzzles, go right ahead, here's the real clew:

A Phoenix death and glorious

Are you a bit scared to begin? Come along, you can start anywhere, why not go back to X, although you may find that wherever you thought you set out from, you will think you have landed up in the same place, at G . . . . y, ready for anything.

Am I insulting you all with this seeming baby talk? Well let's get out our ABC and try again. Hum it after me if you can't quite manage the words.

A re you a B it scared to begin, C ome along you can start anywhere, why not go back to X, although you may fin D that wh E rever you thought you had set out F rom, you will have landed up in the same place, a G ready for A.

You see the idea? If so, well done. You'll be counting next, all the way to seven and eight, even reaching nine, singing beautifully too I'll be bound. Then there will be all those -ographies and -ologies, not to mention the -isms, till you are ready to get back to X and X will be G and G will be X and X will be Goodbye!

You don't want to say Goodbye before you know who I *am*? Oh surely you know me, I am the one whose job it is to Amuse and Amaze.

Recommended Books

Blake, William. 'Jerusalem'.

Borges, Jorge Luis. *Labyrinths*. Penguin, 1970.

Brou, Willy and Marcel. *Le Secret des Druides*.

Burton, Maurice. *The Life of Insects*. Macdonald Education, 1973.

Chatelain, Maurice. *Nos Ancêtres Venus du Cosmos*.

Churchward, James. *The Lost Continent of Mu*. Spearman.

Critchlow, Keith. *Chartres Maze*.

Dee, John. *The Hieroglyphic Monad*.

Dryden, John. 'Ode upon St Cecilia's Day'.

Harvey, William. *Lecture Notes*.

Ivimy, John. *The Sphinx and the Megaliths*. Abacus, 1976.

de Lubict, Schwaller. *Le Temple de l'Homme*.

Michell, John. *The View Over Atlantis*. Sago Press, 1969.

Reiche, Maria. *Peruvian Ground Drawings*. Kunstraum (Munchen).

Roberts, Anthony. *Atlantean Traditions in Ancient Britain*. Rider, 1977.

Saunders, M. W. *Destiny Mars*. Downs, 1975.

Shakespear, W. and Rowley, W. *The Birth of Merlin*. London, 1662.

Temple, Robert. *The Sirius Mystery*. Sidgwick & Jackson, 1976.

Waters, Frank. *Mexico Mystique*. Sage Books, 1975.

Wells, G. Weston. *The Best Kept Secret in the World*. Regency Press, 1975.

Westlake, Aubrey. *The Pattern of Health*. Robinson & Watkins, 1973.

Whyte, L. L. *Accent on Form*. Greenwood (Westport, Ct.).

CHAPTER TWELVE

Glastonbury-Jerusalem, Paradise on Earth:

A Revelation Examined

JOHN MICHELL

The special place which Glastonbury occupies in English sacred geography, a distinction inherited from very early times, is acknowledged in its legendary claim to the title of England's Jerusalem. Set in a mythic landscape, with its sacred springs and holy mountain, the site seems to attract to itself spontaneously the attributes of the archetypal holy city or cosmological world-centre, which in traditional societies is located in the national temple and state oracle. Such places were recognized by ancient rulers as natural control centres, where political authority was sanctified by a magical science involving the fusion of cosmic and terrestrial forces. This fusion was expressed symbolically in every feature of the temple and its environment. The Omphalos or altar within the sanctuary of the temple was a formal image of the whole world; so was the sanctuary, the temple, the surrounding city, and the landscape in which it stood.* The whole complex and each of its parts expressed the idea of paradise on earth. When the unity of the ancient world was lost, the symbol of the holy city, as in St John's Revelation, kept alive the memory of a golden age and of its promised restoration.

The ground-plan of the holy city and of the cosmic structures within it derives from a canon or code of numerology whose origin is mysterious and of great antiquity. It represents an ideal, the perfectly balanced universe, which combines in harmony all the creative powers, symbolized in numerical relationships, and their diverse products. Its magical function, at a natural generation centre was, in accordance with the principle 'like attracts like', to make active in human society the influences of a perfectly ordered cosmos. The priests of the temple, corresponding to the guardians of Plato's ideal city, had exclusive charge of education, initiation and advancement, and were careful that all institutions, crafts, music, ritual, and architecture remained true to the same proportional canon.

In *City of Revelation*, the basic numerical structure of the old cosmic canon and the

---

*A spectacular example of this spiritually organized landscape geomancy is to be found in Peking, where the Imperial Palace, its adjacent mounds, lakes, roads, etc., form a balancing microcosmic pattern laid out to strictly canonical astrological principles. (*Ed.*)

geometrical figure derived from it is set out. It is known as the 'New Jerusalem diagram' because it is developed from the given form and dimensions of the New Jerusalem in Revelation 21. The same secret code is behind Plato's delineation of his ideal Republic, and in a much earlier period it was expressed architecturally in the ground-plan of Stonehenge. All these were based on the same New Jerusalem diagram, representing the ideal

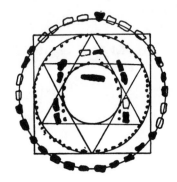

The New Jerusalem diagram applied to Stonehenge. The diameter of the inner ring is 39·6 feet, the same as that of the circle contained within St Mary's Chapel, Glastonbury. The outer circle of sarsen stones has a circumference of 316·8 feet, the same as Bligh Bond's circle of twelve cells, and the square also measures 316·8 feet around its perimeter.

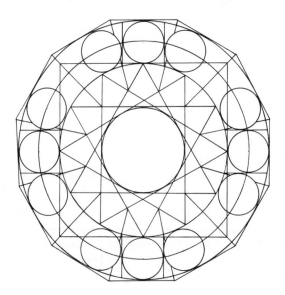

The developed New Jerusalem diagram, here reproduced from City of Revelation, *has since been refined by the mathematician, Robert Forrest, who calculates that the enclosing twelve-sided figure has four sides measuring 3280 feet, eight sides of 3271 feet and a total area of 120 million square feet.*

universe, study of which reveals the cosmology that upheld the ancient world. The subject of this essay is the identification at Glastonbury of this very same cosmological pattern, implying that Glastonbury, like Stonehenge, was a cosmo-magical centre, an English Jerusalem. Details of the matter are given in Chapter four of *City of Revelation*, from which is reproduced the explanatory diagram. In summary, the legendary twelve

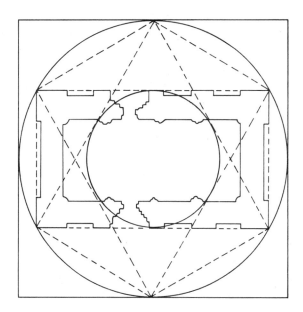

Plan of St Mary's Chapel, showing its relationship to the twelve hides of Glastonbury. Source: John Michell, City of Revelation.

The diagram shows that ground-plan of St Mary's Chapel, Glastonbury, the site of St Joseph's circular wattle church, said to be the first in Christendom, of which William of Malmesbury wrote: 'The Church at Glastonbury did none other men's hands make, but actual disciples of Christ built it.'

The present chapel was built after the fire of 1184 which destroyed the ancient buildings, and its dimensions were set out to conform to the sacred geometry of the original foundation. The surrounding area was known as the twelve hides.

These traditions are combined in the figure above. The dimensions of the existing chapel are 39·6 X 68·6, a ratio of 1 =√3. A property of the √3 rectangle is that the diameter of the circle contained within it is half the diameter of the circle in which the rectangle itself is contained. Here the diameter of the inner circle is 39·6 feet, of the outer circle 79·2 feet.

The outer circle is now enclosed within a square. The side of this square measures 79·2 feet; its perimeter is 316·8 feet and its area 1·44 acres or 0·012 hides. It is therefore a microcosm of the New Jerusalem which is a square of side twelve furlongs or 7920 feet and area 1440 acres or twelve hides each of 120 acres.

hides of Glaston and the actual dimensions of the St Mary's Chapel on the site of the original foundation, form a geometric harmony with measurements corresponding to those of the New Jerusalem diagram.*

In the course of his remarkable work at Glastonbury half a century ago, F. Bligh Bond was led to reconstruct the cosmological plan of the original foundation. In his two books. *The Gate of Remembrance* and *The Company of Avalon*, he describes his sources as a combination of archaeological work and revelation. Messages of 'scripts' purporting to come from Ambrosius, a twelfth-century prior at Glastonbury Abbey, were received by a medium of his acquaintance. These referred to the mystical dimensions of the original Glastonbury foundation. So Bligh Bond interpreted them; and reviewing the affair in the light of modern research, we find evidence of genuine revelation. For the dimensions as Bond's friend received them are the very same as those of the New Jerusalem diagram. Here are the details of this extraordinary matter.

On the day of St Michael and All Angels, 1921, Bond's friend was inspired to take up her pen, which wrote automatically the following message from the monk, Ambrosius:

First let there be a Circle – ronde CXXX paces – gressus: on it XII cubiculi. Ronde outer, CCCLX with fence. In midst of alle, Ronde Chirche, but XVIII crosst: wall of mudd and stane III thick – total XXIV in your measures.

Outer fence in olde measures, by steppes – paces. Celles not all equal in ring: two at sud-linea bifurcata – lo! I have it thee shown aforetyme; because of grunde. But near equal.

This is a very good, accurate description of the New Jerusalem diagram fifty years before it was discovered. Bond recognized it as applying also to Glastonbury, where he had found traces of a ring of twelve cells (the XII cubiculi of the script), conforming to the legend that the twelve followers of St Joseph on their journey from the Holy Land to Glastonbury, had dwelt in anchorites' cells around the central church. Three measurements are given in the script:

> Outer fence, circumference 360 paces;
> Inner ring with twelve huts, circumference 130 paces;
> Circular church in centre, outer diameter 24 'in your measures'.

The length of the Roman pace is conventionally given as between 2·43 and 2·44 feet. Bond, however, proposed an arbitrary length of 2.47 feet because, to fit in with his own numerological theory, he wanted the circumference of the outer fence to measure 888 feet, the esoteric number of Jesus. Bond did not 'bend' the evidence to suit his theory; he admitted that his excessive value for the pace was speculative; and his care in recording the exact words of the original script is rewarded by the exciting discovery that the figure detailed in the script is the New Jerusalem diagram as exhibited in the plan of Stonehenge.

*The 'ideal' dimensions of the chapel are 39·6 X 68·6 feet. Bligh Bond in *Gematria* states that the measured width of the plinth at the western end is 40 ft 1 in, some six inches in excess of our figure, but he noticed that joints have opened in the masonry, on account of which the original measurement would have been slightly less. The length he estimated to be √3 times the original width. Other slightly different measurements have since been proposed. It may be that decay and modern restoration work have made absolute precision impossible. What is certain however, is that the ground-plan of the chapel has always been reputed to preserve the mystical dimensions of the cosmological centre located on that spot at the beginning of the Christian era.

Giving the pace the exact, more conventional value of 2·437 feet, the circumference of the two rings become: outer, 360 paces or 877·3 feet; inner, 130 paces or 316·8 feet. These measures correspond exactly to the mean dimensions of two of the rings at Stonehenge, namely the circle of Aubrey Holes and the sarsen stone circle with the lintels respectively.

There remains the third measure given in the script, that of the original circular church, whose diameter, so Bond supposed, is preserved in the width of St Mary's Chapel. In the script the diameter is given as 'total 24 in your measures', which leaves uncertain the unit of measure referred to. If the circular church had the same width as the St Mary Chapel, its diameter was 39·6 feet, and that means that the unit we must take is the old English and masonic tenth part of a pole or rod, equal to 1·65 feet. This unit is the same as the Sumerian cubit displayed on the rule excavated at Lagash in 1871 (see A. E. Berriman, *Historical Metrology*), and it is inherent in the metrology of the New Jerusalem diagram. Twenty-four of these cubits make 39·6 feet. If this was the diameter of the central shrine at Glastonbury, it is the same as the blue-stone semi-circle which opens out towards the midsummer sunrise at Stonehenge.

Comparison of the New Jerusalem diagram with the figure derived from Bligh Bond's script leaves no doubt that in some extraordinary way Bond and his collaborator received in outline the ancient cosmological formula which was unknown in their time; and the fact that it was unknown and that Bond misinterpreted it makes the whole affair deeply mysterious and intriguing. Elsewhere Bond suggested a link between Glastonbury and Stonehenge, of which there is now more evidence in that the orientation of the Abbey and the axis of the town of Glastonbury point directly towards Stonehenge to the east. This feature is shown in diagrams in this book illustrating contributions by Kenneth Knight, Donald Cyr and Nigel Pennick as well as in *The View Over Atlantis*. Another striking correspondence between Bond's script and the New Jerusalem diagram is in the arrangement of the twelve circles or cells around the ring of perimeter 316·8 feet (this length, which is exactly a hundredth part of six miles, is also the mean circumference of the Stonehenge sarsen circle). In both diagrams they are not spaced evenly round the circle but, as in the words of the script, 'Celles not all equal in ring'.

Our conclusion is that the temples at Glastonbury and Stonehenge, both natural centres of the earth's living energies, were at some remote period designed according to the same plan and to fulfil the same function as the archetypal 'holy city' described by Plato and St John. These political-religious-magical centres operated as centres of fusion between cosmic and terrestrial forces and, according to legend, served to transmit the fertilizing spirit raised there to every other part of the country by means of an underground system of veins and channels. Thus beneath every ancient temple are subterranean chambers, labyrinths, watercourses and other traditional apparatus of the chthonic deities. Elsewhere in this book Ann Pennick summarizes accounts and legends of these nether regions at Glastonbury. A. Watkins and other writers have found correspondences between legendary underground tunnels and the mystical straight alignments of sites (leys) characteristic of the megalithic science. There are also growing indications that the confluence of leys at Glastonbury formed a greater model of the New Jerusalem diagram. Anthony Roberts's montage of sections from the local one-inch map

The landscape of the New Jerusalem. These sacredly geographic points collectively form the tapestry of the 'New Jerusalem' ley alignments. The whole vast structure is significantly orientated towards the magnetic north, the magnetic dimension being integral to the overall interpretation of geomancy. The sacred geometry here emblazoned across the earth is symbolically significant. It represents the fusion of all religions, philosophies and cosmologies, being timeless in form and magically reflective of the Macrocosmos, termed by the Hermeticists as the Empyrean. It is an ultimate expression of the prime geomantic formula, 'as above, so below'. (Ed.)

Map arranged by Anthony Roberts

a. St Joseph's Chapel, Glastonbury Abbey. Market cross at cross-roads (High St and Magdalene St). Ancient chapel in precincts of almshouses (Magdalene St).
b. Peak of Glastonbury Tor.
c. Street parish church (Holy Trinity), site of St Gildas' cell.
d. Butleigh Church (St Leonards, twelfth century).
e. Straight road near Butleigh church leading towards church at Kingsweston.
f. Windmill Hill, south-east of Glastonbury. Cross-roads at Ham Street.
g. Monument on other Windmill Hill, south-west of Glastonbury (Taurus effigy in Zodiac).
h. Peak of Burrow Mount or Mump, mini-Tor near Athelney.
i. Righton's Grave Hill (triangulation point). (Polden Hound effigy.)
j. Burford cross.
k. Small mark stone at Yarley cross-roads. Straight stretches of road each side.
l. Cross-roads near Bleadney with very small mark stone at their centre.
m. Meare Farm (medieval site).
n. Straight road and canal from Meare. This alignment also runs to the left of Brent Knoll summit.
o. Tumulus mound above Cheddar Gorge.
p. Mendip prehistoric camp and linear earthwork on Westbury Beacon, behind Stoke Woods.
q. Gorsey Bigbury henge monument. Possibility of ancient Gorsedd at this site.
r. Burrington church (Holy Trinity, thirteenth century). Straight road, cross-roads and straight track.
s. Church at Brockley (St Nicholas, thirteenth century).
t. Church at Tickenham (St Quiricus & Julietta, thirteenth century). The alignment runs on to eastern ditch of Cadbury Camp earthwork on Tickenham Hill.

u. Wells Cathedral.
v. Wells market cross.
w. Ponter's Ball prehistoric earthwork, north-eastern tip (Capricorn's horn in Zodiac).
x. Cross-roads at Asney; piece of straight road pointing west towards next cross-roads.

(Drawn by Anthony Roberts after the map in John Michell, *City of Revelation*.)

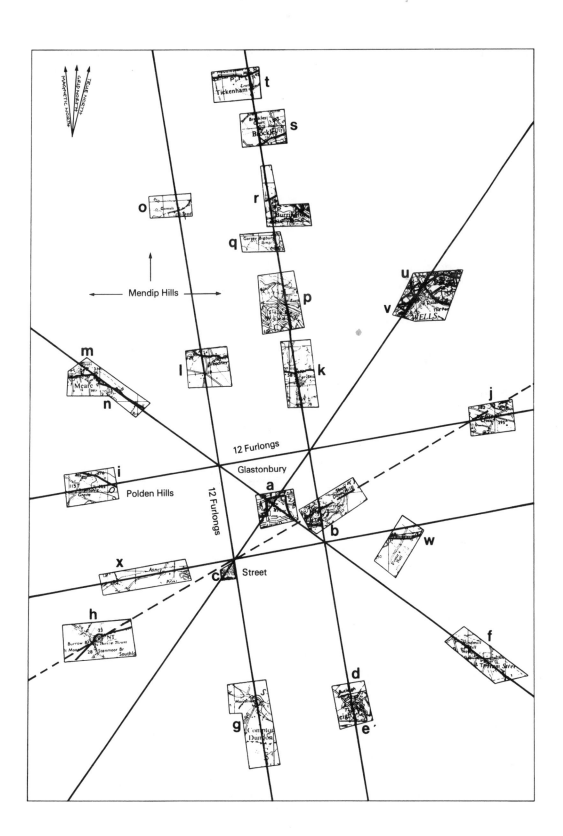

MAGNETIC NORTH
GRID NORTH
TRUE NORTH

o

t

s

r

Burri...

q

Gorse Bigbury...

Mendip Hills

p

u

v
WELLS

m

Meare

n

l

...copney

k

i

117...

Polden Hills

j

12 Furlongs

Glastonbury

a

b

w

12 Furlongs

x

Asney

c

Street

h

NT
Burrow B...
Moor
Stenmoor Br
Southl...

f

Windmill
Hill
Turnham Street

g
Compton
Dundon

d

e

shows a well-defined ley coinciding with the eastern side of a square containing twelve hides (1440 acres) centred on the St Mary Chapel; other alignments, including the Burrow Mump–Glastonbury Tor–Avebury line, appear to contribute to this geometric pattern.* This implies that the New Jerusalem pattern had been imposed on the Glastonbury landscape long before the Christian foundation, when the ideal of Paradise on Earth was reinstituted in the mysteries of the esoterically oriented Celtic church.

ADDENDUM: SOURCES OF THE NEW JERUSALEM DIAGRAM

The cosmic scheme described here, and in more detail in *City of Revelation,* was received from five sources.

1. The precisely measured and published dimensions of the ground-plan of Stonehenge, built during the third millennium BC.

2. The dimensions given of Plato's ideal city in *The Republic,* written in about 500 BC.

3. St John's holy city, New Jerusalem, whose dimensions are given in Revelation 21, dating from the early Christian era.

4. The dimensions, actual and legendary, of the Celtic Christian foundation at Glastonbury, the 'English Jerusalem'.

5. The mysterious revelation to F. Bligh Bond of the measurements in the Glastonbury sacred geometry.

The existence of the same scheme in such diverse contexts is something that demands an attempt at historical interpretation. The earliest and most complete example of the New Jerusalem diagram is at Stonehenge. Astronomers have shown that Stonehenge is a temple of the twelve gods, in that alignments from it indicate the four solstitial rising and setting points of the sun and the eight extreme positions of the moon – twelve directions in all. These alignments fit in with the symmetrical geometry of the Stonehenge scheme in a way that seems almost miraculous. Clearly the final building of Stonehenge coincided with the establishment of a remarkable form of society governed by a caste of philosopher-initiates, of which traditions remain in the heroic legends from the Bronze Age.†

The Stonehenge ground-plan, based on the New Jerusalem diagram, reveals the cosmology of that age. At some time and for reasons unknown the society vanished, but a succession of initiates evidently preserved its cosmology. This ancient inheritance was available to Plato when he came to delineate his ideal society as a proposed reconstruction of the 'artificial golden age' in the remote past. St John, who is said to have been an initiate into the Celtic mysteries, drew on the same esoteric source when describing his

---

*In Somerset a hide of land measured 120 acres. The ancient 'twelve hides of Glastonbury' would have totalled 1440 acres and if this area is reckoned as a square, its side would be twelve furlongs in length. Twelve thousand furlongs is the length given by St John in Revelation 21 as the side of the transcendent New Jerusalem. In the physical Glastonbury landscape the twelve-furlong square forms a perfect, proportional microcosm to its vast heavenly counterpart. (*Ed.*)

†It is thought that much of this prehistoric esoteric science formed the basis of the later Druidical schools in Britain, which of course had links with the Greek Pythagoreans. (*Ed.*)

holy city, and the virtually simultaneous appearance of the New Jerusalem diagram at Glastonbury, the citadel of Celtic esotericism, may be seen in terms of an attempt to give form to St John's idea.

Yet, with the case of Bligh Bond, we have remarkable evidence that the survival of the New Jerusalem scheme of ancient cosmology has not been dependent solely on its transmission over thousands of years to successive generations of philosophers. St John described his receipt of it as a mystical experience, perhaps the climax of his initiation. Bond, as we have seen, had it through the medium of automatic writing, as a spontaneous revelation. This implies that the New Jerusalem diagram is something more than an artificial product of human genius. There is an archetypal or pre-existent quality about it that makes it reappear at various times, suggesting that it is in some way inherent in both the macrocosm and human nature. It occurs typically at times of crisis or renewal, as, for example during the tragic Anabaptist rising at Munster during the sixteenth century. Of the power of its influence on human affairs there can be no doubt; but this power, like that of all archetypes, is amoral, producing either catastrophe or renaissance depending on how it is interpreted by the people receiving it.

Recommended Books

Berriman, A. *Historical Metrology*. Dent, 1953.

Bond, F. Bligh and Lea, T. Simcox. *Gematria: A Preliminary Investigation of the Cabbalah,* etc. RILKO, 1977

Borst, Lyle B. *Megalithic Software*. Twinbridge Press, 1975.

Michell, John. *City of Revelation*. Garnstone Press, 1972.

Michell, John. *The View Over Atlantis*. Sago Press, 1969.

Afterword

COLIN WILSON

A great deal of this book is intended for readers who are already familiar with the notion of ley lines, power centres and terrestrial zodiacs. But there must still be many who have only a nodding aquaintance with such ideas, and who consequently find many of the contributions completely baffling. So let me start by making allowance for these neophytes, and explaining briefly the curious occult philosophy of leys that has begun to emerge in the past ten years and which is still in a vigorous state of development.

Shortly after the war, a retired solicitor named Guy Underwood, who had spent most of his life at Bradford-on-Avon (not far from Stonehenge), decided to devote the days of his retirement to studying some of the prehistoric sites that abound in Wiltshire. His approach to the problem would strike many archaeologists as highly eccentric, for his chief instrument of exploration was a dowsing rod.

Nowadays, it is moderately respectable to talk about dowsing, since authorities like Sir William Barrett have written books on the subject. A century ago, it was widely regarded as a rural superstition, like fairies or wishing wells; Sabine Baring-Gould has a chapter on dowsing in a book called *Curious Myths of the Middle Ages,* where it can be found among chapters on Prester John, the Wandering Jew, and the Holy Grail. In fact, the majority of people nowadays would probably agree that dowsers *do* seem to be able to locate water, and that it is simply another of those unexplained phenomena like flashes of precognition ('I *knew* we'd get a letter from Aunt Jane this morning'), or the fakir's ability to lie on a bed of nails. It is less widely realized that *most* people can dowse – my own estimate is nine out of ten – and that practically all children can do it first time. No one quite knows why a forked twig – or two strips of plastic tied together at the end – will twist downwards when they pass over underground water; but for some reason, they do. Further speculation must wait until later.

Why did Guy Underwood choose to investigate prehistoric sites with a dowsing rod? Because he wanted to test an assertion by two other dowsers, Captain Robert Boothby and Reginald Smith, that most prehistoric sites are constructed over water – either underground streams or blind springs (springs that never reach the surface). A few weeks' investigation convinced him of the correctness of this claim. Above long barrows and hillside figures cut in the chalk, the rod responded negatively, as it always did for water – that is, the left hand took most of the 'pull'. But at this point, he began to detect another force that caused a positive response – a pull on the right hand. It seemed to be some kind of magnetic force, and this came in two distinct varieties, one wide and one narrow. He called the wide variety 'aquastats' and the narrow ones 'track lines'. And all three seemed to play an important part in the placing of holy sites like Stonehenge. In fact, aquastats and water lines often seemed to run together along the same course. When this happened they seemed to play an important part in laying out sacred sites, and for this reason Underwood called them 'holy lines'.

The baffling question, of course, was *why* ancient man should have wanted to construct his sacred sites on underground springs, or whatever.* What difference could it possibly make? But then, this is part of an even larger question. Why did he want to erect so many standing stones anyway? Barrows are understandable, since they are ancient graves or tombs. And a circle like Stonehenge *looks* a little like a temple – one can easily imagine strange torch-light ceremonies taking place there, and crowds of worshippers kneeling to the rising sun. But the average stone circle – like Boscawen-Un in Cornwall or the Rollright Stones in Oxfordshire, or Long Meg and her daughters near Penrith – doesn't look in the least like an ancient temple. It would seem just as logical to think of them as the site of some prehistoric game – perhaps an early form of baseball or rounders . . .

In 1921 a Hereford businessman named Alfred Watkins thought he had discovered an important clue. He seems to have been riding around the countryside on 30 June when he observed that various farm gates, stones, churches and ancient mounds seemed to fall on straight lines. Study of Ordnance Survey maps verified his suspicion; it seemed clear that many sacred sites *do*, for some reason, lie in straight lines. Single upright stones are often used to mark these 'lines' in valleys. Watkins concluded that the lines, which he called 'leys', were intended as trade routes in a land without roads.

If that was so, then the upright stones were little more than milestones. But if Underwood was right, they were rather more than that, for they were placed above areas to which his dowsing rod responded strongly. That made little sense either . . .

In the late 1960s, a scholarly recluse named John Michell combined both ideas into a new theory – although it is unlikely that he had read Underwood's *Pattern of the Past*, published posthumously in 1969.† Michell pointed out that the Chinese also have their own equivalent of ley lines, which they call dragon paths, or *lung mei*; they believe they

---

*It is now generally recognized that underground water plays a vital role in all forms of dowsing. It is equally recognized that most megalithic stones are sited above water (blind springs, streams, etc.). Water generates a vigorous static field, and many contemporary dowsers suspect that the energies of this field are channelled (and amplified) by the stones erected above them. This theory has been enhanced by recent (1977) dowsing experiments conducted upon the Tor near the time of the summer solstice. It is well known that this holy hill is liberally channelled with underground water courses and when a group of dowsers congregated around the broken megalith known as the Living Rock, a variety of geodetic phenomena manifested through their instruments. The earth currents are strongly resonant on the Tor and the editor was an eye-witness to these events! (*Ed.*)

†John Michell included a brief summary of *Pattern of the Past* in an afterword to his *The View over Atlantis*, published in 1969. (*Ed.*)

are the lines of some sacred earth force, and built temples at important intersections. Oddly enough, numerous ley lines in England are associated with dragons, for many churches dedicated to St Michael stand on leys, and St Michael (like St George) is a traditional dragon killer. Another enthusiastic student of these matters, the late T. C. Lethbridge, pointed out that many churches dedicated to St Michael are built on ancient pagan sites dedicated to the sun-god Lugh (a Celtic version of Lucifer); St Michael was Lucifer's leading opponent. The Church took over the pagan site for its place of worship, and replaced Lucifer with his Christian opposite. But then, *why* did the Church want to build its places of worship on the sites of old pagan temples? You would have thought they'd have avoided such 'unholy' places. Could it, Lethbridge wondered, have been something in the earth itself that made the place holy? This is a strange idea to the modern mind, for which holiness is a purely abstract quality associated with faith (i.e. wishful thinking).

There is another basic objection to John Michell's identification of ley lines with the Chinese dragon paths; in China, it is the wandering path – like Chesterton's rolling English road – that is sacred; the straight line is associated with powers of darkness. Yet Underwood himself had provided a king of answer to that one. His awuastats and other geodetic lines often run in straight lines for short distances. And of course, you could quite easily trace a long line, tens of miles long, that *included* 'geodesics' along a great deal of its length.

When Lethbridge visited a stone circle called The Merry Maidens near Penzance in Cornwall, he found that the nineteen stones of the circle seemed to contain *some* kind of force; when he held a pendulum (an alternative to a dowsing rod) in one hand, and placed the other on the stone, the hand resting on the stone began to tingle as if a mild electric current was running through it, and the pendulum in the other hand began to revolve like an aeroplane propeller. Noting that many stone circles have legends of dancing associated with them – girls turned into stone for dancing on the Sabbath, etc. – he speculated that perhaps prehistoric worshippers somehow *charged* the stones with a kind of vital electricity by dancing round them. But as to what the stones were actually used for, Lethbridge could only offer the suggestion (which he admits to be little more than fantasy) that they might have been intended as beacons for flying saucers!

Oddly enough, the suggestion is not quite as mad as it looks at first sight. John Michell seems to have become interested in ley lines because there had been so many UFO sightings over them – particularly in the area of Warminster, not far from Stonehenge. There have also been many in the area of Glastonbury, particularly around the Tor. Both Warminster and Glastonbury are the crossing points of several leys. Moreover, investigators of the supernatural have observed that ghost and poltergeist phenomena often seem to happen at nodal points on leys (i.e. crossings).

In 1976 I made a series of programmes for BBC 2 on various occult phenomena, and one was about Ardachie Lodge, on the edge of Loch Ness. In 1952, a Mr and Mrs MacDonald moved into the lodge as housekeepers and their first night was made highly unpleasant by footsteps, knockings, and the sight of a strange old lady crawling around on all fours with a candle in her hand. The phenomena continued for many months, and were investigated by the Society for Psychical Research. The previous owner of the house *had* been an arthritic old lady, who crawled around the place holding a candle at night . . . But Mrs MacDonald insisted she had never had any psychic experience before. They finally left, and the house was pulled down. After the programme had been broadcast in early 1977, I received a letter from a Mr Stephen Jenkins, a Croydon schoolmaster, who told me that Ardachie stood on a crossing point of half a dozen ley lines, all of which he specified with references to the Ordnance Survey map.

Mr Jenkins, I discovered, was something of an expert on leys, having been investigating them for more than a quarter of a century. His interesting book, *The Undiscovered Country,* gives many examples of rather odd phenomena that have taken place on ley lines – especially at nodal points. At a nodal point in Cornwall, as a teenager, he saw a shimmering 'phantom army' which vanished as he took a step forward. Revisiting the spot many years later, after he had learned something about leys, he again saw the 'phantom army' at precisely the same spot. He seems to feel that this is some kind of 'tape recording' of an actual historical event that has remained impressed on the area because of the ley force. He records several instances of becoming curiously dizzy at the nodal points of leys, and being totally unable to take his bearings. (I have had a similar experience near Boscawen-Un in Cornwall, and have related the incident in my book *Mysteries.*) A party of schoolboys he took to one of the nodal points experienced the same dizziness, although he had taken care not to mention his own experience. Mr Jenkins also mentions a number of 'ghosts' that have been seen on ley lines.

This would certainly not have surprised T. C. Lethbridge. His own experiences of ghosts and poltergeists (described in his book, *Ghost and Ghoul*) led him also to the conclusion that water has some kind of a 'field' (the force to which the dowsing rod responds), and that this field can somehow record strong emotions. These in turn, can be picked up accidentally by anyone who is sensitive to them, especially dowsers. Lethbridge knew nothing about leys, but he believed that there are other kinds of field in addition to the one associated with water, and that these can also record events and emotions. In some cases a whole battle might be recorded (which may explain why so many people have heard booming cannons and the clash of arms at the site of the Battle of Edgehill). All the evidence suggests that crossing points of ley lines provide the ideal conditions for such recordings. This may explain, for example, the ghost that haunts one of the chalets in the back garden of Geoffrey Ashe, at the foot of Glastonbury Tor. The house was once owned by the famous occultist Dion Fortune, who probably used the chalet for magical purposes; now the ghost of an old woman is often seen – or felt – in the chalet. (Mr Ashe tells me that his children pay no attention to it – they feel it is basically benevolent.) Similarly, a Mr John Cox of Highbury has told me of all kinds of curious sights and sounds in an old pub he purchased; perhaps the strangest thing about these phenomena is that he often hears events (i.e. workmen making alterations in a room) *before* they happen, as if the ley – on which the pub stands – causes some kind of 'time slip'.

But perhaps one of the most interesting clues to the actual use of ley lines is offered by Mr Francis Hitching, who remarks that the medicine men of the Sioux Indians in South Dakota renew their powers of healing and second-sight by rubbing their spines against a megalith called Standing Rock. This is almost certainly the kind of use to which the standing stones were put by our Stone Age ancestors. Places like Glastonbury, Stonehenge, and Avebury were holy because the earth forces were unusually concentrated at such points. Our ancestors must have known of various ways of using these forces. The precise details are a matter for speculation. We know that their religion was connected with the fertility of the earth; perhaps at certain times of the year they were able to redirect these forces in such a way as to ensure the fertility of their land, just as a modern farmer in a desert area might canalize his water and direct it to the fields where it is most necessary. *If* they could canalize the forces, then perhaps the standing stones are not intended simply to mark the route of ley lines, but to redirect the energy into straight lines across country. Stephen Jenkins mentions that Air Marshall Sir Victor Goddard told the British Interplanetary Society in 1969 that UFOs could come from 'an invisible world that coincides with the space of our own' – another dimension, so to speak, like the place described by H. G. Wells in *The Plattner Story*. If so, then perhaps the nodal points of leys form some kind of link between the two worlds. Or perhaps they simply provide the necessary energy to bridge the dimensions. Is it possible that the Neolithic priests who built the outer circle of Stonehenge were also able to use this energy to appeal to 'supernatural' beings? In other words, might nodal points of leys be places where prayers might be heard and answered?

Stephen Jenkins has another fascinating remark that brings me to the subject of this piece. Jenkins spent some time in Tibet, studying Buddhism. He speaks of the legendary Kingdom of Shambhala, the Place of Bliss. When Jenkins asked his teachers where Shambhala was located, they replied that it had once been in the Island of Britain, the Celtic Britain of the last centuries before Christ; it was called Gwynfa, the Place of Bliss, and was located at Glastonbury . . .

This curious piece of information fits in rather well with what we know about the ancient history of Glastonbury. In the Iron Age – from around 600 BC – the area around the Tor was mostly under water. In the third century BC, there were two 'lake villages' at present-day Meare and Godney, around three miles north-west of Glastonbury; they were built by Celts. And at about this time, Glastonbury seems to have acquired the name of Avalon, which in Celtic mythology refers to a rendezvous with the dead. So again, it seems that we have a legend of a place that formed a link between two worlds. (The twelfth-century historian Giraldus Cambrensis declares that Glastonbury is Avalon, and that King Arthur lies buried there.) In his book, *King Arthur's Avalon*, Geoffrey Ashe suggests that the area of the Tor was used by these Celtic settlements as a burial place for their dead – hence the name. But Ashe was writing in 1956, more than a decade before the rediscovery of leys. Nowadays, I suspect, he might be willing to concede that the notion of a *rendezvous* with the dead might well indicate a place that stands 'between two worlds', as well as a burial ground.

In due course, Christianity arrived in Britain. And, as one might expect, Glastonbury soon became a centre of this new religion. That was a logical thing to happen, if Lethbridge is correct. The old 'isle of glass' (Yns-witrin) had been a holy centre perhaps for many centuries before the Celts arrived. Modern carbon-fourteen dating has shown that the outer ditch of Stonehenge – with all its astronomical alignments – was constructed as long ago as 2900 BC, in the New Stone Age. From this information, Dr Euan MacKie has argued convincingly that the society that built Stonehenge had a highly organized priestly caste, a religious elite. The same people almost certainly constructed the nearby Silbury Hill (which looks like a smaller Glastonbury Tor). It is therefore perfectly conceivable that Glastonbury Tor was another key centre of the ancient fertility religion. The early Christians took it over because they also felt that its power could be used for religious purposes. Significantly, they built a chapel to St Michael (supplanter of the dragon) on top of the Tor.

To ley hunters it is also significant that the so-called Great Ley runs right through Glastonbury Tor as well as through the Avebury stone circle. The Great Ley is the longest straight line that can be drawn across southern England. It is also – perhaps coincidentally – the line of the midsummer sunrise. It begins at St Michael's Mount in Cornwall, runs across Bodmin Moor and Dartmoor, through many places dedicated to St Michael, and joins the coast of East Anglia near Bury St Edmunds. There are a surprising number of St Michael's churches along this line – at Avebury, Buckland Dinham, the Tor, Othery, Burrow Mount, Lyng, Creech St Michael, Trull, Brent Tor, and St Michael's Mount itself. All these churches also have associations with dragons, which are often portrayed carved into the fabric and in the stained-glass windows.

So what does all this amount to? Basically, the notion that ancient man was far closer to the earth than his modern descendants, and had entered into an altogether more symbiotic relationship with it. His religion was based upon the forces of the earth, upon which his existence depended, and he recognized that these forces varied in strength according to the positions of the heavens. This is why he was also an expert in astronomy and why his temples, like Stonehenge and Callanish (in the Hebrides), were also vast stone computers for predicting eclipses of the sun and moon. He may have known how to use these earth forces in many ways: to bring fertility to the land, to increase his own psychic powers (modern primitive tribes still rely on their shaman or priest to tell them where they can expect to find herds of deer or other animals), perhaps even to perform acts of magic. (Lethbridge suggested, half seriously, that the forces could have been used in erecting the great sarsens of Stonehenge. I myself have noted that Uri Geller often places his foot against some 'earthed' object, like a radiator, in order to gain the power to bend metal or stop watches, and have wondered whether he may not be somehow making use of the earth force.)

All this sounds reasonable enough. But the most surprising part is still to come. John Michell pointed out that many of the landmarks on ley lines seem designed to be seen *from the air*. (The famous snake mound in Ohio is an example.) That curious enthusiast Erich von Daniken has also pointed out many prehistoric sites – like the Nazca lines in Peru – that seem to be designed to be visible from above. Lethbridge, as we have seen, speculated (half jokingly) that the stone circles were intended to 'guide in' ancient spacecraft. If, in fact, we can stretch our imagination to the point of believing that the earth might have been visited by spacemen in prehistoric times, then there is nothing wildly improbable about this theory. The stone circles may not have been *built* to guide in flying saucers, but if the space-craft had instruments that could measure the earth's magnetic field, then they may well have used the stone circles as beacons at night.

Now back in the age of the first Queen Elizabeth, her astrologer Dr John Dee visited Glastonbury, drew a map of some of its principal features, and came to the conclusion that many constellations of the heavens were deliberately reflected in man-made earthworks. He called this 'Merlin's secret', and apparently felt that one of the basic shapes of this pattern was that of a horse. (This would have interested Lethbridge, who felt that many ancient sites are connected with the Celtic horse goddess Epona.)

In the 1920s, another student of Glastonbury, Mrs Katharine Maltwood, studied maps of the area and reached the astonishing conclusion that someone had taken the trouble to draw a vast zodiac on the countryside around the Tor. She knew about the great effigy mounds in America in the shapes of animals, birds and reptiles. She knew that the legends of the Holy Grail have often been connected with Avalon, but rejected the notion that the Arthurian Grail is the *only* one. She spoke of 'an earlier Grail, that "Cauldron of Wisdom" already famous ages before Joseph or Arimathea brought his message here'. (For more detailed comments on these legends I must refer the reader back to other articles in this book.) In short, Mrs Maltwood concluded that men in remote ages of the past had deliberately used certain natural features of the landscape to sketch vast drawings of the signs of the zodiac on the Glastonbury landscape. She seems to have had no clear idea of why anyone should do this, and certainly no suspicion that the whole thing was designed to be seen from the air. When her book about the Glastonbury 'Temple of the Stars' appeared in 1929, it convinced few people; most readers probably thought it an amusing but totally wild theory. In recent years, discoveries about leys have suddenly made it seem altogether less preposterous. As the reader will have discovered, the majority of contributors to this book accept Mrs Maltwood's ideas; some have even added their own interesting elaborations and refinements.

I have to confess that I am by no means wholly convinced. As far as I am concerned, one piece of vital evidence is missing. Dr Michael Dames has argued persuasively that Silbury Hill was built to represent a woman crouching in the position of child-birth, and that at the harvest festival the moon was reflected in a lake between her thighs to give the impression that the baby's head was emerging. He also suggests that this could be *seen* by the whole tribe which stood on the hill. The whole ley theory seems to demand that the temples could actually be used for religious purposes. And I find it very hard to imagine how Glastonbury's Temple of the Stars could have been used in any practical way. I am willing, I should add, to be convinced. But for me, the mere demonstration that various configurations of the land *could* be the signs of the zodiac is no convincing proof. I would need to be told precisely how the worshippers used the Zodiac in their religious ceremonies.*

I am aware that sceptics will dismiss this whole theory about Glastonbury as a tissue of moonshine. They will argue that Glastonbury Tor is a striking landmark that *looks* as if it came straight out of a fairy tale, and that this has simply stimulated the imagination of various writers with a romantic bent. John Cowper Powys set his *Glastonbury Romance* there for no other reason, as far as I can see. But anyone who takes the trouble

*The article by John Michael goes some way towards explaining this dilemma. (*Ed.*)

to start at the beginning – with the works of Professor Thom on the astronomical alignments of the megalithic monuments, and the speculations of historians on their purpose
– will probably end by being convinced that there *is* some strange mystery here, almost
certainly connected with an ancient fertility religion which may date from many
thousands of years before Christ. Even Margaret Murray's astonishing speculations about
the 'old religion' of the witches begin to look like inspired guesses. We may reserve the
right to doubt whether Glastonbury is really the ancient Shambhala, or even whether its
Zodiac was constructed deliberately. But eventually, there can surely be little doubt that
this was once one of the holy centres of England – perhaps of Europe – and that some of
the most important and exciting discoveries about its purpose are still to come.

Jerusalem

And did those feet in ancient time
Walk upon England's mountains green
And was the Holy Lamb of God
On England's pleasant pastures seen

And did the Countenance Divine
Shine forth upon these clouded hills
And was Jerusalem builded here
Among these dark Satanic mills?

Bring me my bow of burning gold
Bring me my arrows of desire
Bring me my Spear! O clouds unfold!
Bring me my Chariot of Fire!

I will not cease from mental fight
Nor shall my sword sleep in my hand
Till we have built Jerusalem
In England's green and pleasant land

WILLIAM BLAKE

MARY CAINE